CAR CARE
Q&A

CAR CARE Q&A

The Auto Owner's Complete Problem-Solver

Mort Schultz

John Wiley & Sons, Inc.

New York • Chichester • Brisbane • Toronto • Singapore

Copyright © 1992 by Mort Schultz

Published by John Wiley & Sons, Inc.

Library of Congress Cataloging-in-Publication Data
Schultz, Morton J.
  Car care Q&A: the auto owner's complete problem-solver /
by Mort Schultz.
    p. cm.
  Includes bibliographical references and index.
  ISBN 0-471-54479-5 (pbk. : alk. paper)
    1. Automobiles—Maintenance and repair—Miscellanea.
  2. Automobiles—Equipment and supplies—Miscellanea. I. Title.
  TL 152.S384 1992
  629.28′7–dc20   91-34887

Printed in the United States of America

10 9 8 7 6 5 4 3 2 1

Printed and bound by Courier Companies, Inc.

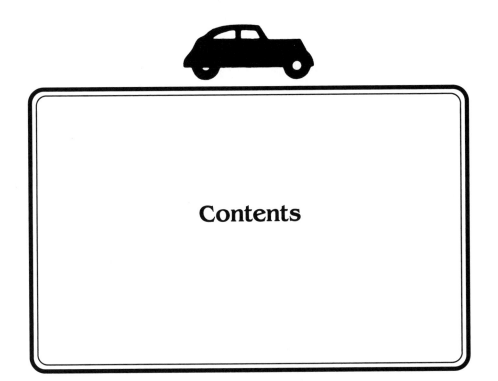

Contents

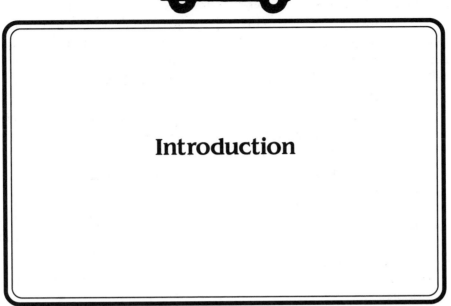

Introduction

In 1963, I started writing the monthly column "Car Clinic" for *Popular Mechanics,* continuing until 1988. In 1984, I started writing "Handyman Garage Service" for *The Family Handyman,* a *Reader's Digest* publication.

The questions I answered in "Car Clinic" and those I currently address each month in "Handyman Garage Service" are submitted by people who have problems with their vehicles, who are spending money needlessly to purchase products and services their vehicle may not need, and who are interested in increasing the longevity of their vehicles by following important maintenance practices. Most of the letters I receive voice the common complaint that trained automotive

technicians failed to resolve a problem. In turning to my column as a last resort, owners are rarely disappointed. With the information provided—information they weren't able to find elsewhere—they can bring their cars, trucks, or vans back to technicians; this time to have a successful repair finally made.

In keeping with this tradition, this book provides answers to some 250 of the most serious, most important, and most complex questions that owners have asked about their vehicles in the more than 30 years I've been at this work. You will (hopefully) find that this book answers most questions you have—or are likely to encounter—about your car, truck, or van.

This compendium of automotive questions and answers provides you with the information you need to get malfunctions repaired properly the *first time* you take your vehicle to a mechanic. There are also answers to questions that will help you in purchasing the products your vehicle actually requires—not those that advertisements urge you to use. Equally important is the information that can guide you in maintaining your vehicle so it can give you satisfactory performance at minimum cost for the life of the car. "The life of the car" is defined as that period between the time you purchase the vehicle and the time you sell it or otherwise get rid of it.

This book is divided into 10 chapters to help make it easier for you to track down the information you need. The Contents includes the specific questions that are addressed in each section.

In the order of presentation, the chapters are as follows:

1. What you need to know about buying *the right* products and services.

2. Maintenance: How to help your vehicle achieve senior citizen status by undertaking important, yet relatively simple and inexpensive, maintenance steps.

3. Behind-the-scenes solutions to engine performance problems—hard starting, stalling, hesitation, lack of power, and the like. Many of the repair procedures offered in this section are not included in the general service instructions technicians use of troubleshoot a glitch in performance. The result in these cases, therefore, is often failure on the part of the technician to resolve the complaint. By using the information contained in this section, however, you will be able to steer your technician to the root of the problem, and have that problem fixed.

4. Simple, inexpensive ways to resolve an annoying noise, vibration, or odor problem.

5. Information that can help you beat the high cost of repairing engine mechanical failures.

6. Your car's brakes, steering, suspension, and tires.

7. What you're facing when a drive train (transmission and differential) repair has to be made.

8. Keeping your vehicle's body in great shape—inside secrets you won't get from a body shop.

9. Getting rid of annoying problems with your vehicle's accessories—heater, air conditioner, defroster, windshield wipers, radio, power door locks, cruise control, and even the digital clock.

10. Information on emergency and safety problems.

If you don't find a solution for your particular problem within the chapter that is most applicable to the question, refer to the index. It will lead you to other pages that may hold the key to solving your problem.

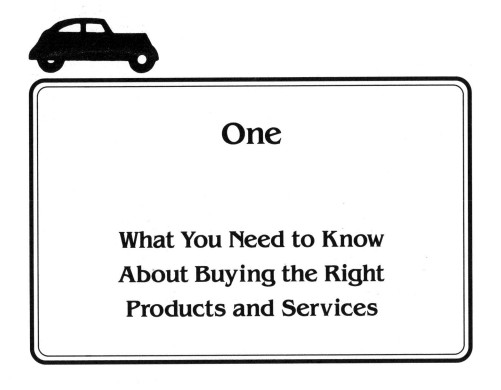

One

What You Need to Know About Buying the Right Products and Services

WHAT YOU NEED TO KNOW ABOUT BUYING MOTOR OIL

Is it true that some brands of motor oil are better than others?

I know of no tests that prove conclusively that one brand of a nationally sold motor oil is any better than another brand. The most important factor in selecting oil is to make certain that the product meets the requirements for oil set by the manufacturer of your car. These requirements, which are spelled out in the owner's manual and are much the same for all cars, are divided into two parts: *Quality Rating* and *Viscosity Rating*.

Quality Rating

When selecting oil, first establish the oil's quality rating. It is printed on the container and should be preceded by the phrase "API Service."

API stands for American Petroleum Institute. Presence of these letters verifies that the oil has passed standards set by API, the American Society for Testing and Materials (ASTM), and the Society of Automotive Engineers (SAE).

Following "API Service" will be a series of letters. For vehicles equipped with gasoline engines, the most significant letters are SG. Oil designated SG has been formulated for gasoline engines designed for vehicles of 1989 or newer vintage.

Prior to the development of oil bearing the SG designation, oil designated SF dominated. It was formulated for gasoline engines designed for 1980 to 1988 models.

As the quality of oil is improved and given a new designation, oil of lesser quality bearing the previous designation is phased out. Oil formulated for gasoline engines in 1970 to 1979 models had the designation SE. Before that, it was SD. You will no longer find oil having these designations or the SF designation by itself in service stations or auto supply stores. You will, however, find oil bearing both the SG and SF designations, as well as some others that refer to using the oil in a diesel engine. It's quite common to find the phrase "For API Service SG, SF/CC, CD" printed on containers of oil. Here's what these letters mean:

- SG and SF specify that the oil meets SG requirements as established by API, ASTM, and SAE, and exceeds the standards previously set for SF oil.

- S stipulates that the oil is formulated to meet the requirements of engines having spark (S) ignition systems—engines with spark plugs, that is.

- G informs consumers of the relative quality of the oil. Oil designated SG is of higher quality than oil designated SF.

- CC and CD indicate that the oil also meets the requirements for engines ignited by compression (C), which is the method of igniting fuel in a diesel engine.

Important: The manufacturers of some engines require that oil used in those engines bear both S and C symbols, for example, SG/CC; SG/CD; or SG SF/CC CD. Oil designated by one symbol—for instance, SG

by itself or CC by itself—should not be used in these engines since damage may result. Also keep in mind that damage caused by using an oil not recommended by the manufacturer of a car that's under warranty *will not* be covered by that warranty. Before you buy another quart of oil for your engine, check the owner's manual to make sure you're using oil the manufacturer wants you to pour into the engine. (See Figure 1.1.)

Viscosity Rating

Oil viscosity (thickness), which is sometimes called an oil's weight, affects fuel economy and cold weather engine starting. If oil has too high a viscosity for the ambient temperature, it will make starting more difficult in cold weather. But more serious is the fact that the thickness of the oil can prevent it from flowing over parts of the engine that need lubrication to prevent premature damage. Conversely, if oil it too thin (low viscosity), for weather conditions, it will flow over engine parts too rapidly, just like water, and not provide adequate lubrication.

The viscosity of an oil, which is printed on every container, is preceded by the letters SAE (for Society of Automotive Engineers). You will see designations such as SAE 5W-30 and SAE 10W-30.

The first number—5 or 10—identifies the cold weather temperature conditions under which the oil provides prompt cold engine starting. If oil thickens too much as it lies dormant in an engine overnight in cold weather, it won't flow readily in the morning when you try to start the engine. It will offer resistance, making it more difficult for the starter motor to turn the engine so it will fire up.

The numerals are comparison figures. An oil having a 5 (or a 10) does not mean that the oil should be used if the temperature is

FIGURE 1.1. The two most important pieces of consumer information printed on the labels of containers of motor oil are the quality rating and viscosity rating symbols. The quality rating is preceded by the phrase "API Service"; the viscosity rating by the initials "SAE." (Courtesy of Mobil Oil Corporation)

going to drop to 5°F (or 10°) above or below zero. The two only indicate that an oil with a 5 flows more readily than an oil with a 10. It offers less resistance to engines starting under more extreme cold temperature conditions.

With present-day motor oil, the 5 and 10 have all but lost meaning, however. Most manufacturers recommend using oil with a 5 designation at all times in most areas of the country to promote greater fuel economy. A 5 oil offers less resistance to an engine, which mens that the engine won't use as much gasoline as it would if it was being lubricated by a 10 oil.

Important: Check your owner's manual to make sure the manufacturer of your car wants you to use SAE 5W-30.

W after the 5 or 10 indicates that the oil is suitable for use in Winter.

The second set of numerals—30—identifies the warm weather temperature conditions under which the oil can be used without becoming too thin to provide the engine with adequate lubrication. There is some discrepancy among manufacturers as to how hot is hot. Some contend that oil having a 30 can be used if the ambient temperature is going to be 110°F; others contend that 100°F is the limit. Check your owner's manual. The manufacturer may want you to switch to an SAE 10W-40, for example, when a particular upper temperature limit is exceeded. Oil bearing the SAE 5W-30 viscosity label will provide prompt cold starting and hot weather protection over a temperature range of approximately 30°F below 0 to about 100°F above 0.

Important: To avert engine damage and keep a warranty in force, you must use oil of the proper viscosity for the expected lowest

and highest ambient temperatures in your region as spelled out by the manufacturer of your vehicle in a chart printed in your owner's manual. If you've misplaced the owner's manual, ask the service manager at a dealership that sells your make of car to get you another copy.

SHOULD YOU USE REREFINED ENGINE OIL?

Recycled motor oil is being sold in the auto departments of several stores in this area, including a couple of nationally known stores. Is this stuff safe to use?

What you refer to as recycled motor oil—the correct term for it is rerefined engine oil—is going to be more widely distributed as time passes. Rerefined engine oil comes from oil drained from the engines of vehicles. The oil is sent to waste management facilities, and from there to companies that specialize in rerefining used oil. The process involves removing impurities and remaining additives from the old oil. Fresh additives are put in, with the end product as unadulterated and as pure as virgin engine oil.

There is, however, a stumbling block to watch out for. Car owners—especially those whose vehicles are still under warranty—should make certain that the rerefined oil they're purchasing has been licensed by the American Petroleum Institute (API) as having met that organization's requirements. The primary concern with a rerefined oil that doesn't meet this criteria is that the old oil used in making the base stock for the rerefined oil may contain oil not suitable for automobile engines, such as industrial machine oil. Techniques employed by some companies for separating auto engine oil from this other oil may not be up to snuff.

Major vehicle manufacturers—Chrysler, General Motors, Honda, Nissan, and Toyota—state that rerefined engine oil is acceptable and will not affect the warranties *if* the oil meets the API requirements and the viscosity requirements established by the particular manufacturer. (Note: As this is being written, Ford is still deciding its policy.)

The API licenses companies to use the API's registered service mark "donut" for products meeting the API engine oil requirements. When an engine oil is licensed by the API, the oil marketer has certified that the oil meets all industry standards. The marketer is then authorized to display the API "donut" on the product's container.

Information printed within the "donut" includes the API service designation (SG, for example) and the SAE viscosity rating, such as 5W-30, 10W-30, or 10W-40. You may also find a statement in the bottom half of the "donut" concerning the "energy conserving" qualities of the oil.

As long as a car owner selects an oil that has this "donut" on the container, and the information within the "donut" corresponds with the API service designation and SAE viscosity grade rating recommended by the auto manufacturer, the warranty will be maintained.

The rerefined engine oils which have been licensed by the API at the time this book is being written are: America's Choice, Ecogard, Mohawk, Spartan, and Canadian Pride. America's Choice is distributed in the United States and Canada by Breslube of Breslau, Canada, a division of Safety-Kleen Corporation. This company has been rerefining engine oil since 1977.

Ecogard is distributed by Ecogard, Inc., of Lexington, Kentucky, which is a subsidiary of Valvoline. This product is also marketed in the United States and Canada.

The other three rerefined oils licensed by API—Mohawk, Spartan, and Canadian Pride—are presently sold only in Canada. They are distributed by Mohawk Oil Company of Burnaby, British Columbia.

SYNTHETIC MOTOR OIL VERSUS NATURAL MOTOR OIL

I would like to use synthetic motor oil in the engine of my new car since I've read favorable comments on its overall superiority vis-à-vis natural motor oil. The service manager at the dealership where I purchased the car, however, has indicated that using synthetic motor oil could render a new car warranty null and void. When I asked why, he gave me some vague response. Do you know if he's correct in what he says and, if so, why?

The service manager was probably alluding to the fact that using synthetic motor oil will render a warranty null and void if you do not follow the oil change recommendations of the vehicle manufacturer. Producers of synthetic motor oil claim that synthetic oil, which costs $2 to $3 more per quart than natural motor oil, can remain in use for as many as 25,000 miles. Car manufacturers, on the other hand, say that to keep warranties in force car owners must change oil much more frequently—in your case once every six months or 7,500 miles (whichever occurs first), if you drive under normal service conditions, or every three months or 3,750 miles (whichever occurs first), if you drive under severe service conditions. (For a discussion of normal and severe service, see page 27–28.)

If you don't follow the car manufacturer's recommendation and something happens to the engine, even if it has nothing to do with motor oil, your warranty can be declared null and void. In short, car manufacturers do not recognize the prolonged oil change span recommendations of synthetic motor oil marketeers.

CONVERTING A CAR TO RUN ON NATURAL GAS

During the gasoline crisis of 1979, I read a series of magazine articles written by you in *Popular Mechanics* **on alternatives to gasoline. One mentioned converting a gasoline engine to run on natural gas. I would like to know the status of this technology. Can I have the engine in my car converted to use natural gas? If so, can I hook a hose to the gas line in my house to fill the fuel tank?**

Natural gas is being used in cars as an alternative for gasoline by an increasing number of companies, particularly natural gas companies (Figure 1.2). Among them are Brooklyn Union Gas Company in New York and Columbia Gas Company in Missouri. Their experience proves that natural gas is a viable alternative to gasoline.

However, there are several obstacles to its use by the general public. Chief among them is the cost of the project. Modifying the fuel system in a car so it will handle natural gas and installing a tank to hold natural gas costs between $1,500 and $2,000 (Figure 1.3).

A more formidable obstacle is finding a technician who is trained in making the conversion. There aren't many around. To locate the one nearest to you, ask a representative from your local gas company. If you strike out there, get in touch with the Natural Gas Vehicle Coalition, 1515 Wilson Boulevard, Suite 1030, Arlington, Virginia 22209, phone number (703) 527-3022. This organization has a list of facilities that are qualified to convert vehicles to run on natural gas. This is not a job you would want an ordinary auto technician to do, no matter how competent that technician happens to be.

The final obstacle you will face in doing a conversion is getting natural gas from the pipeline into the tank of the car. You can't just connect a hose to the gas pipe in your home. You need a compressor that is rated at no less than one cfm (cubic foot per minute) to pump the natural gas from the gas pipe serving your home into the car's tank. It takes a one-cfm compressor from three to five hours to fill an empty tank.

Your local gas company might rent you a compressor, if it has any available. Your only other alternative is to try and buy one, and that will cost you another $3,000 or so.

Let's suppose that money is no obstacle, all potential problems seem to fall into place for you, and you decide to have the conversion done. You now have to decide whether you want to install a bifuel or dedicated system.

Bifuel means you can have the engine converted to run on either natural gas or gasoline. The bifuel engine won't run as well as it would with a dedicated system, however.

Dedicated means you'll be able to use only natural gas to run your car. Natural gas is rated at about 130 octane. Thus, the engine compression ratio will be increased to 13:1 from 8:1 or 9:1, which means that your engine will run superbly. Furthermore, since natural gas is a clean burning fuel, it won't contribute to a buildup of deposits inside the engine as gasoline does. By using natural gas, therefore, you lessen considerably the possibility of having to overhaul an engine during the time you own the car.

1

Compressed natural gas is formed by compressing natural gas to 3,000 pounds per square inch into CYLINDERS installed in the rear, undercarriage or top of the vehicle.

2

When natural gas leaves the cylinders, it passes through a master shut-off valve into a high-pressure fuel line to a REGULATOR to reduce pressure.

3 & 4

Then, the gas passes through a specifically designed MIXER to mix the natural gas with air; it enters the CARBURETOR at atmospheric pressure.

5

Next, the natural gas flows into the combustion chamber in the ENGINE and is ignited to create the power required to drive the vehicle.

FIGURE 1.2.   The future will see vehicles using fuels other than gasoline. One of them will undoubtedly be natural gas. This drawing provides an overview of a natural gas system as employed by a number of United Parcel Service vans. (Courtesy of Brooklyn Union Gas Company.)

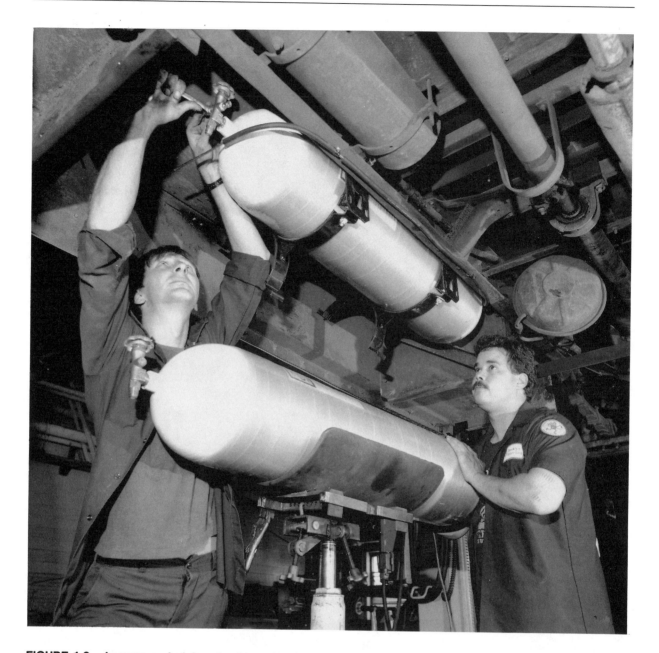

FIGURE 1.3. In vans and pickup trucks, natural gas cylinders can be installed under the vehicle. In cars, they can be placed in trunks. In either case, the tanks are put into a position where they are well-protected from rupturing in the event of a collision. The three cylinders shown in this photograph were installed in a UPS van and supply that vehicle with the equivalent of 15 gallons of gasoline. (Courtesy of Brooklyn Union Gas Company)

Another advantage to using natural gas is that it is practically nonpolluting. Furthermore, it is much less expensive than gasoline. At the time of this writing, a quantity of natural gas equivalent to a gallon of gasoline costs 42 to 80 cents, depending upon the area of the country, as compared to $1.10 to $1.40 for gasoline.

CONVERTING A CAR TO RUN ON PROPANE

Can you tell me where to get parts and do-it-yourself information for converting my car to run on propane?

Converting an engine so it can run on propane is *not* a job to do yourself. It must be done to precise safety and mechanical requirements so those in the car, as well as motorists traveling near that car, are safe. A poorly done job can cause an explosion. Only a technician who has been trained in doing propane conversions should undertake this task.

To find someone in your region who has been trained as a propane conversion technician, contact IMPCO Technologies, Incorporated, 16804 Gridley Place, Cerritos, California 90701, telephone (213) 860-6666. IMPCO Technologies is the major manufacturer of propane conversion equipment in the United States. However, it will sell this equipment only to qualified technicians.

Note: Generally, the advantages that natural gas provides (see page 6) are also provided by propane. Neither presents a danger if the equipment is properly installed. They are comparable in performance. It is easier at this point in time, however, to find technicians who are qualified to install propane equipment than those who install natural gas equipment. Propane (and natural gas) is

a cleaner burning fuel than gasoline, is much less polluting, and costs a little less. There are ample facilities throughout the country that are equipped to pump propane into a vehicle's fuel tank. There aren't many as yet for filling a car with natural gas. The cost of conversion to propane is roughly comparable to the cost of converting to natural gas, that is, $2,000 to $2,500.

USING GASOLINE THAT CONTAINS ALCOHOL

I drive my car, which gets 15 miles to the gallon, 128 miles per week. Gasoline that contains alcohol, which is available in this area, currently costs 20 cents per gallon less than straight gasoline. The savings over a year would be significant, but I'm concerned that alcohol will harm the engine. Will this be the case?

You can safely use gasoline containing ethanol or methanol, which are the two types of alcohols blended into gasoline . . . but you have to be careful.

Ethanol, which is made from a grain product such as corn, alfalfa, or soy beans, is also referred to as ethyl alcohol or grain alcohol. As long as the manufacturer of your car specifies in the owner's manual that it's okay to use ethanol (practically all manufacturers sanction its use), you can safely put a fuel composed of 10 percent ethanol and 90 percent unleaded gasoline into your car's fuel tank.

Methanol, which is made from wood, coal, and even garbage, is also called methyl alcohol or wood alcohol. As long as the manufacturer specifies in the owner's manual that it's okay to use methanol, you can safely put a fuel consisting of 5 percent methanol, 93 percent unleaded gasoline, and a co-solvent of 2 percent into your car's fuel tank.

The cosolvent prevents methanol and gasoline from separating in the fuel tank, as they characteristically do when they are combined. The cosolvent also helps prevent an attack by caustic methanol on fuel system parts. An excessive amount of methanol or the absence of a cosolvent will result in methanol corroding metal parts in the fuel system and causing plastic and rubber parts to deteriorate.

Stations selling gasoline that contains alcohol should have data displayed on the pump concerning the percentage of ethanol or methanol blended into the gasoline. In the case of methanol-gasoline blends, the presence of a cosolvent should also be specified. If labels are not present, it's best not to use the fuel.

WHEN TO REPLACE ANTIFREEZE (COOLANT)

The maintenance schedule for my car recommends draining and flushing the cooling system and putting in fresh ethylene glycol-base antifreeze every 30,000 miles or 24 months, whichever occurs first. The antifreeze now in my car has been in use 30,000 miles, but looks as good as the day I took delivery of the car. Why should I have it replaced?

A margin of safety is built into maintenance schedules, so you can probably get several thousand miles more from this coolant before its corrosion-inhibiting chemicals dissipate. Then again, maybe you won't. If not, the few dollars you save now by not replacing the coolant, plus perhaps a considerable amount more, may have to be spent for a new radiator or heater if the deteriorated coolant condition goes untreated and leads to a restriction of your present radiator or heater. Coolant depleted of corrosion inhibitors may cause an engine to overheat and break down on the road when the radiator clogs with corrosion.

Given these possibilities, you may now decide that it isn't worth your while to put off cooling system maintenance. But if you don't come to this decision, keep a watchful eye on the coolant. "Watchful" means to examine it every week or two for signs of rusty discoloration. If you see rusty-looking particles floating in the solution or if the coolant changes color, inhibitors have weakened and you should install fresh coolant as soon as possible.

Caution: To examine coolant, you have to remove the radiator cap. Be sure the engine is cold and is not running. After inspecting the surface of the fluid for particles and a change of color, see that the radiator cap is secured firmly to the radiator filler neck. Consult your owner's manual for additional information on how to remove the radiator cap in your particular vehicle.

WARNING: DON'T USE RECONSTITUTED COOLANT (ANTIFREEZE)

I found two types of antifreeze on a supermarket shelf. One was called reconstituted antifreeze, and it cost half the price of the other type that is a popular brand of ethylene-glycol base coolant. The less expensive antifreeze claims to be every bit as good and as safe to use as the popular brand. Can this be so?

I'll let an advisory from General Motors answer the question for you. This advisory is similar in wording to advisories issued by other car manufacturers that presently warn against the use of reconstituted (recycled) antifreeze. It says this:

In use as an engine coolant, ethylene glycol becomes oxidized producing a very degraded and deteriorated substance. Contamination by other automotive fluids during draining, handling, and storage is also a major detriment to the reclaiming (reconstituting) process. There is no additive we are aware of that can be merely put into used coolant that will restore it to an acceptable state.

In other words, at present you'll put your car's cooling system and engine at risk by using an antifreeze that is not a fresh ethylene-glycol base coolant.

Note: As this is being written, companies are working on equipment and processes that (hopefully) would allow successful reconstitution of used ethylene-glycol base antifreeze. Although laboratory results are promising, the technology has not to this point been perfected.

THE WIND CHILL FACTOR AND COOLANT (ANTIFREEZE)

What effect does the wind chill factor have on antifreeze in a vehicle that stays outside in winter? Should it be taken into account in establishing the ratio of coolant to mix with water?

The wind chill factor refers to the evaporation of moisture by wind. It affects people—not things. Therefore, it has no bearing on the coolant in a car's cooling system.

To determine how much coolant to mix with how much water, consider only the lowest anticipated ambient temperature for the part of the country in which you're driving. In most parts of the country, a ratio of 50:50 is needed. It will provide protection down to approximately 40°F below zero.

Remember that ethylene glycol-based antifreeze inhibits corrosion and rust as well as protecting an engine from freezing. That's why the mixture and not just plain water should be used in a cooling system year-round, regardless of the ambient temperature in the region. Maintaining the level of ethylene glycol solution is important in a warm climate like Florida's as well as in a colder one like Minnesota's.

INFORMATION ABOUT AN IMPORTANT WARRANTY

Can you explain the emission controls warranty issued by new car manufacturers? What is covered and for how long?

In accordance with federal law, the parts that make up the various emission controls of vehicles are guaranteed by new car manufacturers to perform properly for five years or 50,000 miles, whichever occurs first. If during the warranty period an emission control part fails, the cost of a new part plus the cost of having it installed will be paid by the manufacturer. The warranty is in effect for the original owner of the vehicle and all subsequent owners until the warranty period expires.

Parts that come under this warranty include the catalytic converter, engine electronic control system components, exhaust gas recirculation (EGR) system components, and positive crankcase ventilation (PCV) system components—those parts that have been installed for the sole purpose of reducing emissions. Every car owner should read the warranty and get to know those parts that are covered since these parts vary from vehicle to vehicle (Figure 1.4). If you have misplaced the warranty, write the customer service department of the manufacturer for a copy.

The emission controls warranty also covers nonemission control parts that go bad

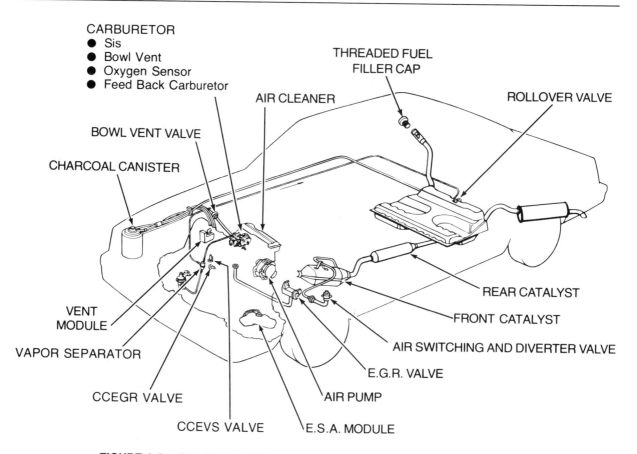

CARBURETOR
● Sis
● Bowl Vent
● Oxygen Sensor
● Feed Back Carburetor

THREADED FUEL
FILLER CAP

ROLLOVER VALVE

AIR CLEANER

BOWL VENT VALVE

CHARCOAL CANISTER

REAR CATALYST

FRONT CATALYST

VENT
MODULE

AIR SWITCHING AND DIVERTER VALVE

VAPOR SEPARATOR

E.G.R. VALVE

CCEGR VALVE

AIR PUMP

CCEVS VALVE

E.S.A. MODULE

FIGURE 1.4.   A typical emissions system. (Courtesy of Chrysler Corporation)

and result in the vehicle failing a mandatory state emissions test. These parts may include spark plugs, ignition wires, and carburetion or fuel injection components.

Whether you are the first or subsequent owner of a vehicle, it is important for you to become familiar with this warranty document. Not knowing for what you are covered under the emission controls warranty can result in your paying out a large amount of money for a repair that shouldn't cost you a penny.

BE CAREFUL OF "LIFETIME" WARRANTY OFFERS

At the time I purchased my new car, I paid $159 to have it rustproofed with Polyglycoat®. As part of the deal, I got a lifetime warranty. I am now experiencing rust-through on both doors. A letter I sent to Polyglycoat Warranty Group in Boca Raton, Florida, came back marked "no forwarding address." Is Polyglycoat out of business? If so, who's responsible for the lifetime warranty?

Polyglycoat Company went bankrupt. The "lifetime" warranty is worthless. A "lifetime" warranty is good only for the lifetime of the company that issues it.

PROS & CONS OF EXTENDED WARRANTIES

My new car dealer has offered me an extended warranty at a cost of $630. I drive my car about 25,000 miles a year. Is it worth buying?

That's like asking me if I think you ought to buy an insurance policy. Stripped of the fancy rhetoric, that's exactly what an extended warranty is—an insurance policy.

When you buy insurance, you're betting (although not hoping) that something is going to happen to make the insurance company pay off. The insurance company, on the other hand, is betting (and hoping) that nothing will happen to the insured. If the company wins the bet, they're going to make money.

The same principle holds true with an extended warranty. If something goes wrong with your car that would cost you more than $630 to have fixed, you'll congratulate yourself for making a wise decision to buy the warranty. Conversely, if you don't get a single dollar returned to you over the term of the warranty, you may regard the money spent for this insurance policy as wasted.

In purchasing an extended warranty, there are other factors to consider—for example, the cost of the policy vis-à-vis the term of the policy. You don't mention how long the warranty offered by your dealer is supposed to remain in force, but let's say it is five years or 50,000 miles, whichever occurs first. At the rate you drive, the warranty will expire in two years. What are the chances of your car sustaining a problem that will cost you more than $630 to repair over the next two years?

There's an even more important factor to consider: What *doesn't* the warranty cover. Keep in mind that some coverage provided by the extended warranty may be redundant if coverage overlaps the warranty issued by the manufacturer of your new car. For example, if power train components are covered for five years or 50,000 miles, you don't need an extended warranty to cover them.

Furthermore, under federal law, the manufacturer is responsible to make all repairs to the emissions control systems of a new (or used) car and to repair nonemissions components if they are the cause of pollution for five years or 50,000 miles, whichever occurs first.

Finally, what company underwrites the extended warranty? Is it the manufacturer of the car or a company you've not heard of? If the latter, how reliable is that company (the reference department of your local library may be able to help you find out). The company may be an independent outfit that sells its product to dealers without any backing from the auto manufacturer. If so, there's no guarantee that the company will be in business when you need them.

RECALL DATA FOR USED CAR BUYERS

I recently bought a used car and would like to know if it's ever been recalled. How can I find out?

A vehicle can be recalled for a safety or emissions-related deficiency. Safety-related recalls are overseen by the National Highway Traffic Safety Administration (NHTSA). An emissions deficiency occurs when a car emits polluting elements in excess of that allowed by law. These elements include carbon monoxide, hydrocarbon, and oxides of nitrogen. Emissions-related recalls are overseen by the Environmental Protection Agency (EPA).

At the time a safety or emissions-related recall is announced, written notices are sent to registered owners of the affected vehicle informing them that dealers will make the repairs free of charge. A recall can involve millions of cars or a few.

If someone who buys a used car wants to find out whether that car has been recalled, he or she should jot down the car's vehicle identification number (VIN) and bring it to a dealer. To obtain the VIN, stand on the driver's side of the car and look through the windshield at the lower corner of the dash. The VIN is stamped on the dash. It may also be printed on a label attached to a side of one of the door posts and is always provided on the car's bill of sale and registration.

The dealer will enter the information into a computerized system to retrieve recall data about the car. The screen will show (1) if the particular model has been recalled for a safety or emissions-related reason; (2) if so, for what; (3) the repair that has to be made; and (4) whether the previous owner had the repair done.

You can also call the customer assistance center of the manufacturer of the vehicle. Every manufacturer runs this type of service. The phone number, which is normally toll-free, is listed in the owner's manual or can be obtained from a dealer that sells the make of car. A customer assistance representative can supply data about recalls as well as other matters by calling up information on a computer screen. When you call, have the vehicle identification number ready.

WHEN AN OWNER'S MANUAL IS OUT OF PRINT

I recently purchased a used pickup truck from a new car dealer. It came without the owner's manual. The dealer gave me an order form that I dutifully filled out and mailed, along with a check, to the vehicle's manufacturer. I got the check back with a letter stating that the manual is no longer available and won't be reprinted. What's a second owner supposed to do?

There's not much that you can do. Manufacturers are obligated by law to supply an owner's manual with every new vehicle. An additional supply is printed to fill requests. Once that supply is depleted, that's it. Another printing is not usually made. The inventory of any one manual is generally sold out in about 18 months.

One solution to your problem is to contact the vehicle's original owner, if that's possible, to find out if he or she still has the manual. An alternative is to buy the factory service manual if your interest in securing a manual is for the maintenance advice it provides. You should be able to order a service manual through the dealer. An ample supply of the manuals is usually available long after the owner's manual sells out. Although written for technicians and containing much more information than you'll probably ever use, the service manual contains maintenance procedures necessary to keep your vehicle in sound condition.

WHERE TO GET OLD SERVICE MANUALS

I'm restoring a 1967 Ford LTD Sport Coupe that's equipped with a 390-cubic-inch V8 engine. I could sure use the car's service manual. I tried Ford, but struck out. Is there any other source?

Try Helm, Incorporated. This company has service manuals for Ford, Mercury, Lincoln, Cadillac, Chevrolet, and Pontiac models built from 1960 onward. To get what you want, write Helm, Incorporated, 14310 Hamilton Avenue, Highland Park, Michigan 48203 or call (313) 865-5000.

FACTS ABOUT BUYING REPLACEMENT PARTS

Are parts sold by auto parts stores and stores such as Kmart and Sears as good in quality as those sold by new car dealers that bear the name of the auto manufacturer? My question is economically motivated. The price charged for a part bearing an auto manufacturer's name is on average 25 to 50 percent higher than the price charged for the same part by one of these other suppliers.

You may be surprised to learn that manufacturers of replacement auto parts supply most of the parts used by U.S. auto manufacturers in the production of their vehicles. Therefore, many of the replacement parts made by these manufacturers for sale by auto parts stores and auto departments of chain stores are the same parts you would buy from new car dealers.

However, the warranties that come with parts bearing the name of an auto manufacturer and parts that don't carry the name of an auto manufacturer are for different periods. Parts that don't carry an auto manufacturer's name generally have a warranty of 30 days or 1,000 miles, whichever comes first. Depending upon the part, auto manufacturers' warranties for replacement parts range from 90 days or 4,000 miles, to as long as 36 months, or 50,000 miles, whichever occurs first. If a new part goes bad within the specified period of time, the part and labor to install another are paid for by the manufacturer as long as the job is done by a dealer who sells the particular make of car.

GETTING "FORGOTTEN" PARTS

I have a 1968 Chrysler Imperial in dream condition. What I need is a check valve for a brake vacuum booster. I've tried Chrysler parts departments and wrecking yards without luck. Please help.

To find a source, I checked out *Hemmings Motor News*. One of the places listed in the publication that I called has the part. It is

Vintage Auto Parts, 24300 Highway 9, Woodville, Washington 98072. The toll-free phone number is (800) 426-5911.

In case this company has sold out all their check valves for the 1968 Imperial vacuum booster by the time you get in touch, write for a copy of *Hemmings Motor News.* The address is P.O. Box 196, Bennington, Vermont 05201. This publication has pages upon pages of places where owners of every make of car can get parts for old models dating as far back as the 1920s.

WHICH SHOCK ABSORBERS ARE BEST FOR YOU

My car needs shock absorbers. Is it worth the extra cost to install shocks filled with gas, or will old-fashioned fluid-filled shock absorbers last just as long? What about shock absorbers filled with air—under what conditions are they used?

All shock absorbers are filled with hydraulic fluid, including gas and air shocks. In those shocks that use it, gas or air is employed *along with* hydraulic fluid as an additional means of tempering the effects of spring action on a vehicle. To understand why, you have to understand the role of shock absorbers.

The use of the word "shock" in shock absorbers is misleading. Shock absorbers don't absorb road shock. Springs do that. What shocks do is counteract the bouncing and vibration of the springs as they absorb shock. If shock absorbers did not stabilize the movement of springs, your vehicle would oscillate and dip, and its wheels would shimmy. (See Figure 1.5.)

Shock absorbers compress and rebound as they absorb spring action. During compression, the piston and piston rod in the shock pressure tube move down and displace fluid, which is noncompressible. Some fluid flows through a valve in the piston to the upper part of the pressure tube. The rest of the displaced fluid flows through the base valve to the reserve tube. The fluid remaining in the pressure tube stops the piston.

During rebound (extension), as the piston and piston rod are drawn up into the pressure tube, displaced fluid in the upper part of the tube flows through the piston valve to the bottom of the pressure tube, and fluid from the reserve tube flows into the pressure tube. The pressure tube is, therefore, filled with fluid. Fluid in the upper part of the tube stops piston movement, cushioning spring movement.

Where does gas come into play? In those shocks that have it, nitrogen is used as a medium to cushion fluid as it surges through the pressure tube. Fluid, as it surges, can affect the stability of some vehicles, but not all. In large-sized vehicles with sound suspension systems, fluid surge has little if any effect on stability. In small cars, surging may contribute to bounce. Gas shocks were devised for small cars.

Why, then, are gas shocks also manufactured for large cars? Because, in time, a suspension system can loosen. Replacing conventional shock absorbers with "stiffer" gas shocks can better stabilize the vehicle . . . so would having a technician service the suspension system. The same effect of stabilization of large vehicles can be obtained by installing heavy-duty shock absorbers.

As for combining air with hydraulic fluid, air shock absorbers are suitable for large vehicles that tow trailers. When a trailer is hitched up, the driver can pump air into air chambers in the shocks to provide firmer support for the car, especially in the rear. When the trailer isn't being towed, air is bled off and the shocks become ordinary units.

There are two types of air shock absorbers. A vehicle that has them as original factory

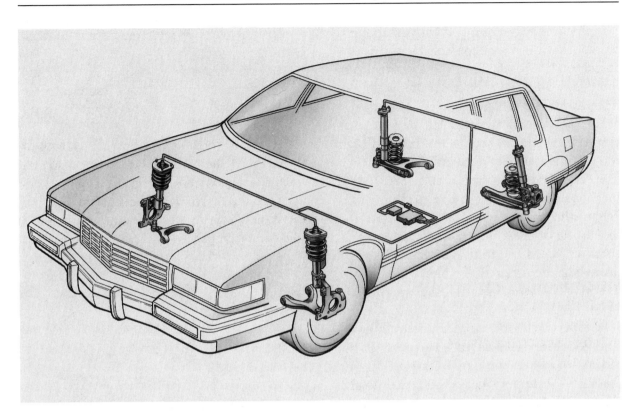

FIGURE 1.5.   There is a shock absorber and spring in each corner of every vehicle. The vehicle illustrated here has what is often referred to as MacPherson struts in the front and shock absorbers in the rear, as well as an electronic control module (computer) to set struts and shocks according to road conditions. (Courtesy of Cadillac Division of General Motors Corporation)

equipment may be equipped with an air compressor that the driver controls by means of a device on the dashboard. This control lets the driver add and reduce air in the shocks from inside the vehicle.

Air shocks that are installed by an owner after the vehicle has been manufactured with conventional shocks have an air hose going from the shocks into the trunk. The end of the hose in the trunk has a tire air valve. When the owner wants to pump up the shocks, he or she pulls up to an air pump at a service station and inflates the shocks as a tire would be inflated. To bleed off the air, the valve is pressed inward just as you deflate a tire.

A type of shock absorber called an overload shock is often installed instead of air shocks to serve the same purpose as air shocks—to support heavy rear end loads, particularly trailers. An overload shock has a coil spring wrapped around it. Like air shocks, overload shocks are placed in the rear of the car, where the load is concentrated; and heavy-duty shock absorbers are installed in the front.

Heavy-duty shock absorbers are units that have larger chambers that hold more fluid than standard shock absorbers. Therefore, they provide more support, but they're stiffer and give a less comfortable ride.

The other kind of shock absorber is the MacPherson strut shock absorber. It combines the shock absorber and spring into a single unit. MacPherson struts have allowed car manufacturers to eliminate some suspension parts, such as upper control arms, that are used on vehicles having conventional suspension design. The result is a reduction in vehicle weight, increased fuel economy, and the advantage of being able to get components into a smaller space.

In most cars that use them, MacPherson struts are placed up front and conventional shocks are installed in the rear. Some cars, however, have a MacPherson strut in each corner.

There is also a new wrinkle in shock absorber technology—the use of an electronic control module (a kind of computer) to set shocks according to road conditions. The computer is constantly adjusting shocks to the road. When the road is smooth and springs are barely bouncing, the computer adjusts the shocks to a less firm position, giving the vehicle a cushy ride. When the roughness (dips and bumps) is encountered and springs start flexing with vigor, shocks are adjusted to firmness by the computer so passengers in the vehicle aren't bounced around.

PLATINUM VS. REGULAR SPARK PLUGS

My dealer claims platinum-tipped spark plugs are recommended for my six-cylinder engine and wants to install a set. The total cost is $45. He says they provide more power and last longer than conventional plugs, which I can have installed for $12. Is he correct?

Only partially. Manufacturers of new cars are outfitting more and more engines with platinum-tipped spark plugs, and more and more service facilities are touting them as the best replacements when plugs have to be changed. But this is not always the case.

You can use either platinum-tipped or conventional spark plugs in any engine. You won't damage an engine by installing conventional spark plugs even when replacing the platinum-tipped spark plugs originally installed by the manufacturer. Contrary to what the dealer told you, your car engine won't deliver any greater power if you have platinum-tipped spark plugs installed. Neither will the engine suffer a loss of any other performance characteristic, including fuel economy without them. That happens when spark plugs, be they platinum or conventional, wear out.

What you do get from platinum-tipped plugs is longer life. This is the reason why manufacturers recommend replacing platinum-tipped plugs every 60,000 miles, while the suggested replacement interval for conventional spark plugs is every 30,000 miles.

HOW TO USE THE TIRE TREAD RATING SYSTEM

I need new tires. The tire dealer is trying to sell me a brand that he contends will last for 60,000 miles. He bases this on a chart that spells out expected mileage vis-à-vis each tire's tread wear grade. Is this chart on the level?

According to the National Highway Traffic Safety Administration, tread wear ratings indicate that "under the same general conditions, one tire *can* be expected to produce more mileage than another. It does not predict what the mileage will be." So, no—any tread wear chart that gives mileage is not an accurate presentation.

Too many variables make it impossible for even experts to predict how many miles any brand of tire will roll before tread wears to an unsafe level. These variables include differences in road surfaces and driving habits. They also involve maintenance habits by owners. If proper inflation is maintained, if tires are rotated according to manufacturer recommendations, and if wheel alignment is kept to specification, the car owner will get more use from a set of tires than someone who doesn't follow a rigid maintenance schedule.

Although accurate predictions cannot be made about the life expectancy of tires, there are tread wear rating charts that provide

buyers of tires with a way of comparing the relative tread wearing capability of one type of tire with others. A tire that's assigned a tread wear rating of 300, say, can be expected to last twice as long as a tire given a tread wear rating of 150 *if* both are used under the same road, driving, and maintenance conditions.

In establishing tread wear ratings, manufacturers test tires on a 7,200-mile course under controlled conditions specified by the federal government. The testing program, which is based on a federal regulation entitled "Uniform Tire Quality Grading System," also calls on manufacturers to provide comparative ratings for tire traction performance and ability to resist temperature.

Tread wear, temperature, and traction ratings are embossed on the sidewall of every tire, using the letters A, B, and C. For example, the tires on your car may have been given an A for tread wear and traction, a B for temperature resistance; or a B for tread wear, A for traction, and C for temperature resistance.

Literature available at tire stores explains the ratings and how to interpret them. Or write for a free copy of the pamphlet, "Uniform Tire Quality Grading System," available from the National Highway Traffic Safety Administration, Distribution Center M443.2, 400 Seventh Street, SW, Washington, DC 20590. You can call to request the pamphlet, if you wish. The toll-free number is (800) 424-9393 (366-0123 if you reside in the Washington, DC area).

PUTTING RADIAL TIRES ON OLDER CARS

Is it true that steel-belted radial tires should not be installed on older cars (mine is a 1971 model), because the suspension system isn't tuned for radials?

Someone told me that radials will damage the suspension.

Whoever told you that is wrong. Suspension systems of older cars will *not* be damaged by steel-belted radial tires. You may, however, notice a difference in the ride and handling characteristics of the car. The ride may seem stiffer, and you may experience tire squirm that is felt as a slight vibration in the steering wheel. You may also hear rattles you've not heard before. Because of these factors, you might want to stick to bias-ply tires rather than radials. You may not get as much mileage from them, but you will pay less for bias-ply tires than you will for radials.

The terms *bias-ply* and *radial-ply* (*radial* for short) refer to the direction in which the cords of the tires lie. The bias-ply is the older construction method. The carcass of a bias-ply tire consists of two or more plies (layers) of rubber-coated fabric. The threads (or cords) of these plies lie at an angle (or bias) to the direction of rotation. A radial-ply tire also has two or more plies of rubber-coated fabric, but the threads lie at a 90° angle to the direction of rotation.

WINDSHIELD WIPER BLADES FOR WINTER

A gasoline station attendant tried to sell me winter-time windshield wiper blades. They are more expensive than regular blades. Is this just a ploy on the part of gas stations to make more money?

Windshield wiper blades for use in snowy regions of the country are a worthwhile investment. They are designed with a protective coating of rubber to keep snow and sleet away from the wiping portion of the blade. The blade maintains its flexibility, unaffected by the elements. Winter-time windshield wiper blades can be kept on the car when weather moderates.

BUYING A COOLING SYSTEM HYDROMETER

How accurate is the inexpensive cooling system hydrometer sold in automotive supply sections of retail stores? The instrument I'm referring to uses small balls that indicate the degree to which the engine is protected against freezing. Expensive hydrometers are almost five times greater in price.

The ball-type hydrometer you're referring to isn't as accurate as instruments used by automobile technicians, but it is sufficiently accurate for use by car owners who wish to keep abreast of the level of protection being provided by coolant. A cooling system hydrometer records the level at which coolant in the engine will freeze. If coolant freezes, it will expand and can crack the engine.

To use the ball-type hydrometer, the engine has to be cold. Remove the radiator cap or the cap from the coolant overflow tank. Draw coolant into the hydrometer until it's about 3/4 full and note how many balls are floating in the fluid.

Instructions accompanying the instrument will stipulate the level of protection indicated by the number of floating balls. With one of the instruments you may come across, for example, if all four balls are floating, the cooling system is protected to 40°F below zero. If three balls are floating, the engine is protected to 20°F below zero. If two balls are floating, the engine is protected to 0°F. If one or no ball is floating, the engine has little or no protection and corrective action should be taken.

TOOLS FOR DO-IT-YOURSELF TROUBLESHOOTING OF A FUEL INJECTION SYSTEM

From 1947 when I bought my first car until now, I have always done most of my own auto repairs. In my repertoire is the ability to service a car's fuel system, including carburetor overhaul. My most recent purchase is a car equipped with a six-cylinder engine that has an electronic multiport fuel injection system. I have a service manual that explains fuel injection clearly enough, but it calls for using expensive instruments to troubleshoot this system. Are there any relatively inexpensive tools available for testing electronic fuel injection (EFI)?

Yes, there are two. One is called an EFI-LITE® and the other is a fuel pressure gauge. You can order them directly from companies that specialize in the manufacture and distribution of automotive tools for professional mechanics and do-it-yourselfers specifically from Borroughs, Kent-Moore, and OTC. Borroughs is at 2429 North Burdick Street, Kalamazoo, Michigan 49007 (the toll-free number is 1-800-253-0138). Kent-Moore is at 29784 Little Mack, Roseville, Michigan 48066 (the toll-free number is 1-800-345-2233). OTC is at 2013 4th Street North-West, Owatonna, Minnesota 55060 (the toll-free number is 1-800-533-5338).

The EFI-LITE, which costs less than $10, indicates an electrical system failure that is affecting the functioning of the fuel injectors. Fuel injectors are electrically activiated solenoid valves. They open on command of an electronic control module (computer) to spray gasoline into the engine. Depending on the extent of an electrical disruption, one or more fuel injectors won't function. If there is a complete electrical failure, none of the fuel injectors will work and the engine won't run.

The EFI-LITE is an easy tool to use. (See Figure 1.6.) Disconnect the main wire harness connector from the connector that extends from the wire attached to one of the fuel injectors by pulling apart the two connectors. Plug the EFI-LITE into the main wire harness connector and crank the engine. If the EFI-LITE gives off a glow that pulsates, the electrical circuit to that particular fuel injector is complete. There is nothing wrong electrically at that fuel injector, so reconnect the two connectors and go on to the next fuel injector. On the other hand, if the EFI-LITE doesn't go on or it gives off a steady beam, there is an electrical malfunction that is keeping the fuel injector out of action.

An EFI fuel pressure gauge costs less than $100. The gauge connects to a fuel pressure fitting on the fuel rail, the fuel line to which all fuel injectors are attached. Gasoline flows under pressure through the fuel rail to the injectors. The fitting resembles a tire valve and, like a tire valve, should have a removable cap screwed onto it.

To use the fuel pressure gauge, unscrew the cap from the fuel pressure fitting on the fuel rail. Then, screw the fitting on the end of the fuel pressure gauge hose to the fitting on the fuel rail. (See Figure 1.7.) Turn on the ignition switch, but do not start the engine. Note the reading on the fuel pressure gauge. Then, turn off the ignition switch (Figure 1.8).

Now, compare the reading you got against the fuel pressure specification in the service manual. If a service manual is not available, the fuel pressure specification can be obtained by calling the service department of a dealer selling the make of vehicle. If the pressure existing in the fuel rail is lower than the specified pressure, there is a problem in the

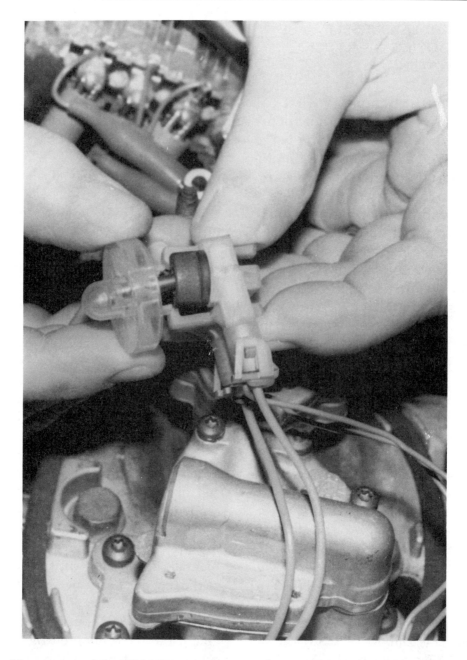

FIGURE 1.6. The purpose of the EFI-LITE is to detect an electric failure in the circuit carrying current to the fuel injectors. The connector attached to each fuel injector is pulled apart and the EFI-LITE is plugged into the main wire harness terminal. The way in which the EFI-LITE glows indicates whether current is or isn't reaching the fuel injector.

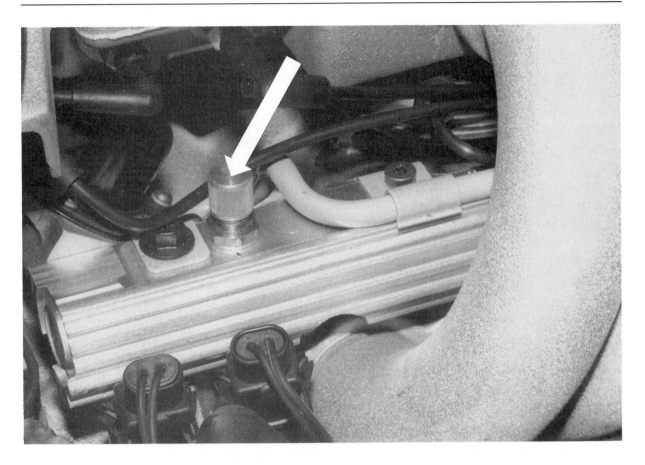

FIGURE 1.7.   An important tool needed for DIY troubleshooting of an EFI system is a fuel pressure gauge. This is connected to the fitting on the fuel rail. This fitting is protected by a cap (arrow), which has to be removed to attach the gauge, but must be screwed back into place after the test is done.

FIGURE 1.8. The fuel pressure gauge is screwed onto the fitting. Notice that readings of the gauge are given in both metric and conventional measurements. The metrics are the larger numbers.

fuel system that's keeping the engine from getting enough gasoline. The reason may be a restricted fuel filter, defective fuel pump relay, damaged fuel pump, or clogged sock. The sock is the filter attached to the intake end of the fuel pump, which is in the fuel tank.

LINERS FOR PICKUP TRUCK BEDS

I recently purchased a pickup truck and want to put in a bed liner, but no local dealer can supply one that fits. The wheel wells sit back further in the bed than in a regular ¾-ton truck. A dealer told me the reason for the screwy arrangement is that my truck is a camper special. Do you know of anyone who can help me?

You'll need a specialist in custom-built bed liners, such as Durakon Industries, the maker of Duraliner®. The company will custom mold a bed liner and tailgate cover for any pickup truck, be it a special or conventional model.

Mail the specifics to the company's customer service department. Include the make of the truck, year, and size of the bed and tailgate. It's a good idea to include a sketch of the bed and tailgate along with the measurements to show the position of the wheel wells in relation to the cab. The address of Durakon Industries is 2101 North Lapeer Road, Lapeer, MI 48446. If you want to call, the phone number is (313) 664-0850.

Two

Maintenance: How to Get a Car to Achieve Senior Citizen Status

HOW OFTEN TO CHANGE MOTOR OIL

Who should I believe when it comes to changing oil in my car's engine? The owner's manual recommends every 7,500 miles. A service station I do business with advises me not to pay any attention to the manufacturer and change oil every 3,000 miles. In this prairie state, there is little traffic and I drive my car most times at speeds ranging from 65 to 70 MPH. Whose advice should I follow, I'm confused?

I don't blame you so let me "deconfuse" you. Your service station adviser is wrong. You won't harm the engine by changing oil more frequently than necessary, but why have the extra expense. The recommendations by auto manufacturers for how often to change oil are based on research done by lubricant and engine specialists. This research is verified and documented by such prestigious organizations as the Society of Automotive Engineers.

Let's talk about your car. The manufacturer recommends changing oil every 7,500 miles or six months, whichever occurs first, if the car is driven under *normal* service conditions. Normal service is defined as driving the car on interstate and other high-speed roads most of the time. If you were driving your car under *severe* service conditions, then according to the manufacturer oil should be changed every 3,000 miles or six months, whichever occurs first. Severe service is defined as driving a car most of the time in city stop-and-go traffic, under extreme cold or hot ambient temperatures (below zero or above 100°F), for short distances, on dusty roads, or if you're towing a trailer.

Other car manufacturers follow the same pattern in recommending oil changes, but specify different intervals. These intervals are given in owner's manuals. If you've lost this important manual, get another copy by writing the customer service department of the manufacturer.

CHECKING MOTOR OIL

Between oil changes, one of the most important parts under the hood insofar as the car owner is concerned is that oil dipstick arrow (see Figure 2.1). If you don't know the location of the dipstick in your engine compartment, ask a technician to point it out. Then use it once a week. When the engine is cold, draw the dipstick from its tube, wipe the stick off with a clean cloth or paper towel, insert the stick all the way back into the tube, and draw it out again. Check the oil on the stick for two conditions: level, which should be between the FULL and ADD marks, and appearance. If the level is on or below the ADD mark, pour in additional oil to bring it up to, but not above, the FULL mark. If the oil has a milky appearance, draw the fact to the attention of a technician and then have the oil and oil filter changed. Don't be concerned if oil looks dirty as long as the oil change interval has not been exceeded. In flowing through the engine, oil has the job of picking up and holding in suspension contaminating elements. Thus, being dirty simply means it's doing its job.

PREVENTING THE DAMAGE TO ENGINES CAUSED BY SHORT TRIP DRIVING

My wife drives her new car to work five days a week—a trip of only 1.1 miles each way. I feel the engine isn't getting hot enough to burn off moisture that forms inside the engine. Won't this cause damage? Other than changing oil frequently, what should be done to get rid of moisture?

Your analysis is correct. The engine in a car driven short distances doesn't get hot

enough to burn off moisture that forms internally, especially in cold weather. Moisture mixes with oil, causing oil to thicken and flow less freely. It then clings to engine parts. If engine parts aren't amply lubricated by a full flow of oil, they will fail prematurely.

Car manufacturers use the term "severe service" to refer to short-trip driving. Short-trip driving is defined by manufacturers as "most trips less than 10 miles, especially when the ambient temperature remains below freezing for a period of time." They advise vehicle owners who drive short distances to change oil and the oil filter every 3,000 to 3,750 miles or three months, whichever

FIGURE 2.1.   The oil dipstick. (Courtesy of Audi of America, Inc.)

occurs first. The exact recommendation for severe service oil change scheduling is provided in your owner's manual. Changing oil and the oil filter at this interval is the only effective method to prevent the damage that short-trip driving can lead to, other than to drive the car on the interstate or a high-speed highway at least three times a week for a distance of at least 10 miles each way.

The following advisory from General Motors to dealers concerning this problem, of short-trip driving is worth mentioning:

"In cold weather, repeated short trips with limited engine warm-up may allow moisture to accumulate in the engine oil. This can cause milky deposits to form on internal engine surfaces (see Figure 2.2). Driving the vehicle for at least 20 minutes dissolves deposits and evaporates the moisture, allowing their removal through the engine vent system. If these conditions persist, the engine oil and filter should be changed at 3,000 miles or three months, whichever occurs first."

SELECTING THE VISCOSITY OF MOTOR OIL

The owner's manual for my car says to use SAE 5W-30 motor oil. An acquaintance who seems knowledgeable about cars claims that SAE 5W-30 oil is too thin for the type of driving I do—that I should be using SAE 10W-40. I average 2,000 miles a month, travel between 55 and 65 mph at least 50 percent of the time and between 60 and 70 mph the rest of the time. Should I follow his advice and switch to SAE 10W-40?

It's not advisable. The only knowledgeable source when it concerns the types of fluids for an engine is the manufacturer of that engine.

Your source is wrong by suggesting that an oil's viscosity should be selected on the basis of the speed at which you drive and the distance you cover. Neither is a valid criterion.

Viscosity means resistance to flow. The critical factor affecting a motor oil's resistance to flow is ambient temperature. Therefore, the ambient temperature anticipated for your part of the country between oil changes is a key factor to consider when choosing an oil. The oil viscosity recommended by your car manufacturer that meets ambient temperature conditions in most parts of the country is SAE 5W-30, which can be used with safety as long as the ambient temperature is not expected to exceed and stay at 90°F for several days running. If it does stay that hot, the oil of choice is SAE 10W-30.

SAE stands for the Society of Automotive Engineers, which is the organization that devised the viscosity rating system. W stands for winter and attests to the fact that the viscosity of the oil will allow for prompt engine starting in cold weather.

Your acquaintance recommended SAE 10W-40 oil, so let's talk about that. In the early 1980s, oil having a viscosity of SAE 10W-40 was the most popular oil on the market. But in the mid-1980s, that changed when GM issued a warning to owners of its cars about the damaging effect SAE 10W-40 oil had on GM engines. Therefore, SAE 10W-40 must not be used in GM engines and those of other manufacturers if there is a warning to this effect printed in the owner's manual. Many owners who chose to disregard the GM warning found out to their dismay that GM wasn't kidding when the engines in their cars needed expensive overhaul. Furthermore, owners whose vehicles

FIGURE 2.2.   Sludge that gums up the parts of an engine, causing need for an expensive overhaul, is the result of not changing oil as often as it should be changed.

were under new car warranty had those warranties declared null and void by GM when an analysis of the oil used in engines that were damaged proved that the oil was SAE 10W-40.

Let me stress that the question asked by this reader concerns a particular car having a 2.5-liter engine. The recommendations that apply in this case might not apply in yours. As I've emphasized, the only authority you should go by when it comes to selecting a type of oil for your vehicle's engine is the manufacturer of that engine. (Additional information about motor oil that will help you understand the recommendation made by the manufacturer is on pages 29–30.)

BETTER WAYS TO REPLACE AN OIL FILTER

When replacing the oil filter, I frequently have a tough time getting a grip on the filter with a wrench. The wrench slips because of an oily film that forms on the filter, making it difficult to unscrew it from the engine. How do I solve this problem?

There are two ways. One is to drive a screwdriver through the filter with a hammer. Then, use the screwdriver as a lever to loosen the filter. This method can get somewhat messy, however, because oil can drip from the penetrated filter onto the floor. Therefore, put a large pan on the floor under the filter to catch oil before you skewer the filter with the screwdriver.

You may prefer instead to fold a strip of sandpaper in half and wrap it around the filter so part of the sanding grit is against the filter and part of it is facing up. Put a rubber band around the sandpaper-wrapped filter to hold the sandpaper in place until you can

tighten the wrench around the filter. Turn the wrench slowly to loosen the filter. The pressure of the grit of the sandpaper against the wrench and filter will help keep the wrench from slipping.

WHERE'S THE OIL FILTER?

I recently purchased a used car made by General Motors. I've always done my own oil and oil filter changes, but this time I'm stumped, because I can't find the filter. Doesn't this engine have one?

It does. It's called an in-the-sump filter, because the filter is installed in the oil pan and is concealed. GM isn't the only manufacturer that has this kind of oil filter. Acura and Sterling also use it.

Here's the step-by-step procedure to replace this filter:

1. After raising the car and making sure it's secure, unscrew the oil pan drain plug. The filter is inside the drain plug hole.
2. Pull the filter from the hole with pliers and let oil drain completely.
3. Slowly turn the filter as you pull it down and out of the hole.
4. Check for the presence of an "O" ring on the used filter. If you don't see it, look for it inside the hole. It *must be* removed.
5. Coat the "O" ring on the new filter with clean motor oil.
6. Press the new filter into the hole by hand.
7. Wipe the oil pan drain plug gasket with a clean cloth and coat it with clean motor oil.
8. Replace the oil pan drain plug and tighten 1/4 turn after the gasket comes into contact with the oil pan.

9. With the engine oil at the correct level, start the engine and let it run at idle as you check around the drain plug for a leak. If there is a leak, tighten the drain plug a little at a time until it stops.

TIGHTENING OIL FILTERS TO PREVENT LEAKS AND DAMAGE

I was at my brother's house watching him change the oil and filter of his car's engine. He screwed a new filter on the engine and then did something I always thought was forbidden. He placed an oil-filter wrench on the new filter and tightened the filter with the wrench. I was taught that you tighten oil filters only by hand. Is he asking for trouble?

Your brother should have used a torque wrench for tightening the filter to the specification required by the manufacturer. A torque wrench is a wrench with a gauge that measures twisting or rotating force. By not doing so, he may indeed be in for trouble.

One reason manufacturers are specific about how tight to make filters is to assure that the filter is tightened sufficiently to prevent an oil leak. A more important reason has to do with the fact that the surface to which filters of most modern engines seat themselves is aluminum. If the filter is over-tightened, which is easy to do when using an ordinary oil filter wrench, the soft aluminum surface may be damaged.

If a torque wrench is not available, then no wrench should be used for the initial tightening. Tighten the filter handtight, start the engine, and check for an oil leak around the filter. If there is a leak, tighten the filter with an oil filter wrench 1/8 of a turn. Check for a leak once again and repeat the process until it has stopped.

HOW TO CHANGE COOLANT IN A MODERN CAR

I've replaced the antifreeze (coolant) myself in every car I've ever owned. Doing so has saved me a considerable amount of money. But now, I'm stumped. When I went to change the antifreeze in my new car, I couldn't get pliers or my fingers on the drain plug in the bottom of the radiator. The plug is recessed in a channel. How do you get it out?

With your fingers, but from a different angle than the angle you tried. I'm assuming you attempted to reach the drain plug by extending your arm down through the engine compartment or by lying flat on your back with the car wheels resting on the ground. This is okay for older cars, but won't let you get at the plug in many newer cars. They require that the front wheels be raised. Here's what you have to do:

1. Equip yourself with a set of drive-on ramps and wheel chocks. You can fabricate wheel chocks yourself. You need two of them. Miter the ends of 2 × 3-inch wood blocks to a 45° angle.

2. Drive the car onto the ramps so the front of the car is raised. Then, push the mitered end of each chock under the back ends of each rear tire.

Caution: Working under a raised car can be dangerous. Unless the car is securely supported, do not get under it.

3. Place an automatic transmission in PARK or a manual transmission in gear, and engage the parking brake.

4. Place a pail or large pan under the radiator to collect coolant as it drains. Don't

let coolant pour onto the ground. It will seep through soil and contaminate ground water.

5. Position yourself under the car, beneath the radiator, and look up. You'll see that you now have clear access to the drain plug in the bottom of the radiator. Reach up and open the plug to let old coolant drain.

6. When all the old antifreeze has drained, pour it from the pail or pan into 64- or 96-ounce glass or plastic containers. Cap the containers and dispose of the stuff in an environmentally safe way (as described on page 35).

PROTECTING ENGINES AGAINST FREEZING

This will be the first winter I'm spending in northern Minnesota, and I am concerned about providing sufficient protection for my car engine in this extremely cold region. When I lived in a moderate climate, I abided by the car manufacturer's recommendation of mixing one part of ethylene glycol-base antifreeze (coolant) to one part of water to get a 50:50 mixture. Since an ambient temperature of 40°F below zero is not uncommon in my new locale, should I use 100 percent ethylene glycol?

No! If you do, the engine block will probably crack. There is a point of diminishing returns with ethylene glycol-base coolant. That point is a mixture consisting of 68 percent antifreeze and 32 percent water. If the percentage of coolant exceeds this, the ability of the mixture to resist freezing begins to fall off.

At the ratio you were using when you lived in a moderate climate—50 percent ethylene glycol-base antifreeze and 50 percent water—your engine was protected against freezing to an ambient temperature of approximately 30°F below zero. This is the mixture recommended for most parts of the country.

A mixture consisting of 68 percent ethylene glycol-base antifreeze and 32 percent water won't freeze until the ambient temperature drops to approximately 70°F below zero. With mixtures consisting of more than 68 percent ethylene glycol-base antifreeze, that protection gets less and less until it reaches only 8°F below zero for undiluted ethylene glycol-base antifreeze. Be guided by this in choosing the ratio for your area. You will have a margin of safety by using a ratio of 65 percent ethylene-glycol base antifreeze to 35 percent water.

DOES YOUR ENGINE NEED PHOSPHATE-FREE ANTIFREEZE

The owner's manual for my European-built sports car recommends use of antifreeze (coolant) that is phosphate-free. I've never heard of phosphate-free antifreeze. Furthermore, labels of coolants I've looked at say nothing about being phosphate-free. Please explain.

Many European car manufacturers suggest using phosphate-free antifreeze in automobile cooling systems to protect the aluminum parts of engines. That's because the water in many parts of Europe contains a high concentration of minerals. When these minerals mix with coolant containing phosphate in the presence of aluminum, deposits are formed that can settle in cooling system passages and block the flow of coolant needed by the engine to prevent overheating. This is not a problem in the United States, because the concentration of minerals in water is much less than in Europe.

If you use a U.S. product that is not phosphate-free while your European-built sports car is under warranty, you may have difficulty getting the manufacturer to pay for repairs if a problem develops with the engine. Therefore, you may want to use phosphate-free antifreeze while the warranty is in effect. You can get phosphate-free antifreeze, which is more expensive than conventional coolants, from a dealer that sells your make of European car.

What about when your car is no longer under warranty? What negative effect, if any, will using a popular brand of antifreeze have? The makers of most well-known U.S. brands say none at all. Automotive cooling system experts seem to agree. This is evidenced by the fact that Chrysler, Ford, and General Motors also manufacture engines having aluminum parts; yet they approve the use of U.S. brands of antifreeze having phosphates in them.

AN OVERLOOKED BRAKE MAINTENANCE PROCEDURE

A mechanic I brought my car to for the first time advised me to let him drain the brake fluid, flush the braking system, and install new fluid. I've never had this done with any car I've ever owned. Is he trying to rip me off? My present car has been driven 50,000 miles.

The mechanic is giving you some very good advice. The service he suggests should be performed every 50,000 miles if the mainte-

nance schedule in your owner's manual doesn't advise you to do it more often. Brake fluid absorbs moisture, which reduces braking efficiency and lowers the boiling point of the fluid. Moisture can corrode the master cylinder and brake caliper bores. (See Figure 2.3.) Corrosion can eat away at seals, which when they fail will result in a brake fluid leak. Nothing holds up forever—not even brake fluid. That's something every car owner should keep in mind.

HOW A DO-IT-YOURSELFER SHOULD GET RID OF CONTAMINATED MOTOR FLUIDS

Throughout the years, I've taken cans of used motor oil and other automobile fluids I've drained from the engines of cars to gas stations that would discard them for me. But I can no longer find a station that's willing to take the stuff. Most stations in my part of the state are self-service stations that don't do oil changes. I've been told by managers at the few stations still servicing cars that recycling companies that once paid stations for used oil and other fluids are extinct. Therefore, those stations and, I guess, other automobile shops that perform oil changes have to dispose of oil as a toxic substance. This means they have to pay to have it taken away by a waste control company. What are car owners who want to save themselves a few bucks by doing this easy job themselves supposed to do—dump the stuff on the ground or flush it down the toilet?

According to the Environmental Protection Agency, do-it-yourselfers generate about 300 million quarts of used motor oil each year,

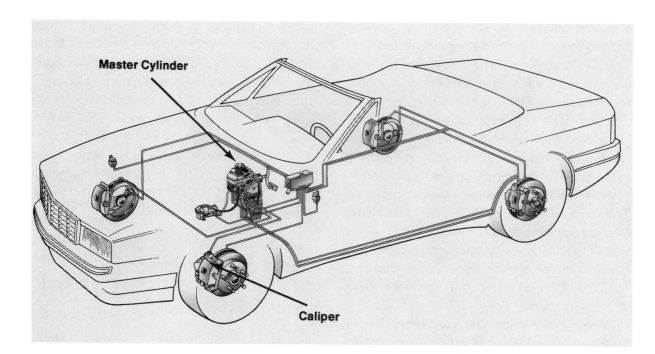

FIGURE 2.3. Even the most expensive braking system, such as this four-wheel disc antilock unit, needs maintenance. In fact, it needs the same maintenance as a nonelectronic conventional braking system. In addition to inspecting pads and linings periodically to detect wear before it reaches a critical point, that maintenance consists of changing brake fluid at a mileage recommended by the manufacturer of the car in the owner's manual. If no recommendation is given, you should have the system flushed and new fluid installed every 50,000 miles. Doing so will help prevent damage to the master cylinder and disc brake calipers. (Courtesy of Cadillac Division of General Motors Corporation)

not to mention millions of gallons of other fluids. This huge amount would pose a serious threat to the ground water if there were no way to get rid of the stuff except to dump it on the ground or pour it down the toilet. But there are ways.

As this book is being prepared, EXXON stations in some parts of the country are announcing themselves as recycling stations where automotive fluid will be accepted free of charge. By the time you read this, the EXXON program, which resulted from the Valdez settlement, may have been extended to your region.

If not, find out if your municipality has a toxic waste control site or call the environmental hot line for your state to locate the state-operated toxic waste control site in your area. The phone number is listed in the phone book under state offices or ask 800-information.

Another way to get rid of contaminated automobile fluids is to canvass service stations that have service facilities and other auto shops that do oil changes, including those at new car dealerships and "quickie" lube shops. Look for one that will dispose of the oil for you if you indicate a willingness to pay a nominal fee to have the facility pour your old fluids into their batch for disposal by the waste management company used by the facility. Ten to 20 cents a quart to have this done is a fair price.

Finally, if you can find no other way to dispose of used fluids, pour them into plastic containers, cap the containers tightly, and mark containers with the words "USED AUTOMOTIVE FLUID" in large letters that can't be missed. Call the trash collection company you do business with to tell them you're going to place the containers alongside your trash cans for pickup. Hopefully, the containers will wind up at a controlled landfill and not on the ground or down a storm drain or sewer where it will cause contamination.

BATTERY FAILURE OR HIGHWAY ROBBERY

On a trip to Florida, I stopped at a service station where the attendant checking the oil asked me to step out of the car. He pointed to the translucent battery case in my Japanese-made car to show me that the water in the battery was below the minimum line on the case. He said he couldn't add water, because this was a maintenance-free battery and was sealed. To make a sad story short, I followed his recommendation and bought a new battery that cost me $80. I have two questions:

1. What caused the original battery, which had seen less than 10,000 miles of use, to lose water?
2. Was I taken for a fool or was the service station attendant on the up-and-up when he said that you can't replenish water if it's a maintenance-free battery?

Just because a battery, maintenance-free or not, needs water doesn't mean it has failed. Furthermore, just because a maintenance-free battery looks sealed doesn't mean it is sealed.

Electrolyte in a maintenance-free battery will rarely dissipate under normal driving conditions until use takes its toll. This doesn't happen for tens of thousands of miles unless a battery is defective to begin with. However, under hard driving conditions, electrolyte can be depleted. Using a vehicle to haul heavy loads, towing a trailer, driving primarily in city traffic, driving in regions experiencing high ambient temperature, or stopping and restarting the engine frequently constitute hard driving conditions.

Let's assume your old battery had to cope with one or more of these abnormal conditions and that it didn't have a manufacturing defect. Could the attendant at the service station have added water to the battery, thereby replenishing the supply of electrolyte and restoring the battery to service? Perhaps—but let's give him the benefit of doubt. He may not have known that he could. Most maintenance-free batteries manufactured in the United States that are installed in vehicles by domestic car makers and those sold as replacements, are sealed and can't be opened to add water. The Delco Freedom® battery is a commonly used battery of this type. (See below.) Once electrolyte is depleted, the battery has to be replaced. On the other hand, most maintenance-free batteries installed in vehicles by foreign car makers can be opened to add water.

Note: Notice the use of the word "most." Whether the battery is made here or overseas, it may be atypical. Therefore, check carefully to make certain a battery is sealed before replacing it.

How can you tell if the maintenance-free battery in your car is one that is able to have the electrolyte level replenished? Some batteries have caps over the cells that are firmly secured to the top of the battery, but can be removed with effort. If these aren't apparent, look for a caution label on top of the battery case that has a perforated line around it. The label may be concealing covers over the battery cells, so strip off the label. If covers (plugs) are revealed, needle-nosed pliers can be used to unscrew them and open the cells so that *distilled* water can be added to

replenish the electrolyte supply. *Caution:* Use only distilled water.

NO WATER FOR A FREEDOM BATTERY

I recently purchased a Delco 72-Month Freedom® battery for my four-wheel drive utility vehicle, which will have a snow plow mounted on it during the winter. The plow is powered by a 12-volt electric motor. Someone told me that because of the heavy demand that will be put on the battery, it will need frequent charging and I'll have to replenish its water level every so often. How do I open the battery to do this?

Although you can open up some makes of maintenance-free batteries to add water (see previous item), you can't open up a Delco Freedom battery. Except for a tiny vent hole on each side, this battery is sealed. But that's okay. The battery should not need "frequent charging" as you've been told. All batteries, not only your Delco Freedom battery, are charged by the vehicle's alternator when the engine is running. You will only have a problem of frequent discharging if the alternator is underpowered. You will find this out if the engine fails to start on mornings after you use the snow plow. If the alternator is underpowered for the electrical demand being put on it, ask an auto electrical specialist to install an alternator that provides greater output.

The electrolyte level in a Delco Freedom battery will drop below the point of no return only when the battery wears out, is overcharged, cracks, or is tipped frequently so electrolyte leaks through its vent holes. If the indicator in the top of the battery becomes clear or pale, it means electrolyte has

---

SERVICE TIP: A BATTERY'S INVISIBLE ENEMY

If you're under the impression that the battery in your car doesn't need tender loving care because it's maintenance-free and has side cable terminals, you may be surprised by some statistics. According to a survey done by Atlas Supply Company, 68 percent of the positive cables and 56 percent of the negative cables of the batteries that were examined were corroded badly enough to have caused a starting problem. However, corrosion wasn't visible, so its presence doesn't indicate gross neglect of battery maintenance by car owners and their mechanics.

Two methods are used to connect cables to batteries. The older one involves two posts projecting from the top of the battery case. The terminals of cables are in the form of clamps that are tightened to the posts. The newer method uses two holes on the side of the battery. These holes are threaded. The cable terminals used with this method are in the form of flat metal plates that have holes in them. Bolts inserted through the terminals are screwed into the holes in the battery to secure the terminals. (See Figure 2.4.)

Unlike corrosion that forms on cable terminals that are connected to post-type batteries—corrosion that is visible to anyone who looks at the battery—corrosion that develops on terminals of side-terminal batteries builds up under the connecting bolts and is not visible. You should, therefore, have terminals unscrewed from the battery every year. Bolts, cable terminals, and holes in the battery should be cleaned with a baking soda/water solution and a wire brush. Cables should then be reconnected snugly and a thin layer of petroleum jelly spread over them to retard corrosion.

---

been played out and the battery is done for. Replace it.

Caution: Never test or try to charge a Delco Freedom battery that has a clear or pale indicator. Doing so can cause it to explode, sending shrapnel flying through the air.

HAVE TIRES ROTATED CORRECTLY

I read your article advising car owners to rotate radial tires by using an "X" pattern. This recommendation is in direct conflict with advice I've gotten from my friend, who is an expert on cars. He says radial tires are never to be cross-rotated—that each tire must be kept on the side of the car on which it was originally placed. He also says that if radial tires are cross-rotated, steel belts can separate and blowouts can occur. Following his advice, I've been having my tires rotated by moving the front tire to the rear and the rear tire to the front on the same side of the vehicle. Do you want to retract what you wrote?

Not a chance. Although there's nothing wrong with doing what your friend suggests, the method he advocates is obsolete in most cases (for the exception, see page 41.) Cross-rotating radials will allow you to obtain

FIGURE 2.4.   The battery shown in this photograph is a maintenance-free unit that can be opened to have the electrolyte level restored. Note the two raised caps. They can be taken off so water can be added to the cells. Distilled water is recommended.

maximum tire life by spreading out tread wear. The exact cross-rotation plan you should use depends on whether you have a front-wheel drive, rear-wheel drive, or four-wheel drive vehicle. That rotation pattern is printed in the owner's manual.

If you have misplaced this manual or drive an older car whose manufacturer once recommended same-side-of-the-car rotation, and you're not sure which plan to follow for your new tires, write to the Tire Industry Safety Council, P.O. Box 1801, Washington, DC 20013. Ask for information about rotating the tires on your particular model car.

WHY THERE ARE ARROWS ON SOME TIRES

Why are there arrows embossed on the tires of my sports car? Do they have some significance?

You bet they do. They are directional arrows, showing how tires must be mounted on the wheels to obtain maximum tire life. Arrows have to point in the direction in which wheels rotate.

The tires on most cars don't have directional arrows, which are embossed only on tires that have to be removed from wheels in order to rotate the tires. The tires have to be taken off wheels, the wheels kept where they are, and the tires remounted on the wheels in accordance with the suggested rotation pattern printed in the owner's manual. Wheels on sports cars such as yours must stay in their original positions, because they have different offsets, which means they are designed to be either rear wheels or front wheels.

Usually, the rotation pattern calls for moving the right rear tire to the right front wheel, right front tire to the left rear wheel,

left rear tire to the left front wheel, and left front tire to the left rear wheel. After rotating the tires, tire and wheel assemblies should be balanced.

Important: If you own a sports car and don't know if tires and wheels meet these criteria, consult the owner's manual or examine the tires for arrows.

HOW TO CLEAN AN ENGINE

I just bought a beautiful used car that is equipped with electronic fuel injection. I washed and polished it so everything sparkles, except the engine. I hesitate doing something that may ruin a part of the fuel injection system. If there a way for me to clean the grimy engine safely and avoid the expense of having it done professionally?

Yes, there is, and you don't have to worry about the fuel injection system. In fact, the procedure to use is pretty much the same for an engine equipped with electronic fuel injection and one that is equipped with a carburetor.

Caution: Wear heavy work gloves to protect your hands and goggles to protect your eyes against the degreasing agent you'll be using. It can cause injury if it splashes and hits you. Engine degreaser can be purchased in a store that sells automotive products.

Here are the steps to follow to clean your engine:

1. Let the engine run for five minutes to get it warmed up. Engine degreaser works best on a warm engine.

2. With the engine turned off, disconnect the battery negative cable, followed by the positive cable. Take the battery out of the car.

Caution: Use a battery holder to avoid dropping and potentially cracking the battery.

3. Take off the air cleaner.

4. Place cling-tight plastic food wrap over the throttle body of an engine equipped with throttle body fuel injection or a carburetor. If your car is equipped with a multiport fuel injection system, envelop the air intake opening with plastic food

---

SERVICE TIP: DON'T FORGET THE PCV VALVE

Practically every American-made vehicle and many foreign cars built from 1964 to the present are equipped with a crankcase ventilation system that features a valve called the positive crankcase ventilation valve—PCV valve for short. (See Figure 2.5.) It's become one of the most neglected parts of an engine. It's also a part that's frequently overlooked as a reason for a performance problem.

The crankcase ventilation system is designed to prevent hydrocarbons from escaping into and polluting the atmosphere. These vapors are routed from the crankcase through the vacuum-controlled PCV valve into the intake manifold, where they mix with the air/fuel mixture and are burned in the combustion process.

Proper crankcase ventilation is necessary if the engine is to perform as it should. If the system isn't purging hydrocarbon vapors from the crankcase, vapors will be drawn up into the distributor through the lower distributor housing and form a film inside the cap. This film causes a condition called carbon tracking, which diverts current needed by the spark plugs away from the plugs. The result is a rough running engine.

A damaged PCV valve can stick in a closed or open position. If a PCV valve gets stuck in the closed position, excessive pressure can build up in the crankcase and cause oil to leak from the crankcase into the air cleaner. If a PCV valve gets stuck in the open position, oil can be drawn from the crankcase into the intake manifold where it can foul spark plugs and result in excessive oil consumption as well as excessive emissions.

A malfunctioning PCV valve can also alter the calibration of a carburetor and cause engine surge, hesitation, and idle fluctuation. The ultimate problem that results from a plugged PCV valve is a buildup of moisture that mixes with oil and forms sludge in the engine. Once this happens, engine performance can be restored only by dismantling the engine for cleaning and repair.

To prevent these things from happening, have the crankcase ventilation system tested and the PCV valve replaced in accordance with the recommendation in the owner's manual provided by the manufacturer of your vehicle. When this is done, be sure to have the PCV system filter replaced as well. In most cases, that filter is to be found in the air cleaner housing. (See Figure 2.6.)

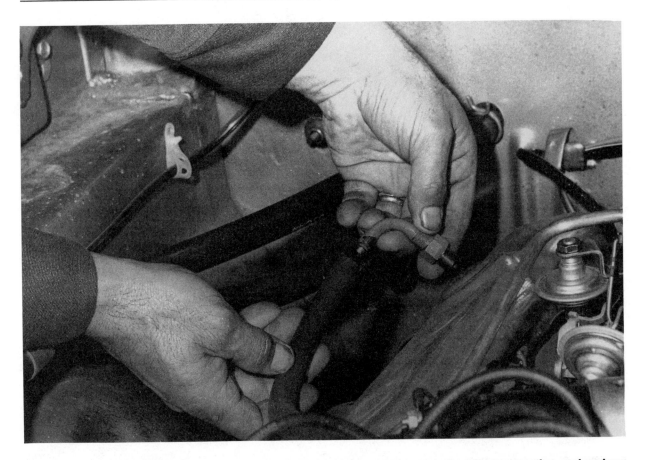

FIGURE 2.5. The hidden and often-forgotten PCV valve can cause excessive oil consumption and various performance problems, such as surging and hesitation. Since the valve doesn't go on forever, having it replaced every 30,000 miles is a reasonable policy to follow. Also have the filter that serves the valve replaced. The filter, which can get plugged and restrict engine ventilation, is usually located in the air cleaner housing. *Note:* Not every engine is equipped with a PCV valve and filter.

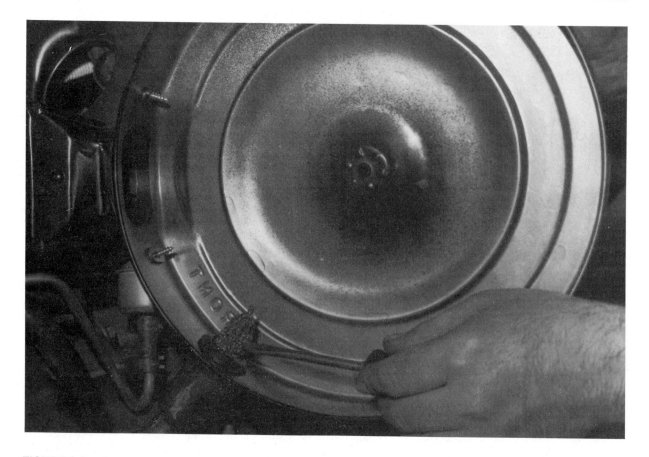

FIGURE 2.6.   On this engine, the PCV filter is a mesh-type bronze wad that is pressed into the air cleaner housing. On other engines, the filter is a flat cotton material that's housed in a plastic holder on the side of the air cleaner housing.

wrap. The plastic food wrap will prevent the degreasing agent from getting into the fuel system and causing damage.

5. Cover the distributor, spark plug cables, and wires and connectors with plastic food wrap.

6. Working forward from the rear of the engine compartment, spray degreasing agent on the firewall, fender housings, battery tray, hood hinges, the underside of the hood, and the engine. Let the agent dissolve grime for the length of time specified by the directions accompanying the product. When that time has elapsed, use a garden hose to wash everything down. Apply another treatment if grime remains, but not if there's only a film or haze.

7. Use a wash mitt, which you can buy in a store that sells automotive products, to get rid of film or haze. Mix a liquid dishwashing soap with warm water, slip on the wash mitt, saturate it in the soapy solution, and swab down the engine and all areas in the engine compartment, including the firewall and fender housings. After they've dried, apply liquid car or furniture polish to fender housings and the firewall. This will make them sparkle.

8. Remove plastic food wrap and reinstall the air cleaner and battery.

9. Reconnect battery cables by attaching the positive cable to the battery, followed by the negative cable.

KEEPING A MANUAL RADIO ANTENNA FREE AND EASY

When I took my car to the car wash and tried to lower the radio antenna, the mast stuck halfway down. I sprayed it with WD-40 and got it loosened up, but this incident got me wondering if there's some sort of maintenance a manual antenna should get to keep it from binding. Yes or no?

SERVICE TIP: LUBRICATE LOCKS

Door, trunk, tailgate, and fuel-tank filler locks can be kept in great shape for years if they are properly lubricated. Improper lubrication, or no lubrication, will cause them to bind or not work at all.

The proper lubricant to use is important. It should be a light household oil, such as sewing machine oil, or a graphite lubricant, such as Lock-Ease. Simply put the thin spout right into the lock and squirt once. It is particularly important to lubricate a lock if you've sprayed it with a lock de-icer. A lock de-icer contains alcohol to melt ice, but alcohol also dilutes the lubricant in the lock.

Important: Never use penetrating oil as a lock lubricant. It will wash out the lubricant in the lock.

Is there a scheduled maintenance period for servicing locks? Not really, but you can set up your own schedule. Or you can apply lubricant to a lock when that lock doesn't turn as freely as it once did, or when you have trouble inserting or extracting the key.

Yes. Raise the antenna to its highest point every so often and use fine steel wool saturated with mineral spirits to wipe the mast clean. Dry it with a clean cloth or paper towel. Then, rub a piece of wax paper over the mast. The paraffin from the wax paper that's deposited on the antenna will act as a lubricant to let you slide the mast up and down with ease.

PREPARING A CAR FOR STORAGE

I own a 1968 Ford Mustang and a 1987 Chevrolet Camaro. I want to store both cars over the winter. Can you offer advice that will keep these vehicles safe from damage?

Do the following to protect your stored cars:

1. Change the oil and oil filter if it's near the time recommended on the service schedules printed in the owner's manuals.

2. If the ambient temperature won't fall lower than 30°F below zero, or if cars are to be kept in a heated garage, make sure engines are filled with a 50:50 mixture of ethylene glycol-base antifreeze and water. If cars are not going to be kept in a heated garage, make certain that cooling system protection is adequate to meet the lowest possible ambient temperature anticipated for the area. For really cold regions, use a concentration of 68 percent ethylene glycol-base antifreeze (use only a nationally known brand) to 32 percent water. (See page 34 for more information about the effects of ambient temperature upon ethylene glycol-base antifreeze.)

3. For this next step you need a fogging oil, which is sold by dealers of outboard motor supplies. Fogging oil clings to combustion chamber parts (cylinder walls, piston rings, pistons, and so on) and will help prevent rust. Spray it into the carburetor of the Ford while the engine is running at idle speed. Let the engine run for as long as directions on the container recommend. This gives fogging oil time to coat parts.

Note: If you were dealing with an engine having a throttle body fuel injection system, you would handle this step the same way. Remove the air cleaner and spray fogging oil into the throttle body, as you would into a carburetor, with the engine running at idle.

For the multiport fuel injection system of your Camaro, remove the air cleaner and spray fogging oil into the engine through the mass air flow metering system with the engine running at idle. (See Figure 2.7.)

4. Following the directions on the can, pour fuel stabilizer into the gas tank. Fuel stabilizer, which you can also buy from a dealer of outboard motor supplies or from a store that sells automotive parts, mixes with gasoline remaining in the fuel system to keep it from forming a varnish-type substance that can build up and clog fuel system parts. Fuel stabilizer is a potent fluid, so be sure to follow directions printed on the container. Usually, a small amount added to the tank is all that's needed.

5. Remove the batteries and store them in a warm location. If you are going to place batteries on a concrete floor, put boards under them. The purpose of the boards is not to keep concrete from "pulling" the charge from the batteries as some may believe. Concrete won't drain a battery. The purpose of the boards is to protect the

FIGURE 2.7.   To protect the internal parts of an engine equipped with a multiport fuel injection system in a car that is being placed in storage, loosen the clamp of the air duct at the mass air flow intake. Pull the air duct off the intake and spray fogging oil into the intake as the engine runs at idle speed.

floor in the event that a battery case splits and allows acid to leak.

6. To prevent tire damage, raise each corner of a car so tires clear the ground. They don't have to be high off the ground—just not touching. If you can't or don't want to raise the cars, inflate tires with 50 pounds of air pressure.

CARING FOR AN ANTIQUE CAR

I've acquired a 1950 two-door Ford sedan that has a V8 engine. During the winter, the car will be in a garage on stands. Since grades of oil and gasoline have changed drastically since 1950, could you suggest the types I should be using in this car—also how often oil, antifreeze, and transmission and differential fluid should be changed? Advice about battery maintenance would also be appreciated. The car will be driven, at most, 500 miles a year.

Gasoline is your chief concern. Leaded premium fuel is needed to prevent damage to this V8 engine, but you're probably not going to find it. You may be able to get leaded regular gasoline, however. If so, fill the tank half full with leaded regular and half full with unleaded premium of the highest octane value you can find.

Lead is needed by older engines such as yours to prevent erosion of the exhaust valve seats. If you can't find leaded regular, use unleaded premium and add a lead-substitute additive, which is sold at auto parts stores. Select an additive bearing the name of a nationally known manufacturer and follow directions on the container.

When you put the car in the garage for its yearly lay up, drain the fuel system or add an antivarnish additive to the gas tank. Varnish from stagnant gasoline can form and clog the fuel system.

Incidentally, if exhaust valve seats eventually do erode badly enough to force an engine repair, the technician who does the work should install hardened-steel seat inserts. These will allow you to use unleaded gasoline without fear of doing harm to the seats.

Oil has gotten so much better since 1950 that it is less of a problem than it was in 1950 for your Ford—so much less, in fact, that no problem exists. Present-day oil will protect that engine for countless miles as long as you follow this simple procedure:

Each year, as you take the car out of winter storage, start the engine and let it run at idling speed for about five minutes. Then, shut it off, drain the oil, and refill the crankcase with a nationally advertised brand of SAE 5W-30 or SAE 10W-30 oil that meets API standards for oil designated SG (see page 1). You don't have to use any additives. All the additives your engine needs are contained in the oil. Also install a new oil filter. In preparation for storage, again drain the oil and refill the crankcase with a fresh supply.

Coolant (antifreeze) should be changed and the cooling system flushed every two years.

There is no need to change *transmission and differential fluid* unless you drive in water deep enough to cause contamination of these fluids. When you change oil, however, check to make sure that both assemblies haven't lost fluid. If they have, there is a leak that should be found and fixed before matters get worse.

Battery maintenance involves removing the battery from the engine compartment in cold weather if the ambient temperature in the garage will fall below freezing. If this is the case, bring the battery into warmer surroundings, such as a basement, and place it on a wooden plank. The reason for the plank is not to protect the battery, but to protect the floor if the battery happens to crack and leak acid.

If the ambient temperature in the garage won't fall below freezing, you can keep the battery in the car. However, disconnect the cables from the battery. Make sure cable terminals are suspended in air and not resting against a part of the car.

HELPING MOTHER EARTH

I try to be conscious of my actions in helping to keep our planet as clean as possible. Among other things, I'm conscientious about recycling, try not to waste water, and discard trash in receptacles instead of on the street. I'm concerned about what my car may be doing to the environment. Has anyone laid down a set of rules that car owners can abide by that will keep pollution from vehicles at a minimum?

Here are 10 simple rules to follow that can make a significant contribution toward purification of the atmosphere by lessening the impact of vehicles on the environment:

1. Maintain your vehicle according to the schedule outlined in the owner's manual. Replacing engine oil on schedule reduces emissions and improves fuel economy. Use SAE 5W-30 oil if the owner's manual recommends it for your engine and climate (see page 30).

2. Keep tires inflated to the pressures recommended on the tire placard, which is probably attached to one of the door posts of the car. You'll also find the recommended pressure in the owner's manual. Doing so will improve fuel economy and thereby cut down on exhaust emissions. It will also get you the maximum mileage your tires were built to give.

3. Drive sensibly to avoid excessive fuel consumption. Avoid jack-rabbit starts, excessive speed, and prolonged periods of engine idling. An example of the latter is if you have to stop at a railroad crossing to let a freight train go by. Turn off the engine until the train passes. It will stop exhaust from your car for that length of time. It will also save you some money in fuel that would otherwise be consumed needlessly.

4. If you do your own maintenance work, properly dispose of used engine oil, coolant, brake fluid, and transmission fluid (see page 35).

5. Have fluid leaks repaired promptly. Letting fluid drip onto the ground can affect the ground water.

6. If the air conditioner has a leak, get it repaired to prevent the release into the atmosphere of refrigerant that is composed of chlorofluorocarbons (CFC). CFC has been identified as a major contributor to the destruction of the ozone layer. Have air conditioner work done by a facility that is equipped with refrigerant recycling equipment, which catches and traps the gas to keep it from escaping. (See Figure 2.8.)

7. Patronize gasoline stations that sell gasoline containing a detergent additive that keeps fuel injectors clean. Oil companies that add detergent to gasoline advertise this fact.

FIGURE 2.8. Protecting the environment necessitates that air conditioning service be performed by a technician who's equipped with proper equipment, especially equipment that can capture refrigerant so it doesn't invade the atmosphere. (Courtesy of Ford Motor Company)

8. Keep a watch over vehicle fluids to make sure they're kept at the recommended levels to maintain efficient performance.

9. Use the air conditioner only when it's needed.

10. Don't ever tamper with the vehicle's emissions control systems.

The Environmental Protection Agency (EPA) says if everyone did these things, emissions would be reduced 25 percent.

Three

Sure-Fire Cures for Those Nagging Engine Performance Problems

Rx FOR HARD STARTING: ENGINES WITH FUEL INJECTION

Why is my car's engine so hard to start in the morning and also after being parked for one hour or longer during the rest of the day? Technicians have given the engine high marks. There are no trouble codes stored in the computer, and the ignition, electrical, and fuel systems have gotten A+ ratings when checked on an engine analyzer. Is it true, as one service manager told me, that this is normal for an engine with electronic fuel injection?

If this were normal for an engine with electronic fuel injection, then all engines with fuel injection would be hard to start. What the service manager told you is not true. However, it is quite possible that the reason for your starting problem is located in the fuel injection system.

Of the various systems that affect starting, fuel injection is the one that is most likely to prevent starting when the engine hasn't been running for awhile, such as overnight. An engine analyzer doesn't often detect the cause of the problem, because there are several fuel injection system malfunctions that can develop and not show up on an engine analyzer.

In tracking down the cause for your problem, a technician should test the performance of the fuel pump electrical circuit, fuel pump check valve, fuel pressure regulator, and the fuel injectors. (See Figure 3.1.) Each can affect engine starting when the engine has not been running for awhile. The following explains these various areas and how they should be tested:

- *Fuel pump electrical circuit.* With many engines, although the fuel pump is experiencing an electrical interruption because of a problem in its main circuit, the engine will still eventually start if it's cranked long enough to build up oil pressure. What some technicians may not realize is that a secondary circuit exists between the oil pressure unit and fuel pump. This circuit goes into action after several seconds of engine cranking to get the pump working and the engine started. The fact that the engine does eventually start causes some technicians to discount the existence of a failure in the main fuel pump circuit as the reason for hard starting. After all, they figure, if an engine does start, the fuel pump must be functioning; therefore, the main electrical circuit to the fuel pump must be intact. But this is not necessarily the case.

  You can determine yourself whether the main fuel pump circuit is working. Squat down at the rear of the car and place an ear as close as possible to the fuel tank. Have someone in the car turn on the ignition key without cranking the engine. If the fuel pump is working as it should, you will immediately hear a whirring noise that will last about four seconds. If you do not hear this noise, ask a technician to test the main fuel pump electrical circuit to determine if there's a breakdown in that circuit.

- *Fuel pump check valve.* The job of the fuel pump check valve is to prevent gasoline

from draining out of the fuel pump when the engine is off for an extended period. If the check valve is malfunctioning, gasoline will drain out of the fuel pump and flow back into the fuel tank. Thus, when you start the engine, the fuel pump will be dry and will have to be primed before gasoline can be delivered to the engine. The time it takes for the dry fuel pump to get itself up to snuff results in longer-than-normal engine cranking.

The fuel pump check valve is tested by connecting a fuel pressure gauge to a fitting on the fuel rail. The fuel rail is the pipe around the engine that delivers gasoline to the fuel injectors. The fuel injectors are attached to the fuel rail. The test fitting on the fuel rail resembles a tire valve and is covered by a cap, which is unscrewed to uncover the fitting, just as a cap covering a tire valve is unscrewed to get at that valve. The fuel pressure gauge is screwed onto the test fitting.

When the ignition switch is turned on, pressure as recorded by the fuel pressure gauge should rise immediately to the specification given in the service manual. Depending on the engine, pressure can be between 10 and 50 pounds per square inch.

When pressure reaches peak level, the technician turns off the ignition switch and keeps the fuel pressure gauge connected for 15 minutes. If pressure does not drop, chances are good that the problem is not in the fuel injection system, but in the ignition system.

If during this period pressure drops significantly, further testing is needed before the technician can definitely pin the cause of the starting problem on the fuel pump check valve. The other two reasons for hard starting of an engine with fuel injection—a faulty fuel pressure regulator or a

FIGURE 3.1.   An engine analyzer may not always reveal the reason why an engine isn't starting properly. Some of the conditions described in the text often escape detection, requiring other troubleshooting techniques. (Courtesy of Ford Motor Company)

defective fuel injector—will have to be checked first, because they can also cause a drop in fuel pressure.

- *Fuel pressure regulator.* To find out if the fuel pressure regulator is at fault, the technician keeps the fuel pressure gauge attached to the test fitting on the fuel rail and turns on the ignition switch. When the fuel pressure gauge again shows that pressure has reached its peak, the technician should pinch close the hose extending from the fuel pressure regulator to the fuel tank. This is called the fuel-return hose. If pressure as recorded by the gauge now drops, it indicates that the fuel pressure regulator is damaged and should be replaced.

  Suppose, however, that pinching the fuel-return hose doesn't affect the fuel pressure reading, which indicates that the fuel pressure regulator is sound. The technician should now test each fuel injector, in turn, to find if they are working normally before pinning blame for the starting problem on the fuel pump check valve.

- *Fuel Injector.* A fuel injector can cause hard starting if it is leaking down. (See Figure 3.2.) A fuel injector is leaking down if it stays open when the ignition is turned off. By staying open when it should be closed, a faulty fuel injector allows gasoline to drip into the cylinder it is serving. This causes the engine to flood, which results in hard starting after the engine has been turned off for awhile.

  One way to find out if a fuel injector is leaking down is to let the engine run until it's warmed up; then turn it off for at least one hour. At that time, spark plugs are removed from the engine for inspection. If the tip of a spark plug is wet or smells of gasoline, it indicates that the injector

serving the particular cylinder is leaking down and that the injector should be replaced.

This leak-down test is applicable to engines that have multiport fuel injection system. If an engine has a throttle body fuel injection system, there are two ways of determining if an injector(s) is leaking down. A throttle body fuel injection system can have one or two fuel injectors.

One way is to have a technician remove the fuel injector(s) for testing on a leak-down tester. If you would like to avoid the expense of having this done, you can try the following procedure yourself:

1. Let the engine run until it's warmed up; then turn it off for one hour before removing the air cleaner over the throttle body.

2. Watch the tip of the fuel injector(s) for about 20 minutes. If gasoline drops from the tip of the injector, the injector is leaking down and should be replaced.

If fuel injectors pass the leak-down test, the trouble you are having is undoubtedly being caused by a faulty fuel pump check valve. The fuel pump will have to be removed from the fuel tank to replace this part.

Rx FOR HARD STARTING: CARBURETOR-EQUIPPED ENGINES

I have an awful time starting the engine of my car first thing every morning. The starter grinds away for 10 to 12 seconds before the engine gets going. After that, it starts normally the rest of the day. The engine is equipped with a standard

FIGURE 3.2. The illustration shows a throttle body fuel injection system. The fuel injector (or injectors) are positioned in a throttle body, which is mounted on top of the engine and looks like a carburetor. You can determine if a fuel injector is leaking down by watching the top of the injector at the spot where the pointer is positioned.

four-barrel nonelectronic carburetor. Can you give me some things I should have a technician look into?

Your situation doesn't sound serious. An engine that starts within 15 seconds is considered by auto manufacturers as an engine that's starting normally. But I can understand how uncomfortable this long a cranking period can be for drivers. Therefore, here are two tips that may help you reduce starting time in the morning:

Be sure to employ the recommended starting procedure. Depress the accelerator pedal to the floor once and release it. Crank the engine for three seconds. If the engine doesn't start, release the key and repeat the procedure two or three times.

Have a technician test the operation of the automatic choke and the choke vacuum break. The choke vacuum break is a chamber on the carburetor that pulls the choke plate open slightly as the engine is being cranked. This prevents undiluted gasoline from entering the cylinders, which will make starting difficult.

REPAIRING A COLD CARBURETOR-EQUIPPED, HARD-STARTING ENGINE

I have a terrible time starting the engine in my car whenever the ambient temperature drops to 35°F or colder. The engine doesn't start by pressing the accelerator pedal once only as specified in the owner's manual. In fact it takes five or six tries, each accompanied by five or six pumps of the accelerator pedal, before the thing responds. In warm weather, the engine starts right up. My technician

is stumped. He's replaced the battery, fuel filter, carburetor float, carburetor needle valve, carburetor accelerator pump plunger, spark plugs, distributor cap, rotor, magnetic pickup, ignition cables, and cooling system thermostat. What's left?

The technician should find out if there's been a service advisory issued by the manufacturer relating to this problem. Then, if there is no advisory, he should check to see that the heated air-inlet system, automatic choke, and fuel pump are working as they should. In one notable case concerning the Chrysler 2.2-liter engine, a thermal bowl-vent valve (part No. 4241223) had to be installed to prevent fuel in the carburetor bowl from evaporating in a car parked overnight in cold weather. An adequate supply of fuel in the carburetor bowl is necessary for prompt cold-engine starting. If that fuel is not available in the bowl, it has to be replenished. This requires pumping the accelerator pedal many times. Maybe the manufacturer of your car has issued a similar advisory. It's worth looking into.

TROUBLE STARTING AN IMPORT IN COLD WEATHER

The engine in the used Japanese-manufactured car I bought a few months ago requires 20 to 30 revolutions of the starter to get going the first start of the day when the ambient temperature is below 40°F. Once the engine starts, it starts promptly the rest of the day. I didn't have this trouble before the ambient temperature dropped to winter levels. My technician is stumped. Please

---

SERVICE TIP: AVERTING COLD WEATHER STARTING TROUBLE

When cold weather arrives, owners of cars that are equipped with carburetors can experience starting problems if dirt is fouling the linkage of an automatic choke and keeps the choke plate from closing. A choke plate that stays open deprives a cold engine of the richer fuel mixture it needs to start instantaneously. To avert this headache, buy a can of carburetor and choke cleaner from an auto parts store. Spray the choke plate and linkage with the cleaner and use an old toothbrush to scrub off dirt.

---

help us out. The engine is equipped with electronic fuel injection.

What you describe is typical of a cold-start injector that is not working properly. This unit is part of the electronic fuel injection system. It is an injector that works only when the engine is started to provide the engine with an extra shot of gas it needs for prompt starting, especially in cold weather. The cold-start injector is connected to a timer that shuts the injector off soon after the engine starts.

Many cars made in Japan and Europe that possess electronic fuel injection have been equipped with a cold-start injector. Most cars equipped with electronic fuel injection manufactured in the United States do not have a cold-start injector.

Reasons for a malfunction with a cold-start injector are a damaged timer, a defective electrical timer circuit, and an injector that has clogged. The reason for your trouble lies only with these possibilities, so ask a technician to check them out. If the technician is not familiar with the cold-start injector,

bring the car to the service department of a dealership that sells your make of car.

HARD STARTING A WARM ENGINE

The V8 engine in my car has been driven 79,000 miles. It runs well and burns no oil. But even with a new starter and battery, the engine is hard to start when it's warmed up. If I let it cool down, it starts beautifully. My options, I'm told, are to live with the trouble or install a new engine. What a choice! Are there any others that you can suggest?

A build up of carbon in the engine will result in an increase in compression when an engine is warm. An increase in compression will put a strain on the starter and make it difficult for the starter to crank the engine. There are two ways of treating this possibility. First, use an engine carbon solvent that you purchase from a dealer or an auto parts store. A product that does a good job of purging carbon from an engine is GM Top

Engine Cleaner®, which can be purchased from a General Motors dealership. Follow the instructions on the container. Try several treatments. Solvent may dissolve carbon and restore normal warm engine starting. If solvent doesn't work, the engine will have to be disassembled to have carbon cleaned out. I doubt that the engine will have to be replaced.

HARD STARTING ONLY AFTER FILLING UP

The carburetor-equipped engine in my car becomes hard to start after I fill the fuel tank. Once a few gallons are used up, starting becomes instantaneous. Technicians mumble, "Very strange," but do nothing. Have you heard of this before?

I have, but I bet the problem is not caused by filling the fuel tank but by *overfilling* the fuel tank. What's probably happening is that excess gasoline—a result of overfilling—flows into the charcoal canister of the fuel evaporation emissions control system. Because of this overload, the canister can't do the job it's supposed to do, which is to absorb fuel vapors that flow into it from the carburetor float bowl. Vapors have to remain in the float bowl, where they expand and force gas into the intake manifold, which floods the engine. The result is hard starting.

The solution, therefore, is not to overfill the fuel tank. See what happens if, when the gas pump clicks off, you count to five and add additional gasoline at a slow rate of speed until the pump again kicks off. But don't add any more.

PREMATURE BATTERY FAILURE LEAVES HIM STRANDED

A few weeks ago, the engine in my car wouldn't start. I had to call for help to have the one-year-old battery jump-started. After I finally got going, I drove the car to a technician to have the battery changed. He unbolted the cables from the side of the battery to reveal a considerable amount of corrosion, which was the reason for my starting problem. The technician advises that I have the battery cleaned every year. I thought modern batteries didn't need maintenance. Is mine an exception?

Many car owners believe that modern batteries are maintenance-free, but the facts prove otherwise. A survey done by Atlas Supply Company revealed that approximately 70 percent of the positive cable terminals and 56 percent of the negative cable terminals in cars having batteries that were supposed to be maintenance-free were corroded. Of these, 22 percent of the positive cable terminals and 24 percent of the negative cable terminals were corroded severely enough to prevent starting.

Terminals that are connected to the side of a maintenance-free battery are devious, because corrosion develops under the bolts that connect the terminals to the battery. The bolts hide the corrosion so it's not visible, leaving car owners to think that everything is okay when it really isn't.

Since the engine starter relies on the battery to supply it with ample voltage to start the engine—a process that will be interrupted by corroded cable terminals—I agree with the technician who suggested that you have terminals disconnected from the battery every 12 months. Bolts, terminals, and pads on the battery to which terminals attach can then be cleaned.

ENGINE STOPS DEAD AT HIGH ALTITUDES

The engine in my 1988 car loses power and stalls when it's run for a few hours at an altitude of about 4,000 feet with the ambient temperature at around 90°F. From then on, it's difficult to stay on the road, because the engine will run for only a brief period until it again stalls. The car operates perfectly at lower altitudes whether the ambient temperature is at, above, or below 90°F. Dealer service departments throughout the country where the trouble has occurred, as well as the dealer from whom I bought the car, have tried and tried without success to solve the problem. No one knows what to check next, because everything that might have an effect has been tested more than once. Do you have any thoughts about this?

Since everything that is obvious has probably been tested, it's time to explore the not-so-obvious. The place to look is inside the fuel tank. The part to look at is the fuel pump strainer.

The greater pressure created in the fuel tank by high altitude and temperature may be causing enough pressure to make the fuel pump strainer expand. This, in turn, narrows the holes in the strainer through which gasoline flows from the fuel tank into the fuel system. Consequently, the engine starves for fuel.

Ask a dealer to contact the technical service department of the manufacturer to find out if a new fuel pump strainer or fuel pump has been issued for your car.

FOREWARNING OF AN ENGINE THAT'S GOING TO OVERHEAT

Is the temperature gauge in my car trying to tell me something? Over the past year it's climbed from just below the 220°F mark to just above 250°F. That's where it rests now. I just had the radiator checked and cleaned, and new hoses, thermostat, and water pump installed. The dealer says there's nothing to worry about. Do you agree?

For the time being, yes. Sooner or later, though, the engine will overheat, because corrosion is closing off the tubes through which hot coolant flows to the radiator where it's cooled before being returned to the engine. A progressive rise in temperature like the one you've experienced can be expected when a cooling system isn't drained and flushed and new coolant installed in accordance with the manufacturer's maintenance instructions printed in the owner's manual.

It would be a smart move to bring the car to a radiator shop now (consult the yellow pages for one) so a technician can determine whether the radiator will benefit from rodding, which is a procedure that has the radiator placed in a chemical bath and treated with extreme heat and rigorous mechanical action to clear corrosion from the tubes. (See Figure 3.3 and 3.4.) If the tubes aren't too badly encrusted, rodding will clear them and avert the only other repair that can be done

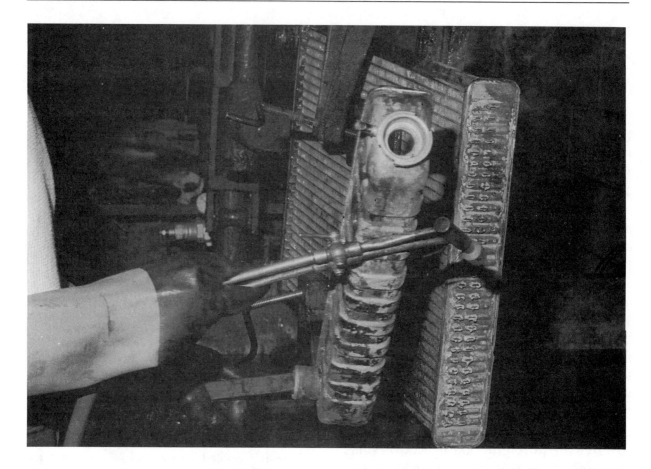

FIGURE 3.3.   Rodding a radiator begins by removing the top and bottom tanks.

FIGURE 3.4.   The core of the radiator is bathed in a chemical solution to loosen corrosive deposits in the tubes. A metal rod is then pushed into each tube to clear the deposits.

to relieve the condition, and that's to replace the radiator.

CAUSES OF AND SOLUTIONS FOR OVERHEATING

My older car has an overheating problem that technicians have not been able to fix. They have cleaned and flushed the cooling system; replaced the thermostat, hoses, and fan; and installed a new water pump. Now, another technician wants to start all over again. The engine overheats only when I drive about 45 mph. I'm just plain frustrated by this guessing game. Can you lead me down the right path?

Let's look at several possibilities that technicians apparently have not covered. The first thing I would have checked is the lower radiator hose. This is the one through which coolant that has been cooled by flowing through the radiator returns to the engine. This hose seldom develops cracks or any other visible sign of damage. So there's a good chance the technician who replaced hoses didn't replace the lower radiator hose.

The lower radiator hose possesses an internal spring that is supposed to keep the hose from collapsing when it's subjected to engine vacuum, which develops at higher engine speed. If the spring in the hose has lost strength, which can happen in time, it can't keep the hose from collapsing at higher speed. A hose that collapses cuts off the flow of coolant to the engine. Thus, the engine will overheat.

Ask a technician to warm up the engine, park the car, and observe the hose as someone behind the wheel speeds the engine.

When the speed of the engine reaches a point equal to above 45 mph, the technician will be able to see whether that lower radiator hose is collapsing. A hose that doesn't maintain a perfectly round configuration, but contracts, is a hose that will have to be replaced.

The next thing to do is to inspect radiator and air conditioner condenser fins for obstructions—they should be clear; then, examine the water pump drive belt for wear and correct tension. After doing these services, the technician should use a cooling system pressure-tester to test the radiator cap. The cap is attached to the tester, which is pumped up until the gauge on the tester records the rating stamped on the cap. After a few seconds, the gauge is checked to see if the pressure reading has dropped. If it has, a new cap will be needed to stop overheating.

Next, the technician should check the exhaust system for a restriction. This noncooling system part can cause the engine to retain hot exhaust gas that causes engine temperature to rise to a point that's too much for the cooling system to handle. Checking the exhaust system involves a visual inspection followed by testing with a vacuum gauge.

The technician should next check ignition timing to make sure it's set to specification. By itself, out-of-adjustment timing won't cause an engine to overheat, but it can cause a rise in engine temperature so that if other factors are borderline, the increase will tip the scales and cause the engine to run hot.

Coolant circulation should then be checked with the radiator cap removed. With the engine warm and running at around 2,000 revolutions per minute, the technician can look into the radiator filler neck to see if coolant is bubbling with vigor. If it's just sitting still, a weak water pump or faulty thermostat is the likely reason for your problem.

These are some other reasons why an engine can overheat or seem to be overheating:

- Faulty fan clutch.
- Malfunctioning temperature sending unit, temperature gauge, or warning lamp. Perhaps the engine isn't really overheating. Instead, a defect in the temperature sending unit circuit or a faulty gauge or warning light may be sending a false signal.
- Clogged radiator tubes. Assuming that a thorough cleaning with a suitable chemical agent and backflushing the cooling system fail to resolve overheating, the radiator should be removed and tested to see if its tubes are clear. Radiator tubes blocked with corrosion will restrict the flow of coolant, especially as a vehicle gets older. A radiator repair shop may suggest a new radiator or may want to try and salvage the old radiator with a chemical flush and rodding of the tubes (see page 61).
- Wrong size fan. If your engine is sporting a five-bladed fan, discuss with your technician the advantage of switching to a seven-bladed fan or installing an auxiliary fan to provide greater air circulation.

ENGINE OVERHEATS ONLY IN CITY TRAFFIC

Ever since I bought it new, my car has overheated in city traffic during hot weather when the air conditioner is on. Technicians have not been able to find out why, so I decided that I'll have to keep the air conditioner turned off and sweat unless you can provide an answer for this problem.

If the technicians who worked on your car tested the cooling system and found nothing wrong, there are two methods to try and overcome the problem. One is to ask a technician to replace the radiator with a heavy-duty model that has greater cooling capacity, and install an auxiliary cooling fan. This is an expensive solution, so you might instead prefer the second choice. That's to shift into NEUTRAL or PARK and press down the accelerator pedal slightly to get the engine to idle faster when you're stuck in heavy traffic with the air conditioner on. This action makes coolant (antifreeze) flow more rapidly, which could bring down engine temperature just enough to prevent overheating.

OVERHEATING IN THE MOUNTAINS

The temperature of my car's engine soars to 240°F whenever the car climbs a mountain or when it's stuck in traffic. The vehicle does this only with the air conditioner running. I've replaced the fan clutch, flushed the cooling system, and installed fresh coolant, a new thermostat, and a heavy-duty radiator. What's left?

An engine that heats up to 240°F is not an engine that's overheating. This is a normal temperature, but if you're uncomfortable in seeing the temperature gauge rise like this, there are two options open to you:

1. Turn off the air conditioner when the car is climbing up a mountain or is stuck in traffic.
2. Install an auxiliary cooling fan. This fan, in addition to the one already serving the engine, will push a greater amount of air through the fins of the radiator to reduce

SERVICE TIPS: WHY ENGINES STALL AND HESITATE

Is your car's engine stalling or almost stalling as you accelerate from a standstill? Does the engine lose power and die or almost die as you try merging with fast-moving traffic at the entrance to an interstate highway? Has the engine stalled and couldn't be restarted?

An engine tune-up may help relieve the deficiency that is causing one or more of these driveability problems. Then again, it may not. So the way to approach the situation is to analyze the circumstances that exist when stalling occurs, and then to tackle the causes which apply to the circumstances. In doing this, consider the following questions:

Note: The conditions described here may also cause an engine to hesitate as you accelerate.

- Does the engine die or almost die only when the engine is cold and the ambient temperature is below 32°F?

  Ice in the fuel system may be the reason. The answer to the problem may be to pour a can of fuel system antifreeze into the gas tank. If you buy the additive from the parts department of a dealer selling your make car, you'll be sure the additive is the right one for your engine.

- Does the engine die or almost die only when the engine is cold and the ambient temperature is below 50°F?

  If the car has a carburetor, the automatic choke may be responsible. But don't think you're off the hook if your car has a fuel injection system. Cars with fuel injection systems don't have automatic chokes, but some have a cold start valve and all have an air flow meter that may not be working right.

  You can probably check the functioning of an automatic choke yourself, but don't fool around with a fuel injection system. Leave that to a technician, but tell him you suspect your problem is related to temperature conditions and that the cold start valve and/or air flow meter should be tested.

  If you are going to test the automatic choke, the ambient temperature must be below 50°F and the engine must be cold—that is, it should not have been started for at least three hours. Open the hood and unscrew the wing nut holding the air cleaner cover to the carburetor. Remove the cover and air filter.

  Incidentally, that air filter is a prime suspect in a car that stalls or almost stalls only when the engine is warmed up, no matter what ambient temperature exists. (See Figure 3.5.) A dirty air filter forces the engine to run on an overly rich fuel mixture. It also forces the engine to use more fuel than necessary. So if the filter is dirty, replace it.

  Now, keep your eye on the top of the carburetor as someone in the car presses the accelerator pedal to the floor and releases it. The choke valve should fall over the carburetor opening. The choke valve is the plate in the top of the carburetor. When it is open, it lies in an almost vertical position, allowing you to look right down the throat of the carburetor. When it is closed, the valve closes over the carburetor throat.

Keep your eyes on the choke valve and ask an assistant to start the engine. The moment that the engine starts, the choke valve should open slightly so there's a little space between it and the side of the carburetor. Air enters the carburetor through this space to mix with and dilute the pure gasoline going to the engine. This keeps the engine from stalling. An engine won't run on pure gasoline.

If you don't see a slight space between the choke valve and carburetor, reinstall the air filter and air cleaner cover, bring the car to a technician, and tell him what you found out so the choke system can be checked. The technician will want to pay particular attention to a part called the choke vacuum break, which is the part that pulls the choke valve open slightly as a cold engine starts.

If you see the space, keep watching the choke valve. As the engine gets warmer and warmer, it should open wider and wider. At the end of three minutes or so, the valve should be wide open.

If things don't work this way, tell a technician about it. The choke linkage, which may be dirty and stopping the choke valve from opening, may have to be cleaned. If not, a faulty part may have to be replaced or the choke may have to be adjusted as instructed by the manufacturer in the service manual.

- Does a well-warmed up engine die suddenly after the car has been cruising along nicely for 10, 20, 30, or more miles?

Usually, you can restart an engine that does die out after 10 or 15 minutes, and it might not stall again for days; then again, it may stall minutes later. There seems to be no rhyme or reason to when the trouble strikes. This is a situation that baffles many technicians, because they often have trouble duplicating the stall as they test drive the car.

If this happens to you, suggest to a technician that one or more parts of the electronic ignition system may be breaking down when subjected for a particular period of time to high temperature in the engine compartment. The parts most likely to act this way are the power transistor (often called the igniter or module), pickup coil, and ignition coil.

A technician can test these components by removing them from the car and heating each, in turn, for 15 minutes in a toaster oven set at a temperature of 350°F. As each part is taken from the oven, the technician tests it with an ohmmeter. If the ohmmeter shows an infinity reading, the part is bad and has to be replaced.

- Does your engine stall or almost stall only when the engine is cold?

It's a good bet that the air control valve of the thermostatic air cleaner system is stuck. This system, which has been installed on most engines having carburetors and throttle body fuel injection systems since 1971, is frequently overlooked as a cause of engine stalling.

To check the system, a technician will make sure the engine is cold and disconnect the duct from the opening of the air cleaner snorkel, if there is a duct attached. A beam of light from a flashlight will be shone into the snorkel. (See Figure 3.6).

The snorkel opening should be blocked by the air control valve. When the engine is started, the air control valve should begin to open and be wide open in two or three minutes. If the system isn't working this way, the technician should test the temperature sensor and vacuum motor which control air valve functioning. One or both are probably defective.

Another possible reason for stalling or almost stalling only when the engine is cold is a manifold heat control valve that isn't working. This valve is inside the exhaust manifold of some cars. Like the automatic choke and thermostatic air cleaner valves, it controls the passage of cool and heated air into the engine.

- Does the engine stall or almost stall when the engine is cold or warm, no matter what the ambient temperature?

    In the case of a cold engine, the reason could be an exhaust gas recirculation (EGR) system that isn't working properly. In the case of a warm engine, the reason could be a malfunction with the positive crankcase ventilation (PCV) system.

    A breakdown in either system upsets the delicately balanced air and gasoline mixture. Have a technician test them.

- Does the engine stall only when it's hot and the ambient temperature is above 85°F?

    A likely reason is vapor lock or percolation, which are two different conditions. With vapor lock, heat causes gasoline to foam in the fuel line and not reach the engine, which dies from lack of fuel. With percolation, heat causes gasoline to overflow from the carburetor into the engine. This causes the engine to flood and stall.

    With vapor lock, the engine won't restart until foam dissipates, which occurs after the engine cools for 20 to 30 minutes. With percolation, the engine can be restarted almost immediately by pressing the accelerator pedal to the floor and keeping it down as you turn the ignition switch.

    Vapor lock and percolation are more likely to occur in engines having carburetors—not in those with fuel injection systems. A technician can insulate fuel lines with insulating foam tape and install a thicker gasket under the carburetor to raise it off the hot engine. These measures help reduce the heat leveled at parts that handle the delivery of gasoline to the engine.

- Does the engine have over 50,000 miles and only recently started to stall or hesitate? Here's what to ask your technician:

  - Is it likely that a weak fuel pump can be causing the trouble? If so, wouldn't it be a good idea to make fuel pump pressure, vacuum, and volume tests?

  - Shouldn't you check ignition wires to see if they're cracked or have developed excessive resistance?

  - What's the chance of a dirty fuel filter or a dirty carburetor being at the root of this trouble? Let's replace the filter and try a can or two of carburetor solvent before going to the expense of replacing the carburetor.

- **Does the engine hesitate as you accelerate?**
  This condition has the following causes:

  - **A vacuum leak because of a disconnected or damaged vacuum hose.**

  - **A vacuum leak because of a bad gasket between the carburetor and intake manifold.**

  - **A carburetor float that's sprung a leak or isn't adjusted correctly. A bad float may also cause the engine to stall as the car turns corners.**

  - **A bad accelerator pump. The accelerator pump is the part in the carburetor that shoots an extra squirt of gasoline into the cylinders as the engine is accelerated quickly to give it the extra fuel it needs.**

  - **A part of the electronic engine control system, such as the throttle position switch, that isn't working properly.**

FIGURE 3.5. Inspect the air filter of a carburetor or fuel injection system frequently. If it becomes clogged with dirt, stalling will result and the engine will begin to consume more gasoline than it should.

FIGURE 3.6.   If the air cleaner on the engine of your vehicle looks like this, with a snorkel (arrow), it is a thermostatic air cleaner. If one of the parts that comprise the system isn't working, stalling will occur either when the engine is cold or when the engine is warm, but not both times. (Courtesy of Chrysler Corporation)

the temperature of the coolant, which is causing a rise in the engine temperature gauge reading.

DANGEROUS STALL

The engine in my car has been stalling under conditions that are putting us in danger. A few times, for example, the engine has died while the car was descending a steep hill. The service manager at the dealership where I bought the car has cleaned the throttle valve, replaced the fuel filter, installed new spark plugs, and checked engine performance on an analyzer. He says as long as the engine runs okay when he has the car, there's no way for him to track down the cause of the trouble. Can you help, please? The car is equipped with an electronic fuel-injection system.

Ask the dealer to have a technician troubleshoot the engine using the step-by-step procedures outlined in the "Driveability and Emissions" section of the service manual. Many of the malfunctions that result in an intermittent stalling condition, which these troubleshooting tests are designed to reveal, don't show up on an engine analyzer. They include a faulty positive crankcase ventilation (PCV) valve, exhaust gas recirculation (EGR) valve, and catalytic converter.

If the technician runs into a dead end, he should refer to the index of technical service bulletins to determine if the manufacturer has issued a service advisory relating to this problem. For example, if your car is a General Motors model, such a service advisory might call for installing a different Programmable Ready-Only Memory (PROM) in the electronic control module of the engine computer control system. PROM is the GM name for the computer programmer that calibrates the electronic engine control system to the engine.

COMBATING SUDDEN ENGINE STALL

I'm concerned because the engine in my car stalls occasionally without any warning. This has happened in traffic, as I've slowed down to exit or get on an interstate highway, and even while cruising along. One of these days someone is going to smack into me. Since the trouble doesn't happen all the time, the dealer hasn't been able to find the cause. Can you suggest something?

The cause of an intermittent sudden stall can usually be traced to the engine's electrical system. A technician should inspect both ends of each ground cable for cleanliness and tightness. There is one ground cable connected from the engine to the body and another from the battery to the engine. The technician should also pull apart every electrical connector and check for bent and corroded terminals. Then, it should be determined if insulation has been rubbed off an ignition system wire. If vibration is causing a bare wire to hit against a metal part, a short circuit will be created that will make the engine stall.

Other causes of sudden engine stall are outlined on pages 66 to 69.

ENGINE DIES ON THE ROAD

The V8 engine of my older car has had the same problem almost from the day I bought it. While driving along, the

engine will suddenly come to an abrupt stop as if the ignition were turned off. This knocks out the power steering and brake systems and forces me to struggle to steer the car to the shoulder of the road and bring it to a stop. Surprisingly, the engine restarts almost at once. The trouble is intermittent. Sometimes it won't happen for several weeks; other times, it occurs several times in a couple of miles. Your suggestions would be appreciated.

The trouble undoubtedly lies in the electronic ignition system—probably with the connector between the distributor and the electronic control unit. This connector can build up resistance. When it does, the connection between the distributor and electronic control unit can be disrupted if there's a vibration, as there would be as the car rolls along the road. When the connection is disrupted, stalling occurs. The vibration as you bring the car to a stop probably restores the contact, which is why the engine always restarts.

Have a technician replace the connector. If the problem is still with you after that, look for a problem with one of the electrical grounds the car possesses. There are two—the battery ground cable between the battery and engine and the body ground strap between the engine and body. These must be clean and tight to maintain the car's electrical service to the engine.

WATERED-DOWN IGNITION MODULE CAUSES STALLING

When the engine in my car started to stall six months after I took delivery of the car from a new car dealer, the technician in the dealer's service department told me moisture had gotten into and ruined the ignition module. So he installed a new one. That was three new modules ago. What's the reason for this excessive moisture buildup that's destroying modules?

Has the technician ever sealed the upper mounting holes and edges of the ignition module with silicone caulk? That's the way moisture generally gets into and damages this part.

ENGINE STALLS WHEN STARTED

The six-cylinder engine of my one-year-old car, which is equipped with electronic fuel injection, starts right up in the morning. But then it stalls when I put the transmission in gear. It will do this once or twice before it finally catches, then runs fine the rest of the day. The dealer has tried his hand at a repair several times, but the only part he's replaced has been the fuel filter. He states that no service advisory about this condition has been issued by the manufacturer. Can you help?

If the dealer's service department followed the troubleshooting procedure to uncover the cause of this problem as outlined in the service manual, the following possibilities were checked: leakage of air into the intake manifold because of a loose or leaking air duct between the mass air flow (MAF) sensor and throttle body, a vacuum leak, loose electrical connectors at the ignition coil and MAF sensor, incorrect engine idling speed, loss of fuel pressure when the engine is cold, and a damaged exhaust gas recirculation (EGR) valve or loose EGR transfer tube.

Once these areas have been inspected, the service department should establish whether engine idling speed is faster than normal for the first couple of minutes after a cold start. The engine computer is supposed to set idling speed at a higher rate until the engine gets a littler warm, then the computer allows the engine to throttle down. Lack of this higher idling speed may mean that the idle air control valve is malfunctioning or the computer has to be reprogrammed. Concerning the latter, the dealer should call the manufacturer's technical service department to determine if a different computer programmer has been issued for your car.

STALLING IN THE CLUTCH

What would cause the engine in my late model car to stall as I depress the clutch pedal in order to shift to a higher gear? The new car dealer's service department has failed in its attempts at fixing the problem.

Check the performance of the idle speed control (ISC). This you can do yourself. As its name implies, the ISC controls engine idling. If it's not adjusted properly, it will cause the trouble you're having.

Important: In doing the test described here, the power steering and power brake systems will become inoperative if the engine stalls. If this happens, press the clutch all the way to the floor and restart the engine as quickly as you can. Perform the test on a road that has little traffic. If you don't feel comfortable doing this test yourself, have a technician do it for you.

To test the ISC, which is also called the automatic idling speed device or some other name that's similar, depress the clutch pedal as you're driving along. As you do, also press down on the accelerator pedal just a little to give the engine a bit more gas. If the engine does *not* stall, the ISC *is* the reason for your problem. Have a technician adjust its setting to the specification given in the service manual or have a new ISC installed.

If the engine does stall during the test, then the reason for your problem may be that the movement of the clutch pedal is causing a short circuit in a component that has a bearing on the engine's ignition circuit. The fault may lie with a defective clutch switch. It could also be caused by an ignition wire whose insulation has been rubbed off, leaving the wire bare. This results in a short circuit whenever the wire comes into contact with the clutch pedal assembly. Ask a technician to look for that bare wire and wrap electrician's tape around it. The technician should then move the harness away from the clutch pedal and secure it with a tie so it doesn't return to its original position.

ENGINE STALLS ONLY WITH AIR CONDITIONER ON

The four-cylinder engine in my late model car stalls or almost stalls only when I turn on the air conditioner. The new car dealer's service department hasn't been able to find out why it does this. What do you think?

The idle speed control (ISC) or its electrical circuit is probably causing the trouble. A technician should test the ISC and electrical circuit using procedures advised by the manufacturer in the service manual. If the ISC and electrical circuit pass the test, then the programmer for the engine computer or the computer itself will probably have to be replaced to stop this air conditioner-induced stalling problem.

CARBURETOR ICING CAUSES THIS ENGINE TO DIE-OUT

Why does my car start to get so sluggish while rolling along until the engine is on the verge of dying out unless I pull to the side of the road where idling for awhile restores its energy? The trouble is cold-weather related. During warm weather, it doesn't do this. I've replaced spark plugs, fuel filters, and carburetor air filters, and have had the engine analyzed. It's been pronounced fit. What are we missing?

Maybe fuel line frosting or a condition called carburetor icing. Have you tried adding a fuel system de-icer to the gasoline in the fuel tank? If the condition is fuel line frosting, it should help.

Carburetor icing, on the other hand, is immune to fuel system de-icer. This condition occurs when condensation turns to frost in the carburetor throat, blocking the flow of fuel to the engine. Manufacturers of vehicles having problems with carburetor icing usually issue service advisories and parts to counteract the trouble. Discuss this with a dealer who sells your make of vehicle.

STALLS WHEN GOING AROUND CORNERS

Can you tell me why my carburetor-equipped engine stalls whenever the car goes around corners or negotiates very sharp curves?

Because there isn't enough gasoline in the carburetor float bowl to keep it going—

that's why. Gasoline in the bowl flows away from the inlet valve because of the tilt of the car while negotiating a corner or sharp curve. Gas is then prevented from flowing through this inlet valve to the carburetor venturi, and from there to the engine. The engine is thus literally left gasless for a moment, so it stalls. The starvation can also occur when a car is brought to an abrupt halt at stop signs and traffic lights.

Ask a technician to raise the level of the carburetor float, which will let more gasoline into the bowl and keep an ample amount of gasoline at the inlet valve during the tilt encountered going around a corner or sharp curve. Also, have the technician check the engine idle speed adjustment to make sure it's in line with the manufacturer's specification.

ENGINE STALLS ONLY WHEN BRAKING

Can you tell me why the V8 engine (with carburetor) in my car stalls only when I apply the brakes? I think it's a fuel starvation condition. Am I right?

I don't agree unless every application of the brake is for a panic stop. If the engine were starving for gas, it would stall all the time—not just when you apply the brakes normally. On the slim chance that you're right, however, make sure the carburetor float is adjusted to specification.

I believe, however, that you're probably dealing with a cracked diaphragm inside the brake power booster. As you apply the brake, the diaphragm leaks vacuum supplied by the engine, which causes a drop in engine power. This, in turn, causes the engine stall.

Have a vacuum test made of the booster. If it won't pass, the solution then would be to replace the booster.

ENGINE QUITS ONLY IN THE RAIN

The engine in my car quits and leaves me stranded when it rains. The dealer has worked on it several times, but has failed to resolve the problem. I would appreciate your help.

Here's what I suggest you have done:

- Inspect the distributor cap, rotor, ignition coil, and distributor pick-up connection for damage.
- Make sure there's a shield over the distributor to protect ignition parts from splash. If one of these parts gets wet, the ignition system can cut-out and the engine will stall.

BLACK EXHAUST INDICATES ENGINE FLOODING

The engine in my car is equipped with a 3-liter engine and electronic fuel injection. It has been driven only 9,000 miles. During that period, it's demonstrated two problems that may be related. First, while driving under 10 mph, engine power drops to 400 revolutions per minute (rpm). If I continue driving at this low speed for long, the engine stalls. Second, after driving the car and parking for awhile, it takes a long period of cranking to get it to restart. As it starts, a puff of black smoke comes out the tailpipe.

The dealer has replaced the engine computer, cleaned the throttle body, set the minimum air rate to specification, adjusted the throttle position sensor, replaced the exhaust gas recirculation valve, and replaced the idle air control and fuel pressure regulator. He is willing to do anything that will solve this problem, but he's at a loss to know what. Do you have any suggestions?

There is obviously something wrong with the way this engine is set up. The tip-off is the fact that it should show a minimum of 600 rpm when the car is moving at low speed. The reason it's not performing as it should is because of too much gasoline in the fuel mixture that's causing the engine to flood. This is indicated by that puff of black smoke.

There are several reasons why an engine having electronic fuel injection system as yours will develop an overrich condition. The dealer has checked some. Others he should look for are a malfunctioning mass air flow sensor, a carbon-coated oxygen (O_2) sensor, a restricted fuel-return line, and a defective crank angle sensor.

THE INEXPENSIVE WAY TO FIX FUEL INJECTORS

I'm the second owner of a pickup truck (22,000 miles) that's equipped with a fuel-injected V8 engine. It hesitates upon acceleration and idles roughly. I've spent a small fortune making compression, fuel-pressure, and fuel pump tests, and installing new spark plugs, cables, distributor cap, and rotor. The fuel injectors have been cleaned twice. Now a dealer is telling me that the fuel injectors should be removed and tested by a special laboratory to see if they are functioning properly. This will cost me another $150. I'd gladly spend it if I knew it would help. What's your opinion?

Fuel injectors don't have to be removed from an engine to be tested. If the dealer doesn't have a fuel-injector balance tester, which allows fuel injectors to be tested with them installed in the engine, take the truck to a dealer who does use this equipment. (See Figure 3.7.)

That's the first piece of good news. The second is that testing, servicing, or replacing fuel injectors are repairs that come under the five year or 50,000 mile (whichever occurs first) emissions control systems warranty. This warranty is passed on from one owner of a vehicle to another owner as long as the warranty period is in effect. It's important to read and become familiar with the provisions of this warranty. They can save you hundreds of dollars for repairs that are the responsibility of the vehicle manufacturer. If you don't have a copy of the warranty for your model car, write the customer service department of the manufacturer and ask for one.

Incidentally, another reason for the trouble you're having with your pickup truck could be a dirty throttle body. Ask the dealer to clean the bore and plate. He should also look for a vacuum leak between the throttle body and intake manifold. These services should be done before fuel injectors are tested.

UNCOVERING THE CAUSE OF ENGINE HESITATION

The engine of my car displays a significant lag when I attempt to accelerate from a speed of between 30 and 40 mph. This occurs whether the engine is cold or warm. The dealer has checked the carburetor, ignition timing, and exhaust system and claims there's nothing more to do. He calls the condition "hesitation on acceleration." I hope you can come up with an answer to this problem.

Maybe one of the following suggestions will help:

- Ask the dealer to road-test the car with the vacuum supply to the exhaust gas recirculation (EGR) valve disconnected. If hesitation is not experienced during the test, the EGR valve is the reason for the condition. It should be cleaned, if possible, or replaced.

- The carburetor may not be responding to the demand of the engine for more fuel as the car is being accelerated. A momentary lean-fuel condition is often the result of a defective accelerator pump or power enrichment device inside the carburetor. The condition can also be caused if the cable from the accelerator pedal to the carburetor is catching as you attempt to accelerate the car.

- If your car is equipped with an automatic transmission, the reason for the hesitation may lie with the transmission and not the engine. A transmission repair may be necessary. It's a good bet that the repair will be to the transmission valve body, but the technician should refer to the service manual for guidance.

A more complete rundown of the reasons for engine hesitation is provided on pages 66 to 69.

FIXING A HESITATING COLD ENGINE

My car hesitates on acceleration only when the engine is cold. The dealer hasn't helped and denies the existence of any applicable service advisory. I hope you can offer a solution. The car is equipped with a carburetor and manual transmission.

FIGURE 3.7. An instrument called a fuel injector balance tester, plus a pressure gauge, is all a technician needs to establish if fuel injectors are performing properly without having to remove each injector from the engine.

The first thought that pops into mind is that the thermostatic air cleaner system has a damaged part. This system uses a plate in an air-intake duct leading to the carburetor to close off the influx of cold air to a cold engine so the engine will get a fuel mixture to burn that is at a suitable temperature. A tear in the accordion-like air-intake duct might be allowing cold air to disrupt the fuel ratio. A technician should spread apart each of the folds of the duct to look for this. Until the engine warms up, this air is supposed to come from the exhaust manifold, which gets hot almost at once when a cold engine is started.

The thermostatic air cleaner system also has a temperature sensor and vacuum motor that controls the plate. If one of these parts is faulty, the plate could be stuck in "open-air" position, which means that cold air will be delivered to a cold engine. This will cause the engine to hesitate until it warms up.

An inoperative or sluggish automatic choke, EGR valve, dirty throttle linkage, inoperative fast-idle cam, and/or malfunction in the ignition timing control system are other causes of hesitation with a cold engine.

HESITATION IN TRAFFIC

At times, but only in stop-and-go traffic, the engine in my car hesitates and hops as if it were starving for gas. It's been this way since I got the car. I've been told that the problem can't be fixed. Do you have any suggestions that I can try?

The facts that the condition happens at times and only during stop-and-go driving are significant. When the fuel supply is less than $1/4$ of a tank, gasoline can slosh away from the fuel pickup in the fuel tank as you apply the brakes. This can cause a momentary period of fuel starvation, which you feel as a flat spot or hesitation in engine performance. Keep the fuel tank more than $1/4$ filled to determine if doing so resolves the problem.

WHY FUEL-INJECTED ENGINES CAN LOSE POWER

Lately, the engine in my car has been losing power. The SERVICE ENGINE light comes on, and the engine acts as if it's not getting enough gas. A technician tapped into the engine electronic control system and could find no trouble codes. What else should we be looking for? The engine is equipped with electronic fuel injection.

Here are several possibilities that won't show up as trouble codes:

- Carbon inside boots that cover the spark plugs. Carbon, a conductor, diverts current away from the firing tips of spark plugs. When this happens, no spark is available to ignite the fuel mixture in the particular cylinder, and a loss of power results. If carbon is found, cables should be replaced and spark plugs inspected for damage. Carbon occurs when a technician who works on an engine fails to press the boots on the ends of cables on to spark plugs securely enough.

- A clogged air filter, restricted exhaust system, or plugged catalytic converter. If the catalytic converter has to be replaced, the repair is covered by the five-year/50,000-mile (whichever occurs first) emissions control system warranty.

- A reduction in fuel system pressure because of a weak fuel pump or fuel pressure regulator. (See Figure 3.8.) The technician should test the fuel injection system with a pressure gauge to make sure pressure is as specified in the service manual (see below).

- Under-the-hood insulation pad that comes loose so it falls over the air intake to the fuel system. To fix this, that section of pad that's directly over the air intake should be cut away.

FUEL-INJECTED ENGINE LACKS POWER

The fuel-injected engine in my pickup truck has become positively gutless. On a hill, I have to floor the accelerator pedal to get over the top, just barely. Yet, the engine starts easily, idles perfectly, and runs well on straight-aways. Can you suggest something that could account for this lifelessness? It wasn't this way for two years after I bought the truck.

Have the exhaust system checked for a clogged or crushed exhaust system pipe or a clogged muffler. A restriction in the catalytic converter can also cause lack of power.

If the exhaust system and catalytic converter are given a clean bill of health, consider the possibility of a contaminated fuel injector. Buy a fuel injector cleaner from a dealer who sells your make of vehicle to make certain the cleaner is recommended for that vehicle and, indeed, if the manufacturer recommends cleaning fuel injectors in your engine with a "canned" product. Some brands of fuel injector cleaners not bearing the name of the vehicle manufacturer can damage fuel injectors. Try a container or two of the cleaner, following the instructions printed on the container.

If this doesn't help, have a technician test the fuel delivery parts of the fuel injection system with a fuel system pressure gauge. The cause of the problem may be in the fuel tank with the fuel pump or fuel pickup filter (called a fuel sock), or with a restricted fuel delivery line, dirty fuel filter, or fuel pressure regulator which is not responding to the engine's demand for fuel under the load imposed when going up hills.

If fuel delivery components get a clean bill of health, the technician should concentrate on the fuel injectors. They may need a more powerful cleaning agent than that provided by the cleaner mentioned above. The technician will use a special tool that injects cleaning agent under pressure through the injectors. (See Figure 3.9.) If this procedure doesn't work, what remains to be done is to determine if a fuel injector is breaking down and not supplying sufficient fuel needed by the engine as your pickup truck negotiates a hill. This test is done with a fuel injector balance instrument. An injector that doesn't pass the test is faulty and should be replaced.

Let's suppose the mechanical parts of the fuel injection system pass all tests with flying colors. Then, an electronic part of the system, such as the throttle position sensor or mass air flow sensor, may be at fault. Testing these should be done by the book. The "book" in this case is the service manual issued by the manufacturer for the vehicle.

REPAIRING A PEPLESS CARBURETOR-EQUIPPED ENGINE

The engine in my 10-year minivan has seen 109,000 miles of service without giving me a problem until now. On slight inclines, it loses enough power to

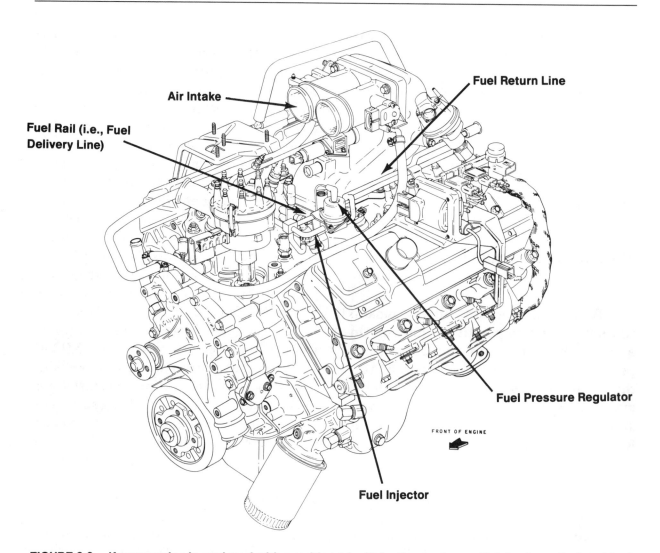

Air Intake

Fuel Return Line

Fuel Rail (i.e., Fuel Delivery Line)

Fuel Pressure Regulator

FRONT OF ENGINE

Fuel Injector

FIGURE 3.8. If your engine is equipped with a multiport fuel injection system, which is also called port fuel injection or multipoint fuel injection, the system is characterized by one fuel injector serving each cylinder of an engine. Therefore, a six-cylinder engine has six fuel injectors—an eight-cylinder engine has eight. (Courtesy of Ford Motor Company)

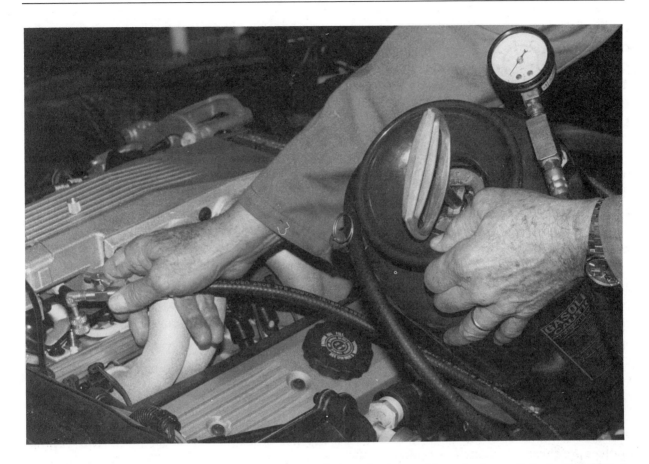

FIGURE 3.9. Force-feeding cleaner through fuel injectors is done with an instrument that resembles a container used for spraying insecticide. The procedure is done by attaching the instrument's hose to the test fitting on the fuel rail and pumping the cleaner through the rail into the fuel injectors.

cause the transmission to shift out of overdrive. Also, when attempting to accelerate, there's a noticeable dead spot. The fuel and ignition systems, including the carburetor, check out okay. What's the reason for this sluggishness?

Wear and a buildup of carbon are probably making this engine unable to handle even light loads. Slight inclines and acceleration on straight roads are considered light loads. This is something to expect with a high mileage engine.

You can usually find out how badly parts are worn by having a technician do a compression test. Spark plugs are removed and the compression tester is inserted into each spark plug port, in turn, as the engine is cranked. Results are checked against the compression specification for the engine that's given in the service manual.

If the compression test shows that the engine has just about bought the farm, your choices are these: (1) Continue operating the minivan this way until the engine finally dies and trade-in or scrap the vehicle; (2) try to regain some power; (3) do an engine overhaul now; (4) sell the vehicle.

Only option No. 2 requires discussion, but be aware that it's a temporary measure that may help if carbon and sludge are contributing factors. Buy a couple of cans of engine carbon solvent from a dealer or auto parts store. A quality product that does a good job is GM Top Engine Cleaner®, which you can get at a General Motors dealership.

Whoever does the job should follow this procedure:

1. Run the engine 15 minutes to get it warm.
2. Disconnect the air injection reaction (AIR) system from the catalytic converter.
3. With the engine running at idle, *slowly* pour half a can of the carbon solvent down the throat of the carburetor. Wait 15 seconds; then pour in the rest of the solvent at a rate rapid enough to get the engine to stall.
4. Turn off the ignition and let the vehicle sit idle for at least six hours.
5. Start the engine and let it run at idle for 15 minutes.
6. After the idling period, have someone press the accelerator pedal about halfway to the floor so the engine is running rapidly as you pour all of another can of carbon solvent into the carburetor. Do this slowly so the engine won't stall.
7. Reconnect the air system.
8. Test the result by going for a drive.

Caution: The one doing this procedure should remember to follow these safety rules when working on a car with the engine running:

- Have the car on a level surface so it won't roll.
- Keep an automatic transmission in PARK or a manual transmission in NEUTRAL.
- Have the parking brake firmly engaged.
- Keep hands away from revolving parts.
- Don't wear loose clothing that can get snarled in drive belts or a belt pulley.

COUNTERACTING A SHARP INCREASE IN FUEL USE

Why have I experienced a 20 to 25 percent fuel economy loss with my car, which is equipped with a fuel injection system? I've gone the usual tune-up

route without any positive results. The dealer has checked for applicable technical service bulletins and has found none. Other than for this, the engine performs flawlessly. What's going on?

This sharp drop in fuel economy in the absence of an engine performance problem, such as misfire or rough idling, is usually the result of a fuel injector that's staying partially open all the time. Fuel injectors are supposed to open and close alternately. If dirt or a damaged part is keeping a fuel injector open when it's supposed to close, gasoline not needed by the engine will drip into the cylinder and be burned.

A technician will be able to check this probability by connecting a fuel injection system diagnostic tester to the engine, but first you may want to try to resolve the problem yourself by adding fuel injector cleaner to the fuel tank. You can buy this product at a service station or from the dealer. Following instructions on the container, try two or three treatments before handing the car over to a technician.

If the technician verifies that a fuel injector is indeed staying open, an apparatus that force-feeds cleaning agent into the fuel injectors should be used. This will work if dirt in the injector is keeping the injector open. But if the results are less than satisfactory, indicating that a damaged rather than dirty fuel injector is causing the fuel loss, the fuel injector should be replaced.

Important: Some auto manufacturers don't want you to use a canned fuel injector cleaner in some engines. The fuel injectors in these engines are designed so they cannot be clogged by dirt. Furthermore, these manufacturers claim that a fuel injector cleaner may damage the fuel injectors. Before using

a cleaner, therefore, check with a dealer who sells your make of car to determine if you should.

STOPPING BACKFIRE

I drive an excellent running American-made car that gives good fuel mileage. My only complaint involves a backfire, which occurs once a day like clockwork after the engine is started for the first time and the car has been driven a mile or two. Can you explain what's causing this? The engine has a carburetor.

Let's make certain that you and I interpret the term "backfire" the same way. A backfire is ignition of fuel in the intake manifold, resulting in a subdued explosion that belches back through the carburetor. The noise, therefore, comes from the engine compartment. This is in contrast to an explosion that takes place in the exhaust system, and which is expelled from the tailpipe, that many drivers erroneously call "backfire." The correct term for this condition is "muffler explosion." A muffler explosion occurs when exhaust, which is unburned fuel, is ignited.

There are several causes of backfire and muffler explosion that are common to both conditions. They include an engine vacuum leak, worn distributor, incorrect ignition timing, dirty or worn carburetor, or worn parts in the intake or exhaust valve train. I have to discount these, because if one of them existed, the backfire or muffler explosion would occur more frequently than once a day.

In your case if the condition is a backfire, have a technician look for gasoline leaking down through the carburetor into the engine because of a worn needle valve or high float level, a defective positive crankcase ventilation (PCV) valve, or malfunctioning exhaust gas recirculation (EGR) valve. If the explosion is out the tailpipe, the technician should look for a sluggish air valve inside the snorkel of the carburetor air cleaner and a faulty air pump diverter valve of the air injection reaction system.

REPAIRS FOR A ROUGH-RUNNING FUEL-INJECTED ENGINE

I own a car with a fuel-injected four-cylinder engine and an automatic transmission. My problem is rough running just after the engine is started. Although operation smoothes out as speed increases, when I let up on the accelerator pedal or bring the car to a stop, the jerkiness resumes. Occasionally, the engine will stall. I've had different technicians try their hand at a repair, but without luck. Can you suggest a solution?

Here are three procedures that may help:

1. Check the engine for a vacuum leak. Most cases involving a rough running engine such as yours have this as the cause.
2. Test the manifold absolute pressure (MAP) sensor, which is a member of the engine electronic control system. If the MAP sensor in your car is being affected by moisture, there will be a disruption in the signal sent by the sensor to the computer. The computer controls the amount of fuel delivered to the engine. If the signal is in error, the amount of fuel delivered to the engine will be thrown off and cause the engine to run rough at slower speeds. The technician should inspect and test the MAP sensor according to the procedure outlined in the service manual

and in any applicable manufacturer service advisories.

3. Make certain the engine idling speed is correctly set according to the latest information from the manufacturer. If the technician uses outdated information, the setting will not be brought into proper adjustment. The correct specification may not be the one on the vehicle emissions control information decal in the engine compartment or even the one in the service manual. It could have been revised by a service advisory. The technician should get in touch with the technical assistance department of the manufacturer to find out if a revision exists.

SMOOTHING OUT A BUCKING ENGINE

My carburetor-equipped engine doesn't run right when the ambient temperature is below 32°F. I use the starting procedure precisely as given in the owner's manual, and the engine does start right up. But when I shift into first gear and engage the clutch to get going, the engine bucks and nearly cuts off. This keeps happening until the engine gets warm. Then it runs fine. The trouble never happens when the temperature is above 32°F. What's wrong?

One of the following is probably causing this problem:

• Water in the fuel system that is turning to ice in cold weather and blocking the flow of gas to the engine. On the chance that this is happening, try a container of fuel system de-icer before going on to the other possibilities. The de-icer is added to gasoline in the fuel tank as directed by instructions on the container. The product is available at service stations and in auto departments of retail stores.

- The automatic choke system to include the choke unloader, which is supposed to open the choke valve and prevent an overly rich fuel mixture that can cause the engine to buck.
- The cold-mix heater, which if present on the engine is in the intake manifold near the carburetor primary venturi tube. If working properly, it will heat the fuel charge before fuel enters the cylinders.
- The heat-control valve in the exhaust manifold, which is supposed to be open when the engine is cold to divert hot exhaust to the engine. If the valve is stuck in the closed position so hot exhaust gas passes through the exhaust system instead of going to the engine, a cold engine will buck.
- Vacuum hoses, vacuum components, and the carburetor-intake manifold joint for a vacuum leak.

ENGINE MISSES ONLY WHEN IT RAINS, PART I

The six-cylinder engine in my pickup truck has a miss when traveling at speeds below 30 mph in rainy weather. Other times it runs great. No technician has been able to uncover the cause. Can you help?

An engine miss is a steady pulsation or jerking that is usually accompanied by a sputtering from the exhaust system. The fact that your problem occurs only in rainy weather points to an ignition system component that is being affected by moisture. The wet component breaks down, preventing the spark plug serving a particular cylinder from firing. The cylinder is said to be misfiring,

which causes the engine to run poorly and more fuel than normal to be consumed.

To pinpoint the faulty component, a technician should have someone sitting in the truck speed up the engine to a level that's equal to 20 to 30 mph. The technician should spray one ignition part at a time with water to see at what point in the spraying operation the engine begins to falter. This procedure pinpoints the part which, when sprayed, brings on the miss.

Parts that should be sprayed are each spark plug cable, each spark plug boot, the distributor cap, and the ignition coil. If this test fails to reveal the reason for misfire, the technician should examine spark plugs and then pull apart every electrical connector in the engine compartment to find any that are corroded or damaged.

ENGINE MISSES ONLY WHEN IT RAINS, PART II

I have a terrible problem with my car when it rains. The engine misses so badly that the car is almost impossible to drive. Two technicians have told me that they can't find a thing wrong with it. The engine has been tuned up, and fuel, ignition, and emissions control parts check out perfectly. Ironically, the trouble started after a tune-up. Can you help me, please?

The fact that the problem began after you had the engine tuned is significant. Perhaps in checking ignition timing the technician used a timing light that requires piercing of a spark plug cable. The point is that if a spark plug cable is mishandled, the damage that results will provide an alternate path for current that is supposed to flow unimpeded to a spark plug. This current would be diverted to ground. In other words, current won't reach the spark plug, the plug won't fire to ignite the fuel mixture, and the engine will miss as badly as yours seems to be missing.

But why only in rainy weather? In your case, the puncture in the cable may be minor and leakage may be nonexistent in dry weather. Therefore, there is no effect on engine performance. In rainy weather, moisture acts as a conductor attracting electricity—literally drawing it out of the cable. Therefore, current leakage occurs even though damage to the cable is slight.

Ask a technician to start the engine and wet down each spark plug cable in turn, to determine if missing occurs. If so, the particular cable which the technician wet down just before the engine began to falter should be replaced.

COLD-ENGINE MISSING AT LOW SPEEDS

The four-cylinder engine in my car hops and almost stalls while driving at low speeds when the engine is cold. Sometimes the SERVICE ENGINE light flashes. Once the engine warms up, however, the trouble disappears and the light doesn't come on. Please tell me what's causing this problem. The engine is equipped with a fuel injection system.

Have a technician tap into the computer with a scanner to retrieve any trouble code being stored. This will usually reveal which circuit and/or sensor of the engine electronic control system is causing a problem. Most vehicles with this control system are equipped with receptacles into which scanners are plugged. In General Motors cars, for instance, the receptacle is located under the dash and is called an assembly line data link (ALDL).

A section in the service manual will interpret any numerical codes the scanner displays. It's then a matter of the technician testing the particular circuit or sensor to verify the finding and making the repair.

If no trouble code is forthcoming when the technician taps into the computer, the cause of missing until an engine warms up usually is centered with the early fuel evaporation (EFE) system or the exhaust gas recirculation (EGR) system.

TURNED-OFF ENGINE KEEPS RUNNING ON

Every so often the engine in my car keeps on running and knocking for a few seconds after I turn off the ignition switch. This is accompanied by a heavy exhaust odor. Please suggest a solution before the engine sustains severe damage.

Relax. The condition, which is called dieseling or engine run-on, will not harm the engine. To some, however, it's frightening; to others, annoying. Dieseling also contributes to air pollution, so let me explain what you can do to stop it.

If your engine is equipped with a nonelectronic carburetor, a technician should clean the moving parts of the carburetor, automatic choke, and throttle linkage. Then, the technician should make certain that the engine idling speed and ignition timing are set to the specifications given in the service manual. Next, the technician should make sure the engine isn't running at a higher-than-normal temperature because of a low coolant level, inoperative cooling fan, or a radiator that's restricted. Have a part called the idle-stop solenoid, which is on the carburetor, replaced. Then, have engine cleaner added to the engine to dissolve carbon.

If the carburetor is electronically controlled, the technician should tap into the electronic control module for any stored codes revealing a troublesome component. One part that is frequently to blame is the idle speed control. The technician should then make sure the engine isn't running at a higher-than-normal temperature because of a low coolant level, inoperative cooling fan, or a radiator that's restricted. Finally, you can have a container or two of cleaner added to the engine to purge carbon from inside the engine.

Suppose your dieseling engine is equipped with a fuel injection system rather than a carburetor. Then, the reason for the problem would be incorrect ignition timing, a malfunctioning idle speed control motor, higher-than-normal engine temperature, carbon inside the engine, or a restricted fuel-return line between the fuel injectors and fuel tank.

Whether the engine has a carburetor or fuel injection system, there is one step you can take to keep it from dieseling until the reason for the trouble is found and corrected. Turn off the ignition switch with the automatic transmission still in DRIVE. If the car has a manual transmission, prevent dieseling by letting out the clutch with the transmission in gear so the engine stalls. Whatever kind of transmission you're dealing with, keep your foot planted firmly on the brake pedal if you use this antidieseling shut-off procedure.

SURGERY FOR SURGING

My car is equipped with a four-cylinder fuel-injected engine and a five-speed manual transmission. I have a problem that has cost me almost $500 to try and get fixed. Upon starting and until warmed up, the engine will speed up; then speed will drop so low that the engine almost stalls. Technicians have used engine diagnostic machines, done tune-ups, and changed the positive crankcase ventilation (PCV) and exhaust gas recirculation (EGR) valves. They swear there's nothing more left for them to check. Can you help?

You don't mention whether the technicians who worked on the car are employed by dealers who sell your particular make of car. If not, they probably wouldn't know if the manufacturer has issued a service advisory covering this problem. Manufacturer service advisories, commonly called technical service bulletins (TSBs), are sent to dealership service departments—not to independent technicians. Therefore, independent technicians often have no idea if a new part or new service procedure has been issued to resolve a problem such as the one you're having.

An example of a TSB that deals with an engine surge like yours shows the importance of this information, for without it chances are the problem wouldn't ever have been resolved. The example concerns the 1986 General Motors 2.5-liter four-cylinder engine, which was manufactured with a shield that protects the throttle position sensor (TPS) from heat. The original heat shield installed over the TPS didn't insulate properly. Consequently, the TPS was damaged, which resulted in the type of surge you describe. The cure for the problem was to replace the damaged TPS and install a differently designed heat shield made of heat-resistant stainless steel. Since neither the original heat shield or TPS showed any sign of damage, who would know this if it weren't for the service advisory?

My advice, therefore, is this: Since the technicians you went to couldn't resolve your problem, ask the service department of a dealer who sells your make of car to determine if there's any applicable service advisories that pertain to a surging condition with the type of engine you have in your car. Car manufacturers also have technical assistance service departments that can be called by a dealer service department to help technicians working on cars solve tough problems such as this one.

ENGINE IDLING SPEED FLUCTUATES

The speed of the engine in my car alternately increases and decreases when the car is at a standstill with the automatic transmission in Drive. This produces a surging effect—that is, a jerky feeling of motion—that is also noticeable when the car is rolling at a slow speed although I'm holding my foot still on the accelerator pedal. I've consulted two technicians, who haven't been able to pinpoint the reason for this problem. Can you help? The engine has an electronic fuel injection system.

Start by making sure that spark plugs and spark plug cables are in good condition, ignition timing is set to specification, and vacuum hoses and vacuum connections are secure and not leaking. Have the air cleaner duct examined for tears and cracks, which frequently show up inside the accordion folds of the duct. They can't be spotted unless the folds of the duct are spread apart and are examined along the bottom surface of the duct, as well as along the top surface. (See Figure 3.10.)

Next, ignition wires and wire harness connectors should be inspected to make certain wires aren't cracked, connectors aren't corroded, and connectors are securely fastened.

There are four components of an electronic fuel injection system that can cause surging. They are the fuel injectors, fuel filter, idle-speed control, and the throttle position sensor.

To try and clear a dirt-clogged fuel injector that may be the reason for surging, pour a container of fuel injector cleaner into the fuel tank if the manufacturer of your car doesn't forbid the use of a fuel injector cleaner. You should, in fact, buy this cleaner from a new car dealer who sells your model to insure that the cleaner you get is compatible with the fuel injectors.

If surging continues after a cleaner is used, see what happens by replacing the fuel filter which may be clogged with dirt. (See Figure 3.11.) Next, test for a malfunctioning idle-speed control. This requires that the technician tap into the electronic engine control system to see if a trouble code is stored. A faulty idle-speed control should be replaced.

Finally, the technician should turn his attention to the throttle position sensor (TPS). The TPS translates the angle of the throttle valve opening into an electrical signal that is transmitted to the computer. If the TPS goes out of whack, the air:gas ratio will be affected. Depending upon the extent that the TPS is disrupted, the engine will surge, stall, throw out black exhaust smoke, and/or use more gasoline than normal. Again, activating the self-diagnosing capability of the computer to see if there is a trouble code will help the technician determine if the TPS is bad. If so, it has to be replaced.

FIGURE 3.10.   A tear inside an air duct that transports air to the fuel system is a devious condition that results in engine performance problems. The additional air disrupts the normal gasoline:fuel mixture. You often can't find the damage without spreading and examining each fold along the top and on the bottom.

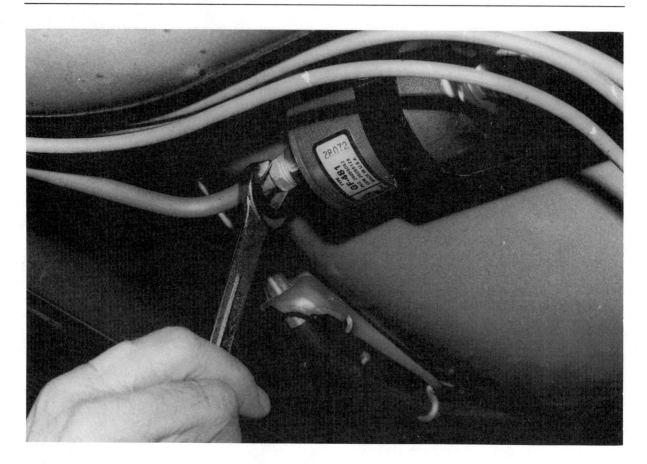

FIGURE 3.11. Whether your engine is equipped with a fuel injection system, as here, or a carburetor, replacing the fuel filter may straighten out surging.

ENGINE IDLES TOO FAST

From the first day I drove it, the engine in my new car has idled very fast even after it's warmed up. At a traffic light, the car tries to edge forward if I don't keep my foot firmly planted on the brake pedal. The dealer has failed to reduce this fast idling speed. He's even installed a new computer. What now?

Since the idling speed of your engine is controlled by a computer based on data it receives from various sensors, the cause of your problem probably lies with a malfunctioning sensor. Replacing the computer isn't going to do any good if a sensor is feeding wrong information to the computer.

In most engines, the three sensors that provide data used by the computer to control idling speed are the coolant-temperature sensor, vehicle-speed sensor, and throttle-position sensor. To pinpoint the sensor or sensors causing the problem, a technician should use the driveability test procedures issued by the manufacturer in the car's service manual.

There could be another reason for the problem other than a faulty sensor. It lies with a part called the idle speed control (ISC), which is also referred to as the automatic idle speed motor or some similar name. In addition to the computer and sensors, the ISC is a member of a team that controls engine idling speed. The sensors gather data and send it to the computer. Based on this data, the computer orders the ISC to set engine idling speed at a particular level. If the ISC isn't working properly, the speed will be at the wrong level—either too fast as in your case or too slow. In addition to testing the sensors, therefore, the technician should use the driveability test procedures provided by the manufacturer in the service manual to test the idle speed control.

Cost of the repair services associated with the parts I've mentioned are covered under the emissions control systems warranty, which is in force for five years or 50,000 miles, whichever occurs first.

WHY A SOUND ENGINE FAILS AN EMISSIONS TEST

I brought my vehicle into an inspection station for a state-mandated emissions/safety inspection. The inspector stuck the exhaust test rod up the tailpipe and flunked me, because pollutants being expelled by the engine were too high. That same day I drove by another inspection station. Because there was no one in line, I decided to have the car reinspected. It passed with flying colors. Why did one inspector flunk the car and another inspector pass it only a couple of hours later?

Assuming that both inspectors were correct in their analysis and the equipment each used was accurate, the reason lies with the temperature of the engine emissions control systems at the time of the test. To get an accurate result, emissions systems must be warmed up when a test is made. Before the first test, you may have had to wait your turn in line. According to what you say, that second test was done right after you rolled off the road into the inspection station.

Car owners who have to wait in an inspection line for a considerable length of time often fall victim to erroneous emissions system test readings. As an engine idles, the temperature of emissions control components such as the catalytic converter and oxygen sensor fall below normal although engine temperature as reflected by the temperature gauge remains at normal. The result will be an increase in exhaust emissions levels although these emissions control components are performing perfectly. One way to get the temperature of these components back to where it should be for testing is to place the transmission in PARK or NEUTRAL a few minutes before your vehicle is set to start the test and pressing the gas pedal down a little so the engine is running at fast idle.

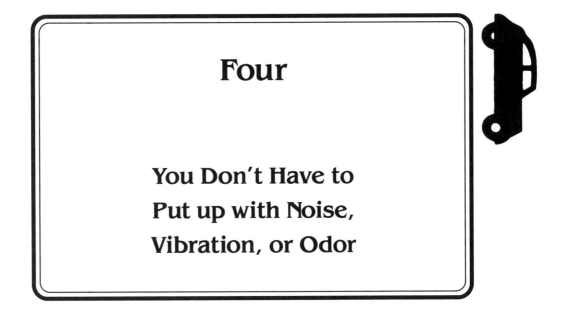

Four

You Don't Have to Put up with Noise, Vibration, or Odor

NOISE DETECTION

The V6 engine in my pickup truck has been making a loud whirring noise, similar to a fan, since the day I bought the vehicle new a year ago. The noise disappears when the engine warms up. The dealer claims it's normal, but I don't believe him. Can you tell me where you think the noise is coming from?

That's a tough question to answer, especially since I don't have the opportunity of hearing the noise. But I can tell you where it's *not* coming from, and that's from inside the engine. Internal engine parts make clicks,

ticks, bangs, slaps, and knocks when they are damaged—not a fan-type whirring sound.

If your dealer hasn't done so, he should have one of his technicians isolate the noisy part by using an automotive stethoscope. With the engine running at idle speed, the tip of the tool is placed on one part after another. When it is placed on the noisy part, the stethoscope will amplify the noise.

Chief candidates that can make a whirring sound are the alternator and power steering pump. The noise may even be coming from the electric fuel pump in the fuel tank. Since sound travels, the whirring noise a fuel pump can make may seem to be coming from the engine compartment.

Once the noisy part is isolated, you and the dealer should decide whether the sound is normal. If you can't come to a meeting of the minds, ask the dealer to call in a factory representative and let that person make the decision. The dealer has nothing to lose by replacing a part under the terms of the warranty since the cost is assumed by the manufacturer.

WHAT TO DO FOR A PINGING ENGINE

I have an old car that has been driven 124,000 miles. It's equipped with a V8 engine and four-barrel carburetor. I am now having a problem with engine ping. If I have the ignition timing set to the specification given by the manufacturer in the service manual, the engine runs great for 30 minutes. But after driving that long on a highway, the engine starts to ping when going up a hill or while cruising along the highway. I can eliminate the ping by accelerating or by letting up on the accelerator pedal. Is there a way to get rid of this noise once and for all? If not, is this a sign of impending engine failure?

If the ping is mild, it's nothing to worry about. On the other hand, if it's a heavy knock that doesn't dissipate after the car crests a hill or doesn't stop when you alter the way in which the car is being accelerated, you would have cause for concern.

In your case, the engine doesn't seem to be nearing doomsday. Still and all, here are causes of engine ping you might want to look into with the idea in mind that a repair may reduce its intensity or eliminate the ping altogether:

1. Although you may be using fuel having an octane rating specified by the manufacturer, it may not be sufficient. As an engine gets older, its octane requirements increase. Therefore, switching to a premium gasoline (92 or 93 octane) might stop the ping.

2. Check to make sure a malfunction doesn't exist that's allowing engine heat to go higher than it should without overheating actually occurring. A loose fan belt, low coolant level, inoperative thermostatic air cleaner system, and a sticking control valve associated with the fuel evaporation emissions system are examples of conditions that can cause a rise in temperature.

3. Loss of vacuum will produce an engine ping. Therefore, test the exhaust gas recirculation system for a malfunction. Also use a vacuum gauge to see if the engine is losing vacuum through a cracked or loose vacuum hose. Another spot where vacuum loss may occur is from the intake manifold-carburetor joint.

4. Although the ignition timing is set to the manufacturer's specification, a problem with components of the ignition system may be the reason for pinging. Check for a damaged diaphragm in the spark advance chamber and weakened springs that control the mechanical advance weights.

5. By this stage in its life, the engine may have accumulated carbon in one or more of the combustion chambers. If carbon gets hot enough, it can ignite the fuel mixture prematurely, which will cause pinging. Use a carbon solvent, such as GM Top Engine Cleaner® to get rid of carbon. Run the car to see if this helps to eliminate carbon and relieve pinging. If the treatment with carbon solvent

doesn't produce positive results, give it up as a lost cause.

DEALING WITH ALTERNATOR WHINE

A whining sound from the alternator of my new car is quite audible and very annoying. The alternator has been tested by the dealer's service department and given a clean bill of health. The technician told me that a whine is common and is no cause for concern. Is he telling me the truth? Should I press the dealer to replace the part while the warranty is still in effect?

The technician is probably giving it to you straight, but find out for yourself by asking the dealer to let you drive a demonstrator that has the same model alternator as your car.

Note: The alternator is also called the alternating current (AC) generator.

Go along with what the dealer says if the noise level is the same in the demonstrator as in your car, but check back with him every so often in case the manufacturer issues a service advisory that authorizes the installation of a differently designed alternator. You might also want to ask the dealer if modifying the alternator bracket would reduce the noise level. For example, placing rubber washers under the bracket bolts or wrapping insulation around the bracket will sometimes reduce the noise to an acceptable level.

RING-A-DING DING FROM UNDERNEATH

A technician who tested my pickup truck couldn't find the source of a ringing noise that seems to be coming from under the truck when the vehicle is accelerated. He claims that all exhaust and suspension parts are secure, and that the noise is not coming from the engine. Can you help us out, please?

The mounting tabs that hold together the two-part shield around the catalytic converter may be causing this problem. If tabs have cracked or broken off, a ringing noise will be produced as the two parts of the shield, now loose, vibrate. Tabs are not visible, so the condition is tough for a technician to find.

The technician can test this theory without taking the shield apart by wrapping two large worm-type clamps around the shield to secure the halves together. If a road test reveals that the noise no longer exists, you can have the shield replaced or keep the two parts of the shield tightened together by leaving the clamps where they are. If the noise is present during the test, a loose cover over the vehicle speed sensor may be causing it.

NOISY WIRE WHEEL COVERS

The wire wheel covers on my car never made any noise until I had a brake job done. Now, two of them squeak as the wheels rotate. What's the reason for this?

Since your wheel covers didn't make a noise before the brake job, the technician who did the brake job may not have tightened the covers sufficiently when they were put back on. Wire wheel covers are heavy. If they aren't secured tightly, they will inch along the wheel and make noise. The first thing to do, therefore, is to use the special wheel cover wrench that came with the car to tighten locking nuts as much as possible.

If the squeak doesn't disappear, remove the noisy covers and spread some silicone grease on the tangs that hold the covers to the wheels. Put them back on the wheels, secure the locks, and drive the car to see what happens. If still not successful, take off the covers, place them face down on a firm surface, and drill four 1/4-inch holes equidistantly around each cover. Then, insert a nylon clip through each hole, reinstall the cover, and tighten each clip along with the cover nut. This should get rid of the noise.

DEFINING "NORMAL SHUDDER"

With people in the car, I get a little shudder when accelerating from a standstill. When I'm alone in the car, I feel nothing. No one has been able to explain why. The car has a four-cylinder engine and front-wheel drive.

The sensation is probably one to be expected when there are people in the car with you. To determine if it falls into the "normal" category, seat a few people in the car, get on a remote road, come to a complete stop, and then accelerate gradually. Note the speed at which you feel the sensation.

Come to another complete stop and accelerate again, but this time so rapidly that tires screech. Really stomp down on that accelerator pedal. If you feel the same "little shudder" at the same speed, you are experiencing what's called lead-pulling. This condition is characteristic of some cars equipped with front-wheel drive cars and all-season radial tires. As long as wheels are aligned and balanced properly and tires are in good condition and inflated correctly, you'll have to put up with it.

FINDING THE REASON FOR VIBRATION

My new car, which is a front-wheel drive model, vibrates terribly. The dealer says it's normal. Is there anything I can do to show him that he's wrong?

Both terrible vibration and vibration that's not so terrible are not normal. To locate the general area where the cause of vibration lies, notice the speed at which the sensation is most pronounced. Then, park the car with the transmission in PARK or NEUTRAL, accelerate the engine to approximately that speed, and let the engine decelerate rapidly by pulling your foot quickly off the accelerator pedal. If you don't get a vibration, you've isolated the cause to the front-drive unit (transaxle) or to tire/wheel assemblies. Ask the dealer to check for loose or defective drive axle shafts, an incorrect drive axle angle, out-of-round tires, unbalanced tire/wheel assemblies, and loose or worn wheel bearings.

If you get a vibration during the procedure, it confirms that the trouble lies with an engine or exhaust system part. A technician should be able to find the part causing the vibration by tracing the exhaust system from stem to stern and testing at brackets attached to the engine to find out which part is loose. (See Figure 4.1 and 4.2.)

TRACKING DOWN A GASOLINE ODOR

At times my car gives off a strong gasoline odor that is noticeable inside the vehicle as I drive along. My technician doesn't see any gas leak. So why do I smell gas? The car has a carburetor.

You state that the smell is present "at times." If those times are after you fill the gasoline

FIGURE 4.1. A loose component beneath a vehicle can transmit sound that can be heard inside the vehicle. A rattle, for instance, may be a loose shock absorber. Tightening the shock to its mount may get rid of the noise, but not if the shock bushing through which the bolt extends is worn. In this case, the shock will have to be replaced.

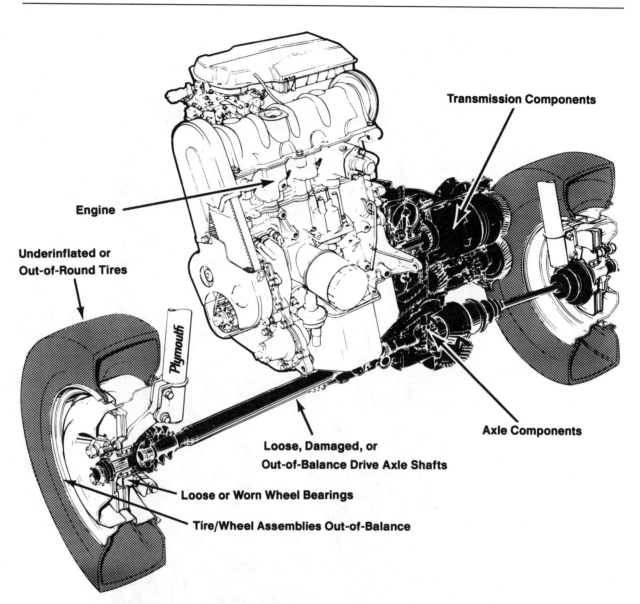

Transmission Components

Engine

Underinflated or
Out-of-Round Tires

Plymouth

Axle Components

Loose, Damaged, or
Out-of-Balance Drive Axle Shafts

Loose or Worn Wheel Bearings

Tire/Wheel Assemblies Out-of-Balance

FIGURE 4.2.   The cause of vibration felt in a car equipped with front-wheel drive is often to be found with front-drive components, especially those pointed out in the diagram. (Courtesy of Chrysler Corporation)

tank, it's possible that you're not tightening the gas cap properly, or you're allowing gas to slosh over the lip of the fuel filler neck (see below).

If these possibilities are discounted, and there is no visible fuel leak, then there is a leakage of invisible fuel vapor. To find the spot where vapor is leaking, do the following:

- Install a new gas cap. The old one may have lost its ability to seal.

- Look for a cracked or bent vapor vent line and loose vent line connections. One vent line runs from the carburetor to the fuel evaporation emissions system canister. Another vent line runs from the fuel evaporation emissions system canister to the fuel tank.

- Service the charcoal canister of the fuel evaporation emissions system. Most canisters contain a filter that can get dirty. (See Figure 4.3.) Or the canister itself might be plugged or saturated with gas. Remove the canister from the car, turn it over, slip the filter out of the base if there is a filter, and replace it. If there is no filter, replace the canister.

- Check the vapor vent valve to see that it's in place and is still tight. This valve is part of the fuel evaporation emissions system.

- Look for an open seam or a perforation in the top of the fuel tank. Unlike a perforation in the bottom of the tank, which would allow gasoline to leak from the tank, a spot in the top of the tank that has corroded away provides a hole through which vapors will escape.

WHAT A CONSTANT ODOR OF ANTIFREEZE MEANS

My car is giving off a strong odor of antifreeze (coolant) when I turn on the heater. The odor is strong enough to take my breath away; yet, the coolant level seems to be holding steady. Can you tell me what's wrong?

Although the coolant level seems to be telling you otherwise, the car is losing antifreeze—maybe not enough for you to notice, but enough to create an odor. This small loss is probably taking place through a

---

SERVICE TIP: GETTING RID OF GASOLINE ODOR

If you get an odor of gasoline only after you fill the fuel tank of your car, make sure the fuel tank cap has been secured properly. Cross-threading the cap to the filler neck will leave a gap that will let gas vapors escape.

Cap threads are designed to go onto the threads of the tank filler neck easily, so cross-threading a cap without being aware of it often occurs. When odor is present, therefore, unscrew and reinstall the cap carefully to see if the odor dissipates.

Another reason for a gasoline odor that prevails only after filling the fuel tank is improper fuel delivery. Letting gas slop over the filler neck will result in an odor that will linger until the gasoline evaporates.

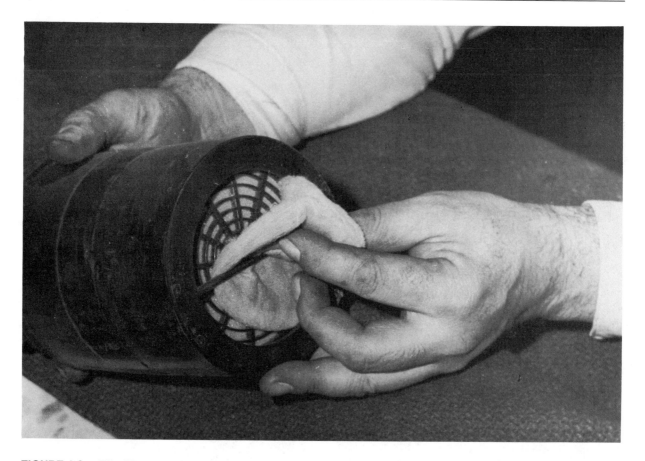

FIGURE 4.3. The filter in the bottom of the charcoal canister will eventually clog and allow a persistent odor of gasoline to be present. This is more likely to happen after the vehicle has been driven about 50,000 miles. If replacing the filter doesn't eliminate odor, the canister may be plugged or damaged and should be replaced. The charcoal canister is part of a vehicle's fuel evaporation control system, which is an emissions control system. Not all canisters have filters, but most of those in cars manufactured in the United States do.

tiny opening in the heater through which coolant is dripping into the heat duct that delivers warm air into the car from the heater. Have an auto-radiator shop technician remove the heater from the car and test it to confirm the existence of a leak. If there is a hole in the heater, it will probably have to be replaced.

EXHAUST ODOR

The dealer says I have to live with an obnoxious rotten egg odor that is emitted from my car's exhaust system. It is most noticeable when coming to a stop. Can anything be done?

What you are smelling is sulfur that forms as fuel is burned in the engine. The emission of sulfur into the atmosphere is not normal and is in violation of the Clean Air Act. The first step to getting rid of the odor is to try different brands of gasoline to find one that has a low enough sulfur content so no odor is emitted. If this doesn't work, the dealer should perform engine diagnostic procedures outlined in the service manual for eliminating exhaust odor. Finally, the catalytic converter should be replaced. The one presently on the car probably doesn't possess a sufficient amount of nickel, which is the element used to offset the sulfur content of fuel.

In doing this work, the dealer will want to check the index of technical service bulletins or call the technical assistance division of the manufacturer. There is reason to believe that the manufacturer has issued a service advisory since, as I said, exhaust odor is a condition that affects air quality and is tightly controlled by federal law. The installation of a new catalytic converter should be done free of charge under the provisions of the five year/50,000-mile (whichever occurs first) emissions control systems warranty.

DEODORIZING A CAR'S INTERIOR

The interior of my car was drenched during a heavy rain, because the windows were left open. Now, there's a musty odor. Can I get rid of it?

A musty odor is usually caused by bacteria that take root in carpet, seats, door trim, and fabric headliner that have gotten wet. Treatment with a deodorizer will mask the smell temporarily. In time, it will return. For permanent relief, you'll have to have a carpet cleaning company use a disinfectant and steam cleaning equipment to kill the bacteria.

The technician who does the work should remove seats, carpet, and carpet underpadding to wash the floor pan with disinfectant. The old carpet underpadding should be discarded and replaced with a new one. Door trim, seats, carpet, and headliner have to be steam cleaned and washed with a disinfectant.

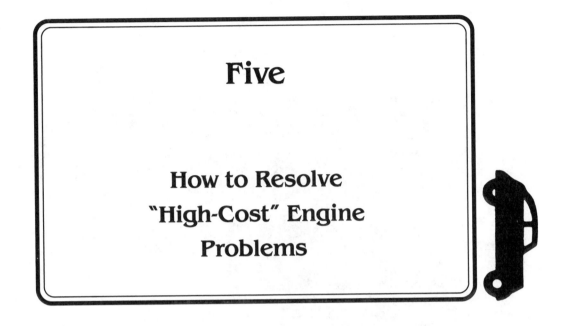

Five

How to Resolve
"High-Cost" Engine
Problems

WHY ENGINES CONSUME OIL

Why do I have to add a quart of oil to the engine of my car every 200 miles? The car's been driven only 15,000 miles. There are no leaks, and the engine doesn't seem to be burning oil. So what's going on?

An engine either burns oil or loses it. There are no other reasons for oil consumption, let alone oil consumption of the magnitude you're describing. However, the reason can be elusive.

For example, oil could be dripping from the oil-pan drain plug because of a damaged gasket around the plug. Replace the gasket and be sure the drain plug is tightened securely. Then, drive the car another 500 miles to see if oil consumption abates.

If oil loss continues, your technician should test the engine for a leak with dye and a "black light." This method is usually successful for pinpointing a hard-to-find oil leak.

Assuming there is no leak, there might be valve guide or valve seal damage. If so, the service manual for the car will tell a technician how to repair damaged valve guides and install new valve seals. (See Figure 5.1.)

Finally, since your car has comparatively few miles on it, the oil rings around the

Valve Seals   Valve Guides

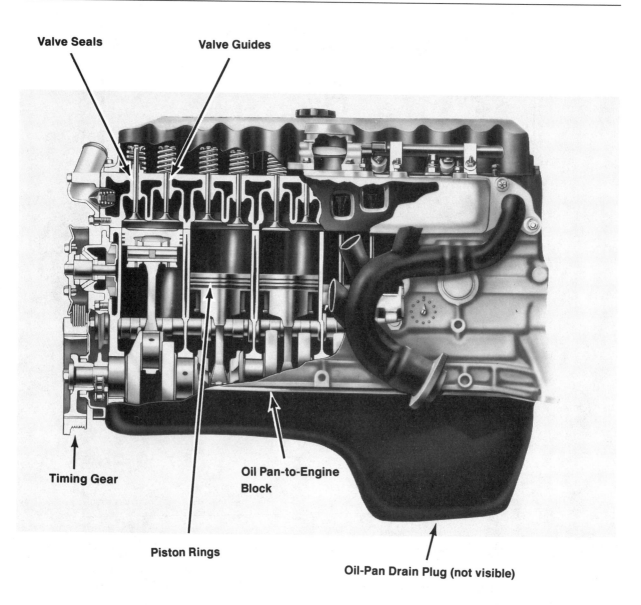

Timing Gear

Oil Pan-to-Engine
Block

Piston Rings

Oil-Pan Drain Plug (not visible)

FIGURE 5.1.   An engine can leak oil externally or internally. External leakage can be at any point where two parts come together, such as where the oil pan attaches to the engine block, where the oil-pan drain plug screws into the oil pan, or where the timing gear cover is bolted to the engine. Internal leakage can be around valve seals, through valve guides, or around piston rings. If leakage is internal, oil enters the combustion chambers and is consumed with the fuel mixture during the combustion process.

pistons may not have seated themselves during the engine break-in period. This frequently happens when a new engine is babied by the car owner and not driven at a reasonable rate of speed (50 to 60 mph) the first few thousand miles. Oil will leak around the unseated rings and enter the combustion chambers where it mixes with the fuel mixture and is burned.

Assuming you bought the car new, maintained it properly, and reported the oil loss to the dealer when the manufacturer's warranty was in effect, the cost of a repair may be covered by the warranty.

UNEXPLAINABLE OIL LOSS EXPLAINED

The engine in my car uses a quart of oil in about 750 miles. The dealer has replaced the oil pan gasket, oil drain plug, oil filter, and O-ring around the distributor shaft—all at considerable cost. Now I'm told, "It's got to be the valve seals." Having this repaired will cost me hundreds of dollars. Please advise if you think the dealer is correct in his analysis.

The reasons for a significant loss of oil are discussed on page 103. If valve seals were shot, the oil loss you'd be experiencing would be much greater than you indicate. What you're experiencing is a minor loss of oil that could be occurring for one of the following reasons:

1. Not using the proper oil-checking procedure. Is the car parked on level ground when you check the oil? If the engine's been running, are you giving oil sufficient time to drain into the crankcase before drawing out the dipstick to take a reading? Three to four minutes are needed before oil that has been circulating in an engine that's been running settles into the crankcase after the engine has been turned off. Checking oil before this period elapses can result in an erroneous reading.

2. Are you using the correct oil for your engine? Is it the proper viscosity for the prevailing ambient temperature? This is spelled out in the owner's manual and also on pages 2 and 30.

3. Do you use your car to haul a trailer or do a lot of mountain driving? Do you load the car with baggage or drive constantly at high speeds? If any of these stressful conditions apply, expect your engine to use a greater quantity of oil than if you don't do these things.

WHEN OIL LOSS IS NOT OIL LOSS

The dealer and I are going round-and-round on what constitutes excessive oil consumption. The problem centers around the four-cylinder engine in my car. It uses a quart of oil every 900 to 1,000 miles. I consider this excessive. My dealer contends that it is within normal parameters. I would like to have your opinion.

An engine that consumes a quart of oil every 900 to 1,000 miles, especially modern power plants such as your four-cylinder, is functioning within normal parameters. Being small and crammed into a confined compartment, your engine develops extremely high internal temperatures. This causes a certain amount of oil to be consumed between oil changes. Other reasons for an engine to burn a quart of oil in 1,000 miles include high-speed driving and the prolonged existence of a high ambient temperature.

SMOKE SIGNAL

My car emits puffs of gray-blue smoke from the tailpipe when the engine is started first time of the day. I bought the car used 1,300 miles ago. During that time, the engine has used less than a quart of oil. A technician found a spark plug fouled with oil, so he thinks oil is trickling into the cylinder served by that plug and is being burned. The engine was misfiring until he changed the spark plugs. Now it isn't. Is the technician correct?

Probably, but what difference does it make? Suppose a valve seal, valve guide, or piston ring serving the cylinder is slightly worn, which would account for oil getting into the cylinder and producing gray-blue exhaust smoke as it's burned in the combustion process. Since the amount of oil loss is negligible, would you want to have a repair done that would cost hundreds of dollars as compared to the couple of bucks it costs every 1,300 miles or so for a quart of oil?

You may be able to prevent spark plug fouling that is causing the engine to misfire by having spark plugs installed which are one notch higher on the heat range chart than the plugs recommended for your engine. Operating at a higher temperature, the hotter plugs might be able to burn off oil as it accumulates on the electrodes and before it has a chance to cause misfire. Ask a technician about this.

Important: Spark plugs of the same heat range must be installed in all cylinders. Don't install a hotter plug only in the cylinder in which oil is appearing.

OIL IN THE AIR CLEANER

Oil keeps depositing on the air filter and in the air filter housing of my car. I, therefore, have to replace the filter and clean the housing more often than the 30,000 miles recommended by the manufacturer. Much more often, in fact—like every 5,000 miles. A technician replaced the positive crankcase ventilation (PCV) valve, but the problem is still with me. He now says it's normal for this to happen, but I don't believe it. Do you?

If oil inside the air filter housing and on the air filter is just a film as opposed to a puddle, the PCV system is a possible cause. However, the PCV valve is just one part that needs attention. A PCV system is also outfitted with a small filter, which if it becomes clogged can force oil into the air filter housing and onto the air filter. (See Figure 5.2.) Therefore, when the technician replaced the PCV valve, the PCV filter should also have been replaced. In some cars, this small filter is inside the air filter housing. In other cars, it's inside the oil filter cap.

The technician should also see to it that the hoses which connect the PCV system to the engine are running straight. A bent PCV hose, as well as a defective PCV valve or a clogged PCV filter, will cause a rise in pressure inside the engine that will force oil vapor or drops of oil into the air filter housing and onto the air filter.

PCV Hose   PCV Filter

FIGURE 5.2. If oil forms a film on the air filter, the cause is usually a problem with the PCV system. The PCV system includes the PCV valve, which cannot be seen in this photograph, and a PCV filter which is located in the side of the air filter in the engine pictured here. The arrow points to the filter, which isn't visible.

If you find a pool of oil lying in the air filter housing, a more serious condition exists, such as a blown head gasket, worn valve guides or valve guide seals, or worn piston rings. Bring your car to an engine specialist who can pinpoint the problem area and make repairs. (See Figure 5.3.)

PROVING THE EXISTENCE OF AN OIL LEAK

At about 8,000 miles, the engine in my car developed a slight oil discharge at the rear main oil seal that the dealer says is normal. Is he right?

He might be. Then again, the presence of oil might indicate a serious problem. It all depends on what you mean by a "slight oil discharge." Here's what I mean.

A haze or film of oil around the rear main seal of an engine is normal. But a leak from around that seal is not normal—even if the engine is leaking only a drop every once in awhile. The cause of the leak could be a defective seal or a cracked rear main bearing cap bolt. In either case, this is major damage that can only get worse as time passes. The repair should be paid for by the manufacturer under the warranty.

Establishing whether a haze or leak exists is not always a simple matter. I suggest you ask the dealer to have the service department do a leak test. The technician will pour a fluorescent dye into the engine, which will mix with oil. After a reasonable period of driving, return the car to the dealer. The technician will scan the outside of the engine with an ultraviolet light. The procedure is called blacklighting the engine. The special light will make an area that's leaking oil look yellow. It will not, however, change the appearance of an area that has a haze over it.

Another possibility is that what you see as a haze or leak isn't oil. It may be a fluid from another source, such as the power steering pump, that's being flung on the engine. Fluorescent dye can be added to all other assemblies that hold fluid, such as the power steering pump, transmission, rear axle, and radiator. The blacklight will cause dye to glow if a fluid from the particular assembly that's being tested is leaking.

REPAIRING VALVE COVER OIL LEAKAGE

My fairly new minivan has been driven only 20,000 miles. In that short time, I've had to have the valve cover gaskets replaced twice because of an oil leak. The dealer told me that since the block of this engine is aluminum, he can't guarantee that the leak won't reappear. He has checked with the manufacturer to make sure the correct gaskets are being used. Is this going to be an on-going problem?

You either misunderstood the dealer or he's wrong. The block isn't aluminum—it's cast iron. The cylinder heads are aluminum. Furthermore, your engine isn't any more prone to oil seepage around the valve covers than millions of other engines possessing cast-iron engine blocks and aluminum cylinder heads. (See Figure 5.4.) That's why I'm doubtful that the valve cover gaskets had to be replaced in the first place. As long as the dealer is certain that the gaskets are the right ones, it's more likely that the valve covers just aren't being made tight enough. The correct specification for the valve cover bolts

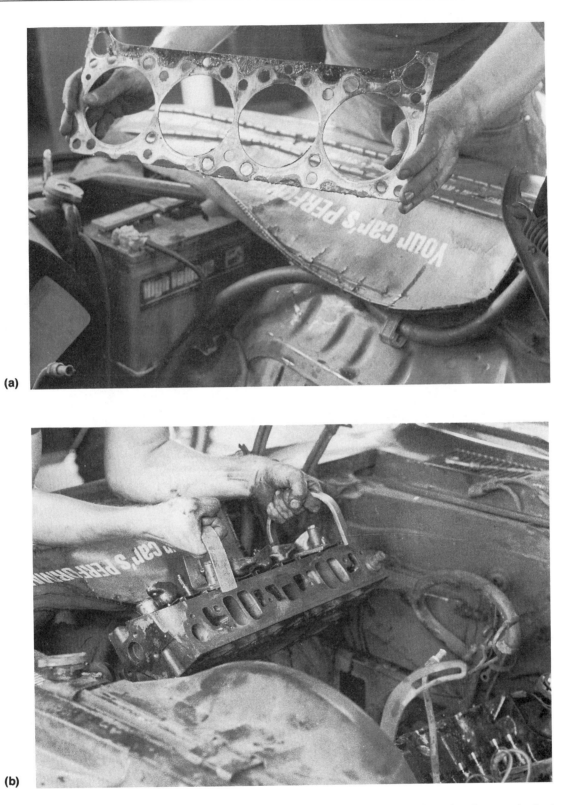

FIGURE 5.3.   A blown head gasket (a) will let coolant leak from the engine without leaving much of a trace, if any. A defective head gasket is replaced by removing the cylinder head from the engine block (b).

Valve Cover Cylinder

Head Point of Contact

FIGURE 5.4. A film of oil that forms between valve covers and the cylinder head (arrow) is normal. But if oil drips from the spot, valve bolts are not tight enough, valve cover gaskets are damaged or not the correct ones, or the valve cover is warped.

may not be the one in the service manual. There could have been a revision to that specification issued by the manufacturer to dealers through a technical service bulletin. Ask your dealer to call the technical assistance division of the manufacturer again to find out if this is the case.

BE SUSPICIOUS WHEN A PART IS REPLACED OVER AND OVER AGAIN

My car is now on its third alternator in less than two years. What happens is that the SERVICE ENGINE SOON light comes on, the windshield wipers operate at what seems to be twice their normal speed, and headlamps alternately brighten and dim. The technician whose been doing the work has been finding a trouble code in the computer that reveals a problem with the charging system. Therefore, he's been installing alternators although tests have indicated that the charging rate is normal. With each new alternator, things are okay for a time. Then the scenario repeats itself. What's going on?

Why are you allowing a technician to install new alternators when the charging rate is normal? A normal charging rate means the alternator and voltage regulator are performing properly. If that's the case, there is another reason why the SERVICE ENGINE SOON light comes on. The reason could be with the engine wiring harness.

It's conceivable that the harness has rubbed through at a point where it drops down from the alternator and runs alongside the air conditioner compressor or engine. When that rubbed-away area comes into contact with metal, a short circuit occurs that causes the SERVICE ENGINE SOON light to

react and electrical components to go crazy. In other words, the alternator may have nothing at all to do with your problem.

Why don't symptoms occur for a period of time after a new alternator is installed? Probably because to install the alternator the technician has to shift the position of the harness, moving it off metal. In time, though, vibration causes the harness to shift back and again come into contact with metal, recreating the short circuit.

Ask the technician to examine the harness closely to see if insulation has been rubbed away, leaving wires exposed. If this is the case, he can repair the harness with electrical tape and tie it back away from the spot against which it's been hitting.

OIL LEAK FROM VALVE COVERS

There is a persistent oil leak around the valve covers of my six-cylinder engine. The dealer replaced the gasket and tightened cover bolts to specification. The covers aren't warped and the cylinder heads are in good shape. Oil started to leak again shortly after repairs were made. Is there a solution or shall I give up?

Ask the dealer to check his technical service bulletin (TSB) index and also with the technical assistance department of the manufacturer to determine if the manufacturer has issued different valve covers or has come up with a different way to install the covers. For example, new covers that are sealed with Room Temperature Vulcanizing (RTV) sealer and special retainers have stopped leaks from valve covers of some models. Manufacturers of other models having the same trouble have issued new gaskets made of a composition material, such as metal and cork, that have proven to be effective in stopping leaks.

CONSEQUENCES OF TOO MUCH OIL IN AN ENGINE

After the prescribed five quarts of oil are added to the engine in my car, the dipstick shows the oil level to be about 1/8 inch over the full mark. Why is this happening? Will this excess amount cause a problem?

Perhaps the oil dipstick was calibrated incorrectly to begin with. Ask the dealer to check with the parts and service department of the manufacturer to determine if a different oil dipstick has been issued for your car.

Another possibility is that the oil dipstick tube has loosened and dropped lower into the crankcase. This will cause deeper penetration of the dipstick into the crankcase and a higher reading.

Assuming that neither of these reasons is valid, then the slight excess you're getting may be caused by not having the oil filter replaced when you change oil. Some oil may be staying in the filter as old oil is drained, thus adding to the five quarts of new oil that are put in. Since most manufacturers recommend replacing the oil filter at every other oil change, what you're seeing as excess is not excess at all, but is normal. So rest easy. That extra 1/8 inch will not cause any problem. However, overfilling the engine by adding 1/2 quart or more over the amount that is recommended by the manufacturer must be avoided. The consequence of doing that could be oil-foaming in which the excess causes oil to form bubbles. This deprives parts of adequate lubrication and can lead to engine damage.

LACK OF OIL PRESSURE

When I start the engine in my pickup truck after it's been off for a few hours, there is no indication of pressure on the oil pressure gauge for 5 to 10 seconds. This worries me, but the service manager at the dealership where I bought the vehicle tells me it's normal. Can I believe him?

Not unless he can prove it to you in the form of a service advisory from the vehicle manufacturer. Oil pressure should be immediate as an engine starts. If it isn't, a problem could lead to major engine damage.

Switching to oil of the correct viscosity for ambient temperature conditions, replacing a clogged oil filter, repairing a sluggish oil pressure gauge, or replacing a malfunctioning oil pressure switch might be all that's needed to correct the problem. More serious and expensive to repair conditions— a weak oil pump, clogged oil pickup screen, defective oil pickup tube, or worn engine bearings—could also be causing the lack of oil pressure.

To get to the bottom of the problem before the engine is harmed, change the oil and install a new oil filter. Make certain that oil of the correct viscosity for the ambient temperature in your region is used (see page 30).

If this step doesn't work, have a technician connect an external oil pressure gauge to the engine and start the engine when it's cold. A quick response on the external oil pressure gauge to a reading that equals the manufacturer specification for normal oil pressure means that your problem is caused by an oil pressure switch or gauge in the vehicle. If the response on the external oil pressure gauge is as sluggish as the response by the gauge in your pickup truck, the dealer should look for one of the more serious conditions.

Be sure to read the manufacturer's warranty that came with your truck. The cost of repairing the problem may be covered.

OVERCOMING COLD-WEATHER INDUCED ENGINE DAMAGE

I have two problems with a new car. The first is a dirty white emulsion that I see in the oil on the dipstick when I check the oil level. The second involves drops of water that drip from the tailpipe after the engine's been started in the morning and the car's been driven a few feet. The service manager at the dealership tells me these conditions are normal and harmless, but I am concerned and would appreciate your evaluation.

I notice that you reside in a part of the country where the ambient temperature hovers near and below zero during the winter. Have you operated your car in warmer weather yet? I'll bet not. I'll also wager that you do mostly short-range driving. Under these conditions—that is, cold weather and short trips—the symptoms your car displays are normal as the service manager says. However, I question the use of the term "harmless." The consequences of what's going on can be quite harmful unless you take precautions.

It's not unusual for a dirty white substance to collect in the oil of a vehicle driven in cold temperatures if the car is used primarily for short trips. Furthermore, the water dripping from the tailpipe is a result of a buildup of moisture that takes place inside the engine overnight. Someone who resides in a cold region such as yours, but makes long trips during which the engine gets hot enough to boil off moisture probably won't experience these conditions.

Combustion of a gallon of gasoline can produce a pound of moisture, which can eventually harm the engine and exhaust system if maintenance steps aren't taken. Moisture can turn oil to sludge, which will damage engine parts. Moisture can also cause the muffler and exhaust pipes to rust prematurely. Here's what you should do to prevent the trouble:

First, during cold weather try to drive the car at a highway rate of speed at least three times a week for a distance of at least 10 miles each way. This will allow the engine to operate at a temperature which will burn off moisture.

Second, change the oil and oil filter frequently. With the symptoms that your car is displaying, once every 3,000 miles or every three months, whichever occurs first, is what's meant by "frequently."

RED MOTOR OIL

I'm concerned about what may be a sign of impending trouble with my new car. When I checked the oil after driving the car a few hundred miles, I noticed that it had a red tint. I had a local gas station change the oil and oil filter since I live pretty far from town and couldn't get the car back to the dealer. So far the new oil looks like oil is supposed to look, but my concern is that the reddish tint may mean that automatic transmission fluid or something else leaked into the engine. Should I complain about this to the dealer?

You probably spent money needlessly to change the oil and oil filter. Car manufacturers often pour a dye along with oil into the crankcases of new engines to aid in detecting oil leaks before labeling the vehicle "ready for market." The dye allows a technician to scan potential leaky areas with an ultraviolet light source. The dye-laden oil shows up on leaking engine surfaces as bright yellow spots, making it easier to spot weak areas. The dye, which gives oil a reddish cast, is not harmful to the engine and drains from the engine when the oil is changed the first time as you have found out.

LOSING COOLANT A DRIP AT A TIME

Several technicians have gone over the cooling system of my car to try and find out why there is a small, but perceptible loss of coolant. This is a mystery that I hope you can shed some light on.

Even if a cooling system pressure tester is used to put the cooling system under enough pressure to force coolant from a small hole in a defective part, such as a hose or radiator tank, a cooling system leak can still be elusive. Let me tell you about one I had to deal with since it might be applicable to your case.

After months of searching for the origin of a coolant loss, I found a pinhole in the bottom of a heater hose which was allowing coolant to leak out a drop at a time. The leak area was hidden and the leak was so sluggish that I was fortunate to spot it. What made it even more difficult to find was the fact that each drop of coolant was falling on the exhaust manifold of the engine. When that manifold got hot, as an exhaust manifold is prone to do whenever the engine is running, the coolant would evaporate instantly.

There is no doubt that there is a coolant leak from the cooling system of your vehicle. The only suggestion I have concerning its detection is that you keep at it until the source is uncovered. Good luck.

A HIDDEN REASON FOR COOLANT LOSS

The engine in my six-year-old car started to lose coolant. Technicians have checked radiator and heater hoses and connections, coolant reservoir tank, radiator, radiator pressure cap, heater, water pump, and thermostat housing without finding any leak. I feared that maybe the engine had developed a crack, but I've been assured that this isn't so. What are we missing?

Technicians have been thorough. There is, however, one spot where a coolant leak can exist that seems to have been overlooked. Have you ever heard of core plugs? Some people call them freeze plugs, but this is a misnomer. Contrary to common belief, these plugs are not installed so they'll pop out of an engine to allow expansion if coolant freezes inside the engine. The purpose of core plugs is to permit access to the interior of the engine block during production for the purpose of removing dust that may have been deposited during the manufacturing process.

Core plugs can corrode and start to leak as an engine ages. Since core plugs are located in the bowels of an engine, a leak can be difficult to detect since coolant falls on the road as the car rolls along. However, the leak usually reveals its existence in the form of corrosive deposits around the defective plug.

To locate and examine core plugs (there are usually two or three on each side of the engine block), the vehicle has to be raised. If one core plug is corroded, the technician should replace all of them. If one plug is leaking, chances are that others will soon follow suit.

When a technician installs new core plugs, the threads and sealing surfaces should be cleaned, and a sealing compound such as Loctite Pipe Sealant® used to seal the plug and prevent leakage. Plugs must be tightened to the specification given in the service manual.

COOLANT DISAPPEARS INTO THIN AIR

I've got a problem with my fairly new car that's worrying me sick. The trouble started six months after I took delivery. One morning while checking under the hood, I noticed that the coolant recover tank was empty. The upshot is that since then I've had to add six gallons of coolant and no technician I've been to, including those in the dealer service department, has been able to find out why I'm losing the stuff. All swear there are no leaks. So what's happening to the coolant?

The engine may have developed an internal crack that is allowing coolant to drip into the oil delivery system. Has anyone checked for this by warming up the engine and withdrawing the oil dipstick? An elevated oil level will reveal if coolant has invaded the oil delivery system.

Another way to test for the presence of coolant in oil is to let oil drip onto a hot exhaust manifold after the engine has been run a few minutes. If the fluid sizzles, it indicates the presence of coolant and, therefore, a crack in the engine. As long as nothing you did caused that crack, you should be entitled to a new engine under the terms of the warranty.

If the dealer's service department discounts the existence of an internal crack in the engine, the loss of coolant may be the result of a defective head gasket. When

replacing a head gasket, a technician should make sure the engine block and cylinder head on which the gasket rests aren't warped or eroded. This repair should also be covered by the warranty.

UNEXPLAINABLE COOLANT LEAK EXPLAINED

Every so often I see a few drops of liquid under the front of my car. I think it's coolant, but the coolant level in the radiator never falls below normal. Neither does the oil, power steering fluid, or any other liquid. So what are these drops, and where do they come from?

As you suspect, they're probably drops of coolant and they're probably coming from the water pump. Most water pumps have a weep (drain) hole that allows coolant to drain under high pressure conditions that build up in the cooling system. If some fluid didn't drain off to relieve pressure, water pump seals could be damaged and the water pump bearing could corrode. This would ruin the pump.

Coolant can also get into the bearing housing when there's a sharp differential in temperature. This occurs when cold coolant in an engine that has just been started comes into contact with the hot metal of the pump on a hot day. The metal can contract to allow a slight leakage of coolant into the bearing housing. Over a period of time, this leakage can be enough to kill the bearing if not for the fact that coolant leaks out of the pump through the weep hole before it can reach the bearing.

As long as you see only a few drops of coolant on the floor now and again, you have nothing to worry about. A water pump bearing that corrodes will make an audible grinding noise that few drivers can ignore. Take prompt remedial action if you hear that kind of noise coming from the engine compartment to avert a breakdown on the road.

CONSTANT WATER PUMP FAILURE

The engine in my car is on its third water pump in less than 50,000 miles. What's causing pumps to fail over and over again?

Have you been replacing water pumps, because they start to leak coolant? Or have you been replacing water pumps, because they start making noise and you feared an on-the-road breakdown?

Most water pumps have two seals—a housing seal and a center shaft-bearing seal. If housing seals are being damaged so coolant leaks from the pump, there is usually no need to replace the pump. Just install a new seal. Housing seal failure can be determined by having a technician unbolt the two halves of the pump to examine the seal.

Failure of the center shaft bearing seal is another story. When that goes bad, coolant leaks into the bearing housing and attacks the bearing, which then starts making noise. There is no external leak of coolant until the bearing breaks down completely. There is no repair to make once this seal fails and noise is heard. The pump has to be replaced.

Whether it's a housing seal or center shaft bearing seal which has been causing your trouble, a technician shouldn't just keep replacing the pump. It's important to find out why it's happening. One reason could be a buildup of too much pressure in the cooling system. The specific amount of pressure the system should maintain is specified in the service manual. For most cars, it's between 14 and 18 pounds per square inch (psi). To find out if the cooling system in your car is exceeding the maximum allowable pressure, have a technician test the radiator pressure cap using a cooling system pressure tester. If the cap is causing pressure to rise above 18 psi, say, that amount is probably too much for water pump seals in your car to endure. Replace the cap with one of the specific value required by the cooling system.

Another reason for premature water pump failure is overtightening the timing belt if that belt relies on the water pump for maintenance of tension, as it does in some cars. An excessively tight belt will have an adverse effect on the center shaft bearing and seal. Ask the technician to use a timing belt tension gauge to tighten the belt to the specification in the service manual and to make certain the belt-adjusting mechanism is functioning properly.

A final cause of water pump failure is use of a poor quality coolant. Are you using a nationally known brand of ethylene glycol as the cooling agent? Use of a less costly, off-brand product can affect the water pump adversely. Bootleg coolant may contain contaminants that attack seals and causes them to fail prematurely. Drain and flush the cooling system and have coolant of known quality installed.

ELECTROLYSIS CAUSES SEVERE DAMAGE

The water pump in my car failed suddenly so I had it replaced, but the new pump didn't last long. That's when the technician got suspicious and tore the pump apart. He found the inside pitted and corroded. Do you know what caused this water pump to fail so quickly? The technician doesn't.

It may have failed because of electrolysis. If so, then damage to the radiator and engine are also possibilities, so I suggest you have this looked into as soon as possible.

Electrolysis occurs when an electrical component is damaged and allows stray electric current to seek a ground (return path) back to the battery. The offending electrical culprit is usually a bare wire in contact with a metal part of the radiator. The coolant provides the ground.

To detect whether electrolysis caused your water pumps to fail, have a technician make the following test:

1. With the engine off, connect the ground (negative) test lead of a volt/ohmmeter (VOM) or digital voltage meter (DVM) to the battery negative terminal.
2. Dip the meter's positive test lead probe into the coolant in the radiator, but make sure the probe doesn't touch the radiator.
3. With the engine and all accessories off, take AC and DC voltage readings with the meter set on the low voltage scale. The reading should be zero (0). If not, the circuit of an accessory that runs with the engine off, such as the clock, is damaged.
4. Start the engine, check to see that the test probe hasn't moved into contact with the radiator, and again take AC and DC readings.
5. Keep the engine running and turn on all lights and accessories, including the heater. Again, take AC and DC voltage readings.

If the vehicle is equipped with a cast-iron engine, the maximum allowable voltage reading is 0.3 volt. More than this can damage the engine. One-half this voltage, or 0.15 volt, can damage an aluminum engine.

If voltage readings exceed the maximum allowable limits, turn accessories off one at a time until voltage drops and isolates the circuit that's causing electrolysis. If the high reading is still present when all accessories have been turned off, the trouble is confined to the electrical system. Electrical troubleshooting techniques now have to be used to zero in on the damaged area so a repair can be made.

SERVICING THE COOLING SYSTEM CAUSES ENGINE TO OVERHEAT

I recently had the radiator of my foreign car drained and flushed. New hoses and a new thermostat were also installed as part of this service. Before this work was done, I didn't have a problem with overheating. Since it was done, I've had nothing but trouble. The technician who did the work and two others have gone over the car, but find nothing wrong. Can you give us some clue as to what may be wrong?

It's possible that the new thermostat was installed backwards which with a foreign car, in particular, will result in overheating. It has to do with a tiny air-bleed hole in the body of the thermostat. If the thermostat is installed with this hole in the wrong position, the thermostat valve will stay partially closed when the engine gets warm. The engine will then start to run hot.

Have a technician remove the thermostat from the engine and look for that little hole. It's just above the thermostat valve. When the technician reinstalls the thermostat, the air-bleed hole should be facing toward the engine. Drive the car. Chances are overheating will no longer be a bother.

CAMSHAFT FAILURE

I own an eight-year-old car with a V6 engine. At 38,000 miles, three years after I bought the car new, the camshaft had to be replaced. The manufacturer paid half the cost. A few months ago I began hearing a clacking and had the engine torn down again. A technician found two lobes of the camshaft rounded off and two worn valve lifters. The repair cost me hundreds of dollars. I would like to know why this type of failure occurs. Is it because camshafts used by manufacturers are less than adequate to begin with?

The number one cause of camshaft failure is inadequate lubrication. (See Figure 5.5.) Preventing camshaft failure, therefore, could be in the hands of a vehicle owner. The owner should have engine oil changed at least as often as the manufacturer recommends, and use a popular brand of oil that is known to be of high quality. For a discussion of how to select oil and how often to have it changed, turn to pages 1 and 27, respectively.

The other reasons for camshaft failure are a misalignment between valve lifters and camshaft lobes, and improper hardening of the camshaft during production. From the way you describe the failure with your engine, it appears that your worn camshaft probably falls into the misaligned category, but let's hold our discussion of this for a moment and talk about inadequate hardening.

From your question concerning the use of "less-than-adequate" camshafts by manufacturers, are you referring to the experiences many owners of General Motors cars had from 1975 through 1982? The soft cam issue, as it was called at the time, affected 1975 through 1982 GM 305-cubic-inch V8 engines. It led to an agreement between GM and the Federal Trade Commission that extended GM's warranty on 305-cubic-inch engine camshafts to five years or 50,000 miles, whichever occurred first.

As I said, I doubt if your situation falls into the "soft cam" category. Although improperly hardened camshafts aren't confined to 1975 through 1982 GM 305-cubic-inch engines alone, they haven't shown up in great numbers on other engines. Besides, improperly hardened camshafts usually start to make noise, reflecting the onset of a breakdown, before 38,000 miles.

The problem you've experienced with two camshaft failures in 98,000 miles was more likely caused by those two worn valve lifters you mention. They probably weren't detected the first time you had the camshaft replaced and, therefore, caused the replacement camshaft to fail. If one or more lobes of a camshaft don't line up perfectly with one or more valve lifters, the camshaft and lifters will sustain abnormal wear.

When a vehicle owner is faced with engine camshaft failure, that owner should ask the technician to inspect every valve lifter for wear and not just replace the camshaft. Those valve lifters that are worn should be rebuilt or replaced. Furthermore, once installed, the replacement camshaft should be checked for front-to-rear free play. If this measurement is not in accordance with that in the engine service manual, it should be brought into line by installing shims on the face of the timing gear.

BATTERY DRAIN IS A PAIN

If I don't drive my car for about a week, the battery goes dead, and I have to get a jump-start. The dealer checked out the electrical system, including the theft alarm. He didn't find any short circuits or anything wrong with the battery or

FIGURE 5.5.   This photograph points out the parts of the engine that are involved in camshaft failure.

alternator. I don't drive the car much. In the last 15 months, it's only gone 5,300 miles. Can this be the reason?

You can bet on it. Driving the car an average of only 90 miles a week is probably not allowing the alternator enough time to charge the battery. But there may be a contributory reason for a sound battery to keep discharging. It concerns that theft alarm. Was it installed after you bought the car? If so, the aftermarket unit (as nonoriginal equipment is called) could be drawing 100 or more milliamps of electricity from the battery when your car is not being driven. This is enough of a drain to discharge the battery in a week's time. Theft alarm systems installed as original equipment by auto manufacturers are designed to draw only about 30 milliamps of current, which is a rate that won't drain the battery if the vehicle isn't driven for 30 days.

In any event, you don't have many options. Whether battery discharge is being caused by lack of driving, an aftermarket theft alarm, or both, driving the car more often is necessary to solve the problem. If you can't do this, disconnecting the theft alarm may help.

ELUSIVE REASON FOR BATTERY FAILURE

Although a technician has given my car's entire electrical system, including the battery, high marks, the battery has gone dead on several occasions. He says the reason is that I don't drive the car enough, and all the electronic gadgetry in the car puts a drain on the battery even when the engine is off. I told him I drive a minimum of 300 miles a week. Isn't that enough?

It should be. Therefore, if the electrical system is as sound as the technician says, some hidden defect is draining the battery. Maybe it's a short that is allowing a bulb to glow all the time. To find out, open the trunk, glove box, and hood. Feel each light bulb. If one feels warm, a short circuit or a defective switch and socket is causing the bulb to remain on all the time. Naturally, this puts a drain on the battery, so have a technician repair the trouble.

CONVERTING THE EMISSIONS SYSTEM OF A CALIFORNIA CAR

I purchased a car that was built for sale in California and, therefore, is set up to meet that state's special emissions requirements. I live and drive in Minnesota. Can I have the car switched over to meet Minnesota emissions requirements? The reason for doing this involves fuel economy. My friend has an identical car and gets 30 to 32 miles per gallon (mpg). I get only 26.

The emissions requirements for vehicles in Minnesota are the same as they are in every state except California, where the laws are the toughest in the nation. As a result, every car built for sale in California differs from every car built for sale elsewhere when it comes to emissions control systems.

According to the Environmental Protection Agency (EPA), there is no law prohibiting you from removing the special controls that make California cars unique and having them replaced with federal emissions control equipment. But be prepared to pay a hefty price to make this modification if you can find someone who is qualified to do this difficult job. That's a big "if."

If you consult a dealer, chances are that he'll refuse to do the job. The policy of new car manufacturers is not to do anything that will alter the original emissions controls or settings of a vehicle.

Another drawback to doing what you suggest is that emissions control systems just aren't hung onto an engine. They are integrated into and are part of the fuel, ignition, and electronic engine control systems. Modifying them means ripping apart these systems and starting from scratch.

As for your complaint about poor mileage, according to the EPA mileage guide, your California-equipped car is rated at 23 mpg city and 26 mpg highway if it's equipped with an automatic transmission. In other words, you are getting excellent fuel mileage with your California-equipped car.

CAN'T FILL 'ER UP

My car was delivered with just under a quarter tank of gas, so the first thing I did after driving it off the dealer's lot was to stop at a gas station. That's when my trouble began. I soon learned that I have to hold the gas pump nozzle at precisely the correct angle and feed gas into the tank gently as if I were feeding a baby or else the pump kicks off. All I get from the dealer is advice to try another gas station. Help—I'm running out of stations.

Have a technician inspect the vent line between the car's fuel tank and the tank filler neck. It is probably pinched, kinked, or clogged, which is preventing air from passing freely through the line. Unless the fuel tank is properly vented, gas will bubble and cause the gas pump to kick off. A faulty vent line should be replaced.

Six

How to Avoid if You Can, Resolve if You Can't Brake/Steering/ Suspension/Tire Trouble

BRAKE SQUEAL MAY BE NORMAL

The brakes in my new car occasionally give out with a squeal when I apply the pedal. The dealer claims it's normal and cannot be repaired. I can't believe that. Please help.

Although it is advisable to get a second opinion when a brake noise appears, you'll probably find that a brake system technician will tell you what your dealer has told you. Let me try to put your mind at ease by quoting a service advisory about brake squeal that's been issued by General Motors. This explanation puts brake squeal/squeak into perspective—not only for owners of General

Motors cars, but for owners of all makes. (See Figure 6.1.) Here's what it says:

The design criteria (for brakes) includes government requirements, service life, space limitations, noise level, heat transfer and cooling, stopping ability, pedal effort and feel, fade resistance and environmental effects. The choice of brake pads is ultimately a balanced choice, but priority must be given to those criteria which affect braking performance under the federal Motor Vehicle Safety Standards. As a result, a certain amount of brake noise can result.

The brake pads used on today's vehicle may cause an occasional and intermittent high-pitched squeak or squeal when brakes are applied with light or moderate pressure. If the brake system is functioning correctly and it is

123

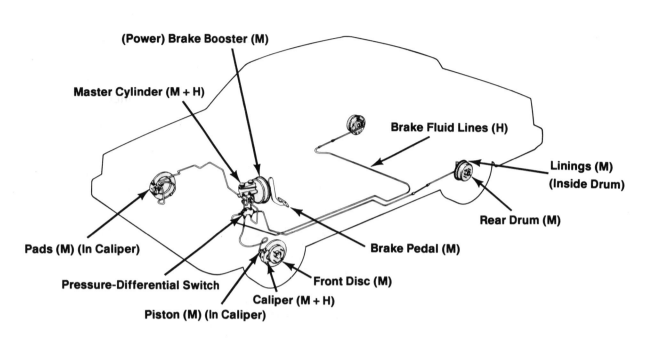

(Power) Brake Booster (M)

Master Cylinder (M + H)

Brake Fluid Lines (H)

Linings (M)
(Inside Drum)

Rear Drum (M)

Pads (M) (In Caliper)

Brake Pedal (M)

Pressure-Differential Switch

Front Disc (M)

Caliper (M + H)

Piston (M) (In Caliper)

FIGURE 6.1. This drawing illustrates the different components that make up a modern automotive braking system which doesn't have antilocking capability. It will help you identify components described in this chapter. Although most vehicles have disc brakes in the front and drum brakes in the rear, as shown here, others are equipped with disc brakes in both the front and rear. Note that each component is designated M or H. M identifies mechanical parts that do or help do the job of bringing wheels to a stop. H identifies parts that supply hydraulic fluid. H parts activate M parts. Parts labeled M and H have a dual role. The purpose of the pressure-differential switch—the only part not labeled M or H—is to detect a difference in hydraulic pressure that is created when there's a fluid leak and to warn of the problem by turning on a warning light in the instrument panel. Warning lights, however, burn out, so it's a good idea to check for a loss of brake fluid periodically using the procedures described in the text. (Courtesy of Chrysler Corporation)

SERVICE TIP: BE BRAKE CONSCIOUS

In a survey conducted by the National Highway Traffic Safety Administration, 36 percent of 125,000 cars (45,000 vehicles) that were examined demonstrated a braking deficiency. In a similar study, 6 percent of 10 million cars (600,000 vehicles) checked by the New York Department of Motor Vehicles over a 12-month period had braking system defects.

If these two studies are even partially accurate, there are thousands upon thousands of cars on the road in danger of having a brake failure. To find out whether your car is in this class, have a technician remove the wheels and examine braking system components. Then, stay aware of brake performance on a day-to-day basis.

A braking system that has developed a deficiency will usually emit a warning in the early stages, which should prompt you to consult a technician before the defect becomes deadly serious. The warning is given in one or more of the following ways:

- The brake warning light stays on or goes on after you start the engine.
- The vehicle pulls to one side when you apply the brakes.
- The brake pedal grabs when you press down on it lightly.
- There's noise (screech, grind, groan, or chatter) when brakes are applied.
- The brake pedal almost hits the floor before brakes engage.
- The brake pedal requires heavy pressure applied to it for brakes to engage.
- A shudder, vibration, or pulsation is felt in the brake pedal, steering wheel, or throughout the vehicle when brakes are applied.

---

the judgment of the dealership's service department that the demonstrated condition is normal brake noise, the customer should be assured that this is an operating characteristic of disc brakes and no repair should be attempted. Efforts to eliminate completely the occasional and intermittent noises that are judged to be normal are frequently temporary.

An occasional brake squeal is characteristic of metallic brake pads and linings, especially in damp weather. Metallic brake pads and linings have been installed by automobile manufacturers since the mid-1980s. They are used in preference to asbestos brake pads and linings, which present a health hazard to technicians as they work on braking systems.

WHY NOISE FROM AN ANTILOCK BRAKING SYSTEM

I just bought a new car that has an antilock braking system. A whirring sound is heard only when I step on the brake pedal while driving at a slow speed after I start the engine. The dealer calls it normal, but I'm concerned and would like your opinion. Is this noise something I have to expect with antilock brakes?

The noise you describe is probably a normal sound and is characteristic of an antilock braking system (ABS) that's going through a self-test called initialization whenever the engine is started. During this test, the ABS

SAFETY TIP: MAINTAIN BRAKING EFFICIENCY

Every few months, have the cover over a metal brake master cylinder taken off, or look through the translucent housing of a plastic master cylinder, to check the brake fluid level. If that level is more than ½ inch below the top of the cylinder, brake pads and/or linings are probably starting to wear or there's a leak.

Consult a brake specialist, because if pads or linings wear excessively, brake discs (also called rotors), and drums will sustain damage. At this point, then, what would have been a relatively inexpensive replacement procedure becomes a very expensive repair. New pads and/or linings will have to be installed—that's the "relatively inexpensive" repair. But if neglected, the pads or linings will wear away, allowing the metal on which they are placed to come into contact with and eat into the discs or drums. This will add the expense of new discs or drums to the repair.

If a fluid leak exists and is allowed to continue, it will cause a drop in braking performance and eventually, a complete loss of brakes.

---

motor, solenoids, and valves perform predrive tests that are monitored by the computer that oversees ABS operation.

Initialization takes place at a speed of 3 to 10 mph during the first application of the braking system following an engine start. The noise that results varies in intensity from car to car so some people may not be aware of it.

Let me add a caveat to this explanation: Since I don't have the opportunity of hearing and evaluating the noise made by the ABS in your car, I suggest you have the system evaluated by another dealer or an independent brake system technician. In all probability, as I stated, the noise is normal. Then again, maybe it isn't. Get another opinion.

GRABBING BRAKES

When I apply brakes the first two or three times of the day, the rear wheels grab and cause the tires to slide. After those first few applications, braking becomes normal and stays that way for the rest of the day. I bought the vehicle new in the mid-1980s, and it's been this way since then. The dealer has gone over the braking system time and time again. So has an independent brake shop. Neither can find anything wrong. So what is causing this problem?

As long as no mechanical defect is present, I can think of only one reason for brake grabbing. Your car was probably outfitted with one of the first types of nonasbestos semimetallic rear brake linings ever used. If you've not had the brake linings replaced since the day you bought the car, you should have them replaced now. The brake grabbing problem will probably disappear with the old linings.

These early version semimetallic brake linings were sensitive to moisture that formed on them during the night. Moisture on linings can cause linings to grab against the brake drums until the heat generated by a few brake applications dries things out.

SERVICE TIP: WHAT YOU NEED TO KNOW ABOUT BUYING A BRAKE JOB

The term "brake job" can mean replacing disc brake pads that cost a few dollars a piece, or doing a complete overhaul of the brake system that will run several hundreds. In between the two extremes are other types of brake work that cost varying amounts.

It's important for you to understand what kind of brake job a technician wants to do on your car and why. You obviously will want what's needed, because safety is involved. But on the other hand, unnecessary repairs are a waste of money—sometimes a lot of money.

A fact you should realize is that most costly brake system damage is often avoidable. I'll explain how in a minute. First, however, an understanding of the makeup of the automotive braking system will provide you with the knowledge needed to buy the kind of brake job your car actually requires.

Practically every car manufactured since 1970 has disc brakes on front wheels and drum brakes on rear wheels. (See Figure 6.2.) Disc and drum refer to the part of the system that rotates with a wheel. It's the part that is brought to a halt and which, in turn, brings the wheel to a halt when you press down on the brake pedal. Each wheel of a car is served by a disc or drum. A few cars, primarily sport models such as the Chevrolet Corvette and Toyota Supra, have discs on all four wheels.

A car's braking system uses hydraulic pressure to push a friction material into contact with discs or drums. This friction material stops the disc or drum from rotating. The friction material used with a disc brake is called a pad; along with a drum brake is called a lining. Whether it's a pad or a lining, the material and what it does are the same.

Other terms you may hear are rotors and shoes. A rotor is another name for a disc. A shoe is the metal plate to which the friction material is attached.

As indicated, pads and linings stop discs and drums, respectively, from rotating. Serious damage occurs when a car owner allows pads and linings to wear down to where shoes are exposed and come into contact with discs and drums. When this critical point is passed, the cost of a brake job soars. That's because the metal shoe presses against the metal disc or drum when you apply the brakes. Metal eats into metal, scoring it badly so you have to replace the discs or drums.

Usually, the pads of front wheel disc brakes wear out before the linings of rear wheel drum or disc brakes. Therefore, being aware of when front pad wear has reached the critical point will enable you to avoid extensive and costly damage.

There's no secret about when disc brake pads have worn to the point at which they should be replaced. If you drive a Ford or General Motors vehicle, you'll get a warning in the form of a high-frequency squeal as the car starts off and moves at a slow speed. The squeal, which is made when built-in metal sensors attached to the shoes come into contact with the discs, will cease or change pitch as you apply the brakes. When this happens, have the pads replaced as soon as possible. If you ignore the warning, discs will be damaged.

Most Chrysler and imported vehicles don't have wear sensors. To check the pads, the front wheels should be removed at 30,000 miles, and every 15,000 miles thereafter, to measure pad thickness. Have pads replaced when $\frac{1}{32}$ inch of material remains at the thinnest point.

Usually, rear drum or disc brake service is not needed when front disc brake pads have to be replaced. Generally, rear brake linings or pads outlast front brake pads by $1\frac{1}{2}$ times. But you should have the rear wheels and drums or discs removed to measure rear brake linings or pads when front pads are being replaced. If rear linings or pads are still sound, have them inspected every 15,000 miles after front disc replacement until they finally need to be replaced. This should be done when linings or pads are worn down at the thinnest point to $\frac{1}{16}$ or $\frac{1}{32}$ inch, respectively.

Note: Rear brake units don't usually have audible brake wear warning devices.

When a technician installs new pads and/or linings, a suggestion may be made to have discs and/or drums receive a light "cut" (also called turning or grinding) to remove irregularities. This is good advice, because minor disc and drum surface irregularities can cause pads and linings to wear prematurely. The disc or drum is put on a brake lathe and is rotated to make the cut. In the case of discs, the manufacturer of the vehicle may recommend attaching a brake grinder to discs mounted on the car. The disc is then rotated against the grinder.

There is a minimum dimension stamped on every disc and drum. Usually, after being ground twice, a disc or drum reaches this dimension. When it does, it should be replaced. As part of doing a brake job, a technician should measure the thickness of the disc or drum metal with a micrometer or brake gauge to establish that the metal is of a sufficient thickness. Driving a car with discs and drums ground to a thickness less than that recommended can cause these essential parts to fall apart during braking. The consequences are not pleasant to contemplate.

A brake system uses hydraulic pressure to push pads and linings into contact with discs and drums. The parts holding hydraulic brake fluid are not immune from damage, so you should know what can cause them to malfunction. Fluid loss resulting from a hydraulic part gone bad can cause loss of braking power more quickly than worn pads or damaged discs.

If parts that handle brake fluid never spring a leak, a brake system will never need additional fluid. Be aware, however, that as pads wear and move closer to the discs, the fluid channel in back of the piston in the caliper is filled with a greater amount of brake fluid. The caliper is the part of a disc brake system that contains the piston that pushes the pads into contact with the disc as fluid pushes against the piston. With more fluid in the caliper, less is left in the master cylinder (fluid reservoir). Therefore, if you replenish the fluid in the master cylinder to compensate for what appears to be a loss and it maintains that new level, you can assume that no leak exists.

Master cylinders in many cars are translucent, so you can see the fluid level without removing the cover. If the master cylinder in your car is metal, remove the cover once every six months to check fluid level. Wipe the cover and cylinder clean before taking off the cover to keep dirt from falling into the fluid. If dirt gets into the master cylinder, the whole system will have to be drained and flushed. The fluid level should be no more than $\frac{1}{2}$ inch below the rim of the master cylinder.

The owner's manual for your car will specify whether the manufacturer recommends the use of fluid that meets Department of Transportation (DOT) specification 3, 4, or 5. Usually, for normal driving conditions, No. 3 fluid is suitable. No. 4 or No. 5 brake fluid is for cars used under extreme conditions of, say, trailer hauling or operating in subzero weather.

When you need brake fluid, buy a new can. Use as much as needed and dispose of the remainder. Brake fluid in an open can is easily contaminated by air-borne moisture. A fresh can is a cheap investment in safety.

As indicated, one way to tell if a part that handles brake fluid has sprung a leak is by watching the fluid level in the master cylinder. If that level ever drops much more than one inch from the top of the rim, there's a leak.

Another way is by testing brake pedal firmness. If the car has power brakes, start the engine. If the car's brakes are not power-assisted, leave the engine off. Put your foot on the brake pedal with moderate pressure. Keep it there for 30 seconds. If the pedal sinks to the floor, there's probably a fluid leak. You should have a leaking hydraulic system repaired at once.

If your car is equipped with an antilock braking system (ABS), be aware that from a troubleshooting and repairing viewpoint the parts that make the system antilocking have nothing to do with the braking system per se. The mechanical braking components and the electronic components that control the mechanical components should be viewed as two separate sets of parts.

Manufacturers now use brake linings that are more resistant to moisture.

LOSS OF POWER BRAKING ONLY IN COLD WEATHER

In cold weather, my power brakes fail to work when the engine is first started. I have to run the engine at idle for about five minutes until brakes start acting as they should. To try and find the problem, a technician disconnected the vacuum line at the power brake booster and placed his thumb over the end of the line as an assistant started the cold engine and pressed down on the brake pedal. There was no vacuum to the power brake booster—not until that five-minute warm-up period passed. Does this indicate that the brake booster has to be replaced?

No, it doesn't. If the booster were defective, you wouldn't have any braking assist—not only when you started the engine, but also after the five-minute warm-up period passed and for the rest of the day.

What the technician's test proves is that something (ice, I would guess) is forming overnight in the vacuum hose attached to the booster. I say ice, because once heat builds up in the engine compartment vacuum to the booster is restored and braking normalizes. Heat then melts the ice and clears the vacuum hose.

Ice can form in the vacuum hose if the hose has a hole in it that's allowing moisture

FIGURE 6.2. There are two pads inside the caliper of a disc brake unit. The caliper sits over the disc, with a pad facing each side of the disc. When you press down on the brake pedal, a piston which is also in the caliper exerts pressure to bring the pads into contact with the disc and bring the disc and the wheel attached to it to a stop. Pads wear. To avoid costly repairs, have pads inspected and, if necessary, replaced before wear reaches the critical stage.

EXPLAINING ANTILOCK BRAKES

An antilock braking system is a conventional braking system outfitted with electronic components. Follow along with Figure 6.3 to get a good idea of how this marvelous safety system works. Suppose the brake pedal is pressed, sending fluid pressure from the master cylinder (4) to mechanical braking components at each wheel (2). One wheel hits a wet or ice patch on the road and begins turning at a speed that's different from the other wheels, a condition that causes cars to skid. An electronic sensor (1) serving the off-speed wheel transmits data to the electronic control unit (5). The electronic control unit then orders a hydraulic pump and valve assembly (3) to apply more or less pressure to the out-of-synch wheel in order to bring its speed into line with the speed of the other wheels, thus averting the skid. All this is done in half-a-blink of an eye. The single lines in this drawing illustrate the flow of electronic data from the sensors to the electronic control unit to the hydraulic pump and valve assembly, and also to a warning light (6) on the dash that will begin to glow if something goes amiss with an electronic part of the system. The double lines illustrate the hydraulic fluid arrangement from the master cylinder to the braking components through the hydraulic pump and differential valve assembly.

---

to enter the hose. It then turns to ice as the car sits idle in cold weather. Replacing the vacuum hose, therefore, should solve your problem.

PREVENTING REAR DISC BRAKE FAILURE

My sports car was rejected by a state inspection station, because the rear disc brakes weren't working. As she was making the repair, which cost me $115, a technician found that the self-adjusting mechanisms and caliper pistons were badly corroded and caused the problem. Why did this happen? Is there a way of preventing a recurrence?

It happened because the self-adjusting mechanisms in the rear haven't been in use. Since the self-adjusters activate the pistons, the pistons also corroded because they haven't been exercised. This, in turn, caused the entire rear braking setup to go down on you.

To avoid a recurrence, engage the parking brake whenever the car is being parked. By setting the parking brake of a car equipped with four-wheel disc brakes, you cause the ratchet-type self-adjusting mechanisms in the rear brake calipers to move the pistons that move the brake pads into contact with the discs (rotors) when brakes are applied. If this doesn't happen, pads will wear to a point where they no longer engage the discs. In other words, the rear brakes won't engage and the full strain of stopping the car will fall on the front brakes.

Once self-adjusters and pistons corrode, they have to be replaced. Therefore, to avoid this very expensive repair every few years, remember what I said: Always engage the parking brake before you turn off the engine.

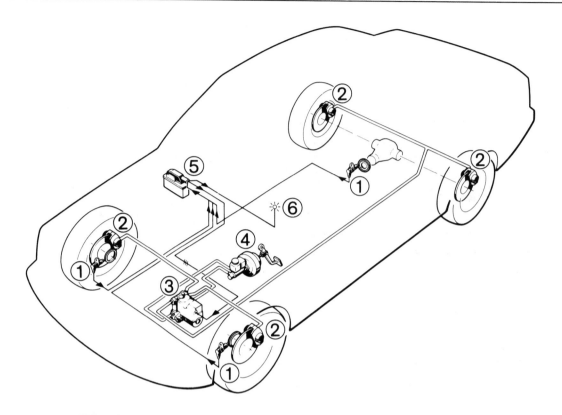

FIGURE 6.3. Antilock brakes. (Courtesy of Robert Bosch Corporation)

UNLOCKING REAR BRAKE LOCKUP

In stop-and-go traffic, there are times when the rear brakes of my car won't release for a few seconds as I accelerate from a stoplight. This happens only in hot weather. I've had the rear brake shoes and wheel cylinders replaced. Now, a technician tells me that a relief valve in the master cylinder is sticking and that the cylinder should be replaced. Another technician tells me the proportioning valve is bad. I'd like some sound advice as to what is wrong before I let someone try out theories that can see me getting nickel-and-dimed to the poor house. Help!

I'm going to throw another log on the fire, because I doubt if either technician is correct. The circumstances under which this condition is occurring point to rear brake drums that are expanding because of extreme heat created by stop-and-go driving under high ambient temperature conditions. I suggest you get a technician who specializes in brakes to make a simple test that will verify whether I'm right. To find a brake specialist, consult your phone book under the heading "Automobile—Brakes."

The technician will use a drum-to-shoe clearance gauge to measure and adjust the gap between drums and shoes according to the procedure and specifications outlined by manufacturer service instructions. If this gap is smaller than it should be, it's causing brake shoes to lock against rear brake drums which have been expanded by the heat.

If the drum-to-shoe measurement is in line with specifications, the brake specialist will look for the cause of the problem with these other possibilities: Contaminated brake fluid, a loose backing plate, weak actuator and return springs, corroded self-adjusting mechanisms, and warped drums. Notice that neither the master cylinder nor proportioning valve is mentioned.

BRAKE RATTLING

I drive a four-wheel drive vehicle that I frequently take over rough backroads when I go hunting and fishing. The vehicle has developed an annoying rattle that seems to be coming from the front, but none of the technicians I've consulted have been able to locate the cause. This is not a body rattle, the suspension system has been given a clean bill of health, and the entire braking system has been gone over as well. Technicians advise that I not worry about the noise. I'd still like your opinion; is it something to be concerned about?

Probably not, but maybe you don't have to put up with it. Ask one of the technicians to replace the front disc brake caliper bolts. The bolts in four-wheel drive vehicles that are driven on rough roads often wear themselves into a groove that causes the caliper to vibrate just enough to produce a rattling sound. The condition doesn't affect safety so you might not want to pay the cost of trying out new caliper bolts.

WHY BRAKE DISCS DEVELOP RIDGES

I recently watched as a technician rotated the tires of my station wagon. As he took off the front wheels and tires, I was surprised to see symmetrical ridges etched into the brake discs. The technician told me this is a common condition

and advised that I have discs turned when I have new brake pads installed. The car has been driven only 15,000 miles. What is happening here?

What's happening is nothing to be concerned about, since the technician didn't advise that brake repairs be done now. Those ridges are caused by the semimetallic brake pads which come into contact with discs to stop the car. It is a normal condition that doesn't affect braking effectiveness.

The technician is correct in suggesting that you have discs turned when new pads are installed. Turning discs, which is standard operating procedure when doing a brake job, refers to mounting the disc on a brake lathe and shaving off surface metal to remove ridges and other minor defects in the discs. (See Figure 6.4.) A turned disc presents a smooth surface for new pads. If left untreated, ridges and minor defects could slice into the pads and result in reduced pad life.

RUSTY BRAKE DRUMS

My question concerns a new car that was taken for a state-mandated safety inspection. When the inspector saw that the rear brake drums and wheel lugs were covered with rust, he said I should have rust removed before it causes trouble. Is he right?

No, he's not. Surface rust on brake drums and wheel lugs is normal and won't cause any problem. These parts are made of cast iron, and cast iron develops surface rust. If you removed the rear wheels from 20 new cars, you would find that drums and wheel lugs of most, if not all, had rust.

STIFF STEERING

Both of my General Motors cars have the same problem of unresponsive power steering for a few seconds after I start the engine, especially on cold mornings. After this, the steering in both cars is normal for the remainder of the day. Do you have any idea what's causing this?

Sure do. Millions of General Motors front-wheel drive models manufactured from 1982 to 1985 experienced this condition. So did thousands of other cars built by Chrysler and other manufacturers that purchased steering components from General Motors' Saginaw Steering Division.

There is no power steering assist for a period of several seconds to as long as two minutes when starting a cold engine in cold weather. When the problem became apparent, General Motors offered to make repairs free of charge. No other manufacturer I know of made a similar offer.

The repair involves installing new seals in the steering assembly to prevent loss of pressure when the steering system is cold. If this doesn't help, the steering assembly has to be replaced—a repair that was done by General Motors, again free of charge.

The General Motors offer had a time/mileage limitation of five years or 50,000 miles, whichever occurred first. By this time, your cars have exceeded the limits, but it still wouldn't hurt to contact the General Motors regional office in your area or to get in touch with the customer service departments of the particular General Motors divisions which manufactured the cars. You might be lucky and get General Motors to assume part of the repair cost.

If General Motors turns a deaf ear to your plea, you can either pay for the repair—the cost will be several hundred dollars—or live

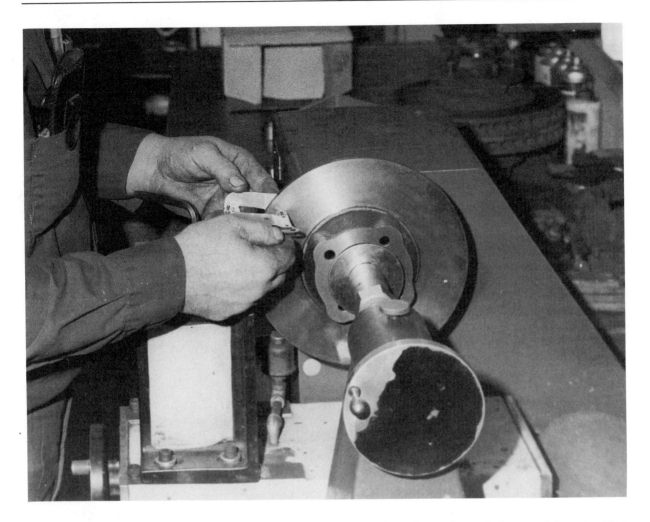

FIGURE 6.4. Having a brake technician remove irregularities from the surface of discs and drums with a brake lathe when you have new pads and linings installed will contribute to the longevity of those pads and linings.

with the condition. If you decide on the latter, the problem probably won't get any worse than it is now. Just be sure to allow an ample warm-up period for steering to free itself before taking to the road.

POWER-STEERING LEAK DILEMMA

It cost me $70 to try and get a power steering fluid leak repaired in my 10-year-old car by replacing the power steering high-pressure hose. It didn't work. Now, the technician says the pump assembly is shot and must be replaced. This will cost me $400, which is too much to spend on an old car. Steering doesn't feel hard and isn't impeding my control of the vehicle. So why must I install a new assembly?

Fluid is the medium that provides power assist to steering. As long as some fluid is still in the system, there will be steering assist. That's why steering doesn't feel hard to you although much of the fluid has been lost.

Fluid, however, has another important job—to lubricate the steering gear. If fluid presently trapped in the system is lost, the steering gear won't be lubricated. Then, not only will steering become much more difficult, but the lack of lubrication will wipe out the steering gear. A new one will cost you far more than a pump assembly.

You could add power steering fluid to the system as often as you lose it, but this will soon become a nuisance. Besides, in time, that leak is going to get worse. So the best solution is to replace the pump.

Now for the good news. The technician seems to be quoting you a hefty price for a pump assembly. A brand new one, if you can get it for a car this old, shouldn't cost more than $150, and the cost of installation shouldn't be more than $100—a total of

$250. There's even a less expensive way to proceed, and that's to install a remanufactured assembly, which is readily available. One should cost you about half the price of a new unit.

SHAFTED OVER A RACK-AND-PINION STEERING FLUID LEAK

My three-year-old station wagon has a leak in the rack assembly of the rack-and-pinion steering system. The dealer says it will cost $1,000 to repair. I contend that a steering rack which goes bad in three years is a steering rack that was poorly manufactured to begin with. Do you know of any secret warranty covering this situation?

What is referred to as a secret warranty is usually a technical service advisory that dealership service personnel fail to implement for one reason or another. Even if there isn't a service advisory that tells the dealer to make repairs, installing new seals in a steering rack should cost you about $150, not $1,000. In short, I think the dealer is trying to take you for a ride. Go to another dealer or take the case directly to the customer service department of the manufacturer.

CONDEMNING SOUND STEERING SYSTEM IDLER ARMS

During a state-mandated vehicle safety inspection, I was told by an inspector that the steering idler arm was too loose and had to be replaced. The inspector who told me this had raised the front of the car, grabbed hold of a front wheel, and tried to shake it. It seems to me that anyone who does this can get a wheel to move. Am I right?

You are indeed. This testing method used by some state motor vehicle inspectors is condemning sound steering idler arms to the scrap heap, not to mention the amount of money it's costing car owners for unnecessary repairs.

The following passage taken from General Motors service instructions concerning steering is applicable to all makes of cars that have steering systems that possess idler arms. I suggest you return to the inspection station and take the matter up with the inspector in charge. If this gets you nowhere, contact the State Department of Motor Vehicles, Inspection Division. Here's what General Motors says:

> The idler arm assembly should be replaced when an up-and-down force of 110 Newtons (25 pounds) is applied at the intermediate rod end of the idler arm and the vertical lash exceeds 3.18 millimeters ($1/8$ inch). Jerking the wheel and tire assembly back and forth, thus causing an up-and-down movement of the idler arm, is not an acceptable method of checking the idler arm, because there is no control on the amount of force being applied.

Note: This question and answer refer to vehicles that possess parallelogram steering systems. They do not apply to vehicles having rack-and-pinion steering systems, which don't have idler arms.

DOING WHEEL ALIGNMENT THE MODERN WAY

In the two years that I've owned my car, I've had to have the front end aligned six times. What's the reason for this? Are the front ends in most cars that weak?

A front suspension system is not likely to lose adjustment unless it is badly jarred. Something like this happening six times in two years is doubtful. That's why I think your wheel alignment isn't being done correctly.

The reason may lie with the fact that "front-end" alignment (also called "front-wheel" alignment) is obsolete. Whoever has been doing your alignment work should be doing four-wheel alignment. (See Figure 6.5.) Another term for it is *total alignment.*

Four-wheel (total) alignment means that the front wheels of a car are adjusted in relation to the rear wheels. If alignment isn't done this way, the thrust of the vehicle will be off-center and the front wheels could track off-kilter to the rear wheels, causing the vehicle to drift or pull to one side. Front tires will wear abnormally, and you may also get a sensation that the car is wandering over the road.

If the shop you're patronizing has been using computerized four-wheel alignment equipment, then it may not have up-to-date alignment specifications for the vehicle. Often, new specifications that supersede those in the service manual or in general repair manuals are provided in service advisories from the manufacturer. Manufacturer service advisories are not sent to nondealership facilities, so your chances of getting an accurate alignment performed may be increased by taking the vehicle to a dealer who sells the particular make of car that you own.

Finally, if the four wheels of your vehicle cannot be aligned to specification, parts of the suspension system are damaged and will have to be replaced.

WHY "PERFECT" ALIGNMENT MAY NOT BE SO PERFECT

I brought my car to a shop to have its wheels aligned, because the car was drifting to the left. When I got it back, drifting was still apparent, so I returned it at once. The service manager told me

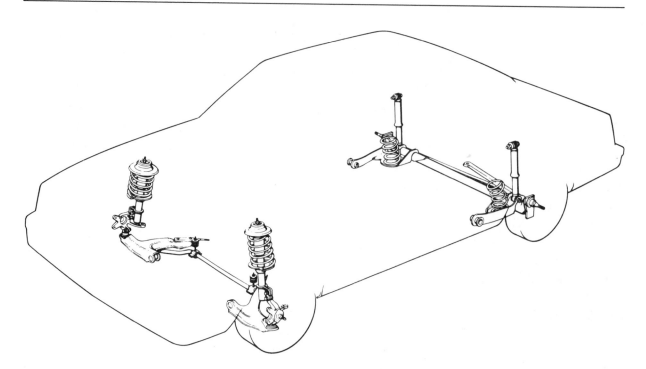

FIGURE 6.5. The front and rear suspensions of a vehicle possess a number of rods, control arms, shock absorbers, wheel spindles, and springs. The suspension system also includes the wheels. If any of these parts is damaged, it won't be possible to correctly align the four wheels of the vehicle. Tire life will suffer. So will handling performance and safety. This is why you should make certain that a technician you bring your car to for a wheel alignment carefully inspects every single component for damage before doing the alignment. (Courtesy of Chrysler Corporation)

that the wheels of the vehicle were in perfect alignment, and that my particular model car was known for a drifting condition. Since I had driven this car 15,000 miles without it drifting, I didn't swallow this excuse and brought the car to the service department of a new car dealership that sells the particular make. The technician who checked alignment said the wheels were way off. He did another alignment and the drifting has disappeared. I'm mad as hell, and I'm going to take the shop owner to small claims court. How do they get away with this kind of nonsense?

Let's give the shop the benefit of doubt by conceding that the manager and technician who did the work believed that it had been done properly, and that four-wheel alignment equipment (see page 137) was employed. There could be two reasons, unknown to them, why the wheels of your car weren't re-aligned correctly.

The first reason could have been a change in the wheel alignment specifications by the car's manufacturer. Ask the technician at the dealership to jot down the specifications that were used to align the wheels so you and the technician at the shop can compare them with the specifications he used. Are they the same?

The second reason is insidious, but much less likely. A section of the concrete floor on which the shop's wheel alignment equipment sits may have been affected by variations in ambient temperature, throwing the equipment off-level. If this happened, the camber and caster settings of your car may have been adjusted inaccurately. Facilities that are equipped with wheel alignment equipment should periodically test side-to-side and end-to-end level at each corner of this equipment with a carpenter's level to determine if an uneven condition exists. If it does exist, it can be corrected with shims placed under the equipment.

CURE FOR A DRIFTING PICKUP TRUCK

My pickup truck has a mind of its own. It drifts to one side on a straight road when I take my hands off the steering wheel. I've varied the tire pressure, rotated tires, and had wheel alignment checked without success at getting rid of the condition. What else can cause this?

Other reasons for drifting include unevenly worn tires and caster split. Uneven tires are those that are worn more on one side than the other, becoming more cone-shape than cylindrical. The condition is usually caused by wheels that are presently or have been out of alignment. If rotating cone-shaped tires (see pages 145–146) doesn't eliminate the drifting condition, installing new tires should.

Caster split refers to a vehicle's suspension system being designed to have more caster on the right side than on the left side to compensate for crowned roads. When the vehicle is rolling along on a flat road or on a road that doesn't have much of a crown, the vehicle may drift.

Ask a technician to check specifications for the caster setting of your truck to determine if the specification for the right front wheel is different from the specification for the left front wheel. If they differ, then caster split is probably the reason for drifting and there's nothing that can be done about it.

There is still another reason for drifting, but it applies only to some makes of pickup trucks. It's related to a part called a ball-joint adjuster slug, which is used to adjust front wheel camber. If your truck has two ball-joint adjuster slugs—one on each side of the front suspension—one of the slugs may not have been installed properly when the truck was manufactured. The ball joint on that side of the truck could be binding and causing the vehicle to drift in that direction.

Have a technician examine the ball joints to see if they are outfitted with adjuster slugs. If slugs are present, the technician should refer to the service manual to determine whether these parts are installed properly.

OVERCOMING A BUMPY RIDE

Passengers tell me that riding in the rear of my new van is uncomfortable, because the rear end bounces so much. Will a different type of shock absorber help make driving more pleasurable for those sitting in the rear?

You can spend hundreds of dollars to try and smooth out the ride of a vehicle by installing one type of shock absorber after another, so don't be too hasty. Your van may benefit most by having a set of rear cargo coil springs put on instead. These are heavier than the rear springs now on the vehicle and will give it greater support and more stability.

To determine what will give you the most benefit for the least amount of money, solicit the opinions of two or three automotive suspension system technicians. Ask them if replacing the springs, shocks, or both will provide the kind of rear-seat driving comfort you're seeking. For example, they might tell you after driving the van that a combination of cargo coil springs and air- or heavy-duty shock absorbers in the rear might be necessary. Install the springs first and use the van for a few hundred miles to determine if the ride is more comfortable. If it's improved, but still not what you want, you always have time to install the new shocks.

KNOWING WHEN TO REPLACE SHOCK ABSORBERS

My car is getting on in years and the ride doesn't seem as firm as it once was, so I'm considering installing new shock absorbers. However, I don't want to replace units that are still sound. Is there any way of telling when a shock is worn out?

Shock absorbers don't wear out. Although shock absorber bushings may. There are only two conditions that cause shocks to lose their ability to absorb the bouncing of springs (see page 16). First, there's the seal that closes off the pressure chamber in a shock absorber. It contains fluid that allows the shock to dampen spring motion. When this seal fails, fluid leaks from the shock. That's one reason for replacing the unit.

The other reason involves road salt, moisture, and heat. These cause one or both rubber bushings at points where a shock attaches to the vehicle to eventually disintegrate. Then, the shock literally hangs loose from the chassis and is useless. Bushings can't be replaced, so new shocks have to be installed.

Note: The same conditions and observations apply to MacPherson struts, which are shock absorbers.

How do you determine whether these conditions have taken place? By doing the following:

- Look to see if there is fluid on the surface of the tube, if the tube is dented, or if bushings are cracked and crumbling. If so, replace shocks.

Note: If one shock absorber is bad, replace the other one on the same end of the car—front or back—to maintain balance. It is not necessary to replace all four units.

- Drive over railroad tracks at 30 to 35 mph. If there's shimmy, noise (clunking), or the vehicle dips, shocks may be bad. The only way to tell for certain is to remove each shock absorber, clamp its lower mount in a vise, and extend and compress the unit. If you don't meet resistance or if you feel a skip in the action, the shock is bad and needs to be replaced.

SHOCK ABSORBER REPLACEMENT FOR DO-IT-YOURSELFERS

I want to replace the shock absorbers of my car. Would you consider this task to be within the scope of a do-it-yourselfer?

Yes, but only if you make sure that the front or rear of the car, which has to be raised, is well supported when you're beneath it. The following describes how to replace both front and rear shock absorbers.

Note: This information does *not* apply to MacPherson struts (see page 143).

To replace front shock absorbers, follow this procedure:

1. Determine if the top mount is reached from under the car or from inside the engine compartment. Engage the parking brake and raise the front of the vehicle; then, place jack stands beneath the lower suspension arms and lower the vehicle onto the jack stands. Put wheel chocks behind the rear wheels to make sure the vehicle won't roll back.

2. If the top mount is reached from below, remove the wheel and tire. You may be able to get at the mount through the wheel well. If the top mount is reached from inside the engine compartment, there may be a dirt shield over it that

must be removed. Then, remove the nuts holding the top mount. Be aware of how you take off hardware so you can reinstall it properly. Usually, a retainer cap goes over the shaft, followed by a bushing and then a nut.

Note: If the nuts are rusted, you may not be able to budge them. Apply lots of penetrating oil and let it seep in. Then, try again.

3. Remove the lower mounting bolt(s) and nut(s). A shock is held by one bolt and nut or two bolts and nuts. You can now withdraw the shock from the vehicle. (See Figure 6.6.)

4. Mount the new shock in a vise, being careful not to damage the case. Pull it out and push it in a few times to expel air that may be trapped inside.

5. Extend the new shock and install it on the car. Attach the upper mounting hardware and screw on the nut fingertight. Next, install and tighten the lower mounting bolt(s) and nut(s). Now, tighten the upper mounting nut. Make sure all fasteners are as tight as you can get them.

To replace rear shocks, follow this procedure:

1. Determine if the top mount is reached from below the vehicle, from inside the trunk, or from under the rear seat.

2. Place wheel chocks in front of the front wheels, lift the rear of the vehicle and place jack stands under the rear axle as close as possible to each shock. Lower the vehicle so the axle is supported.

3. If you can't budge hardware, apply penetrating oil and let it soak in. Then, remove the lower mounting bolt and nut, followed by the upper mounting bolt(s) and nut(s). Remove the shock.

FIGURE 6.6. In this car, shields (one on each side) that protect fasteners from dirt cover the top of front shock absorber mounts. To remove the shock absorbers, the shields have to be pried off. They should be reinstalled after new shock absorbers have been installed. Rear shock absorbers may have a similar setup, with the top mounts being loosened from inside the trunk or passenger compartment.

4. Expel air from the new shock by pulling it out and pushing it in a few times. Install and tighten hardware securely.

As for MacPherson struts, special tools are required to replace them, so it's not a task you would want to tackle. In dealing with a technician you've hired to replace struts, keep in mind that the entire unit does not usually have to be replaced. The shock absorber and coil spring around it are taken off the vehicle as a unit. The special tool is used to retract the coil spring so the shock absorber can be opened, and a replacement cartridge is inserted. By avoiding replacement of the entire strut—that is, the spring and shock absorber case in addition to the mechanism—you save about $1/2$ of what the job would otherwise cost.

Rx FOR A DIPPY FRONT END

The dealer replaced the MacPherson struts in the front of my three-year-old car under the extended warranty, because one was leaking and because the front end of the car was dipping and almost hitting bottom when the car went over bumps. The new struts haven't helped the dipping, but the dealer says nothing else can be done and I'll have to live with the condition. Isn't there any kind of MacPherson strut to use up front that can help prop up this car?

The only one that may do that is an adjustable MacPherson strut made by Koni America, Incorporated, 111 West Lovers Lane, Culpeper, VA 22701. These units can be set to give a degree of support from firm to soft. Set at firm, you may eliminate the bouncing. The ride, however, will be less cushy and you might not like it.

But why are you placing the blame for this problem on the new struts? More plausible reasons for the condition would be weak front coil springs or springs that were installed incorrectly by the technician who replaced the struts. In most cars, the strut (shock absorbing) part of the unit fits inside the coil spring. When a leaking strut is replaced with a new strut, the coil spring is usually kept in service. The technician could have accidentally reversed the spring so the top of the spring is attached to where the bottom should be and the bottom is where the top should be.

Another reason for a car bottoming is that the technician may have left off the jounce bumpers that are supposed to go between the strut and spring. There could also be an insulator needed between the strut and the top of the spring seat to lessen the chance of bottoming.

From the way you describe it, the dealer replaced the leaking strut and the strut on the other side of the front of the car. This is the way it should be. Struts should be replaced in pairs. Therefore, what is applicable to the new strut which replaced the leaking strut is also applicable to the other new strut.

HOPE FOR TIRE HOP

Is there a cure for the front-end bounce I'm getting from my new utility vehicle? The sensation occurs between 25 and 35 mph. The dealer has balanced the wheels, and replaced and rotated the tires without being successful. He then turned the matter over to the vehicle's manufacturer whose representative said that the condition was caused by "frame-beaming," whatever that means. He says, "All utility vehicles do it." I'd appreciate your opinion since the

representative offered to try anything that would satisfy me.

The representative is not accurate in his analysis. Frame-beaming refers to a slight deflection of the frame that gives a sensation that the vehicle is flexing. It's a sensation you can feel when driving at slow speeds—up to about 10 mph—not between 25 and 35 mph as in your case. In addition, frame-beaming is characteristic of pickup trucks and large vans, not smaller utility vehicles. Where does this leave you?

Tire hop or bounce is symptomatic of unbalanced wheel assemblies. Even though you've had wheels balanced, the job may not have been effective.

A wheel assembly consists of three interrelated parts. They are the tire, wheel, and brake disc or drum. The accepted present-day method of balancing wheel and tire assemblies is to take a tire and wheel as a unit off a car and mount that unit on an electronic balancing machine that spins to determine where an unbalanced spot exists. Weights are added to the wheel to counterbalance the imbalance.

This method often does the job, but sometimes it doesn't. That's why I suggest you ask a technician to forget about electronic balancing and do balancing in two stages: static and dynamic.

Static balancing involves placing each tire and wheel as a unit, in turn, on a leveling machine which is called a bubble balancer. This is done with the unit off the vehicle. The machine holds the unit stationary as the point of imbalance is found so a counterbalancing weight can be added.

Dynamic balancing is done after static balancing is done. It requires using a machine called a spin balancer. The tire and wheel unit is mounted on the car so it's in contact with the third element of the assembly; that

is, with the brake disc or brake drum. With the car raised, the spin balancer is pushed against the tire. When turned on, the spin balancer can be brought up to a speed that equals highway speed to spin the tire-wheel-brake assembly. An out-of-balance condition will be revealed by a flashing stroboscopic light that's part of the spin balancer.

There may be another reason why you're experiencing tire hop. Maybe the surface of the roads on which you drive are affecting tires, causing them to hop. In other words, are you getting the bounce only on roads that were recently paved? If so, there's obviously no solution other than to stay off those roads.

A GOOD RADIAL TIRE THAT CAN'T BE REPAIRED

I'm engaged in an argument with the manager of a tire store and need some facts. Something punctured the inside shoulder of one of the new radial tires I purchased from him. The manager refuses to repair the damage. He contends that a patch won't hold. He wants me to scrap the tire and buy a new one, which is a heck of a note for a tire that just cost me $65. Help. I need the truth to put this guy in this place.

You ought to thank him instead. He's keeping you from making a mistake. No repair should ever be made to an injured part of a radial tire that's beyond the belted area of the tread. These are the shoulder and sidewall, which flex as a tire rotates. Flexing will cause a patch on the shoulder or sidewall to pull away from the tire. The result could be a blow-out and loss of control.

You may be able to retain the use of this tire, however, by installing a tube. But the tube has to be one that's specifically designed for a radial tire. Discuss this with the manager of the tire store. Remember, though—a tube manufactured for use in an old-fashioned tube-type bias-ply tire should never be put into a radial. It won't hold up.

Here are a couple of other tips concerning radial tire repair that can help you avoid a problem:

1. Never repair a radial which has a puncture or cut that's more than $1/4$ inch in diameter.

2. Don't repair a radial which has tread worn down to a depth of $1/16$ inch. Replace it.

PREVENTING REAR TIRE WEAR

The rear tires of my car—not the front, mind you—have developed an irregular wear pattern over the face of the tread. The manager of the service department at the new car dealership contends that the tires were not manufactured properly. A tire dealer who sells the brand blames the problem on an inherent defect with the car. Meanwhile, I'm stuck in the middle. I don't want to install new tires if they're going to start wearing because of a defect with the car. Any suggestions?

Abnormal wear of rear tires in cars equipped with front-wheel drive units (transaxles), as yours is, is not an uncommon complaint. The condition has affected several makes of cars. Automobile manufacturers have devised procedures to correct the problem and prevent the abnormal wear. In the case of some General Motors models, for example, the procedure is to have shims installed to change the alignment of the rear wheels. Ask your dealer to check with the manufacturer to find out if this or a similar procedure has been developed for your car.

Whether there is or isn't a mechanical procedure that will offset irregular tire wear, rotating tires on a regular basis is a time-proven method that will certainly help prolong tire life. If tires presently on the car are in such poor condition that they have to be replaced, the new tires you buy should be mounted on the front wheels and the tires now on the front of the car should be moved to the rear. After driving 7,500 miles, rotate tires using a modified X pattern. If you're going to keep your present tires in use, have them rotated using this modified X pattern.

The modified X pattern calls for moving the left front tire to the left rear, the left rear tire to the right front, the right front tire to the right rear, and the right rear tire to the left front.

To get maximum mileage from tires, have them rotated every 7,500 miles.

DEALING WITH CUPPED TIRES

My new car came equipped with steel-belted all-season radial tires that developed depressed spots over the tread after about 5,000 miles. I had them rotated periodically, but still they gave a rough ride for the 48,000 miles that they lasted. When I bought a new set of all-season radial tires, I thought this problem was at an end. But sure enough, the same thing is happening—the tires are starting to cup. Why is this happening?

The factors that cause tires to cup are improper inflation, abusive driving, failure to rotate on a regular basis, and excessive toe-in. Toe-in is the amount, measured in inches or degrees from zero, that the wheels point inward.

SERVICE TIP: PRESSURE-CHECK THE TIRES OF YOUR NEW CAR

Not many buyers of new cars check the air pressure of tires when they drive the vehicles out of new car dealer showrooms. They usually wait for hundreds or thousands of miles to pass. During that time, it's possible that those new tires are sustaining unnecessary wear. It's also conceivable for an owner to wonder why a new vehicle isn't driving as comfortably as expected. The reason may be that during the manufacture of the vehicle, tires were overfilled with air to get them seated properly to the wheels and were shipped to the new car dealer this way.

Before the dealer delivers a vehicle to a customer, tire pressure is supposed to be reduced to a normal level. Sometimes it isn't. The above-normal pressure than results in unnecessary tire wear and also a harsh ride.

By this time, the message should be clear: Check tire pressure soon after you get your new car to make sure it's at the level specified on the tire pressure placard attached to a door jamb of the vehicle or printed in the owner's manual.

I suggest you have a wheel alignment specialist check the suspension for damage and then set the toe-in of all the wheels of your car to zero. Tell the technician to disregard the toe-in specification given in the service manual and other service literature. Make sure tire inflation pressure is maintained at the specified amount. The specification is given on a placard pasted on the driver-side door.

If your car has front-wheel drive, have tires rotated every 7,500 miles using the modified X pattern. This means moving the left front tire to the left rear, left rear tire to the right front, right front tire to the right rear and right rear tire to the left front.

If your car has rear-wheel drive, rotate tires every 7,500 miles by placing the left-front tire on the right rear, right-front tire on the left rear, left-rear tire on the left front, and right-rear tire on the right front.

If cupping worsens or wear appears to be greater over one area than the other areas, have toe-in set to 1/32 inch. Test the results for a few thousand miles more. If this proce-

dure doesn't help, I suggest that next time you have to buy tires you purchase units having a conventional tread design.

DIMPLES IN NEW TIRES

Two of the four radial tires I just bought for my car have dimples in the sidewalls. I can even feel how uneven the surface is when I run my hand over it. The manager of the tire store claims that dimples are normal and refuses to replace the tires. I intend to take him to court, but before I do I need expert testimony in writing that he's wrong. Can I rely on you for that?

No, because the manager is correct. Dimples, ripples, waves, undulations—call them what you wish—that are apparent in the sidewalls of a new tire do not indicate a defective tire. The uneven surface is made where the fabric (cord) beneath the sidewall is spliced together. These splices do not affect the durability of the tire. Neither do they alter handling or riding comfort. All they may do is make dimples. In other words, a tire with dimples performs as well and lasts as long as a tire that doesn't have dimples.

FACTS ABOUT STUDDED SNOW TIRES

The tires on my car are studded snow tires. According to the law in my state, I can keep them on the car from October 15 until April 1. My question concerns the laws in other states, because I want to make a trip this winter to Florida that will take me through Delaware, Maryland, Virginia, the Carolinas, and Georgia. Will I run into a problem with the authorities in these states?

It depends on the state and when you'll be traveling. The law concerning studded snow tires differs from state to state and changes from year to year. As this is being written, the Carolinas and Georgia don't have any restrictions concerning studded snow tires, so you can have them on a car any time of the year. You can drive through Delaware and Virginia with studded snow tires on the car from October 15 until April 15. Studs in these two states are prohibited at other times of the year.

That leaves Maryland and Florida. In Maryland, as this is being written, you can have studded snow tires on a car from November 1 to March 31 as long as the car is used in five counties (Alleghany, Carroll, Frederick, Garrett, and Washington). In all other counties, studded tires are prohibited the entire year.

Studded tires are prohibited all year long in the whole state of Florida. If you get caught with studded snow tires on your car when they're not supposed to be there, you will be fined.

ON WHICH WHEELS TO PLACE STUDDED SNOWS TIRES

What's the story on where to place studded snow tires? Should they go on all four wheels or only on the wheels driven by the car's differential? My car, a 1990 model, has the differential in the front.

It doesn't matter whether the differential is in the rear or front. For maximum traction, place a studded snow tire on each wheel.

AVOID YUCKEY ALLOY WHEELS

When I had new tires installed on my car several months ago, the tire and wheel units were balanced. Now I notice that the stylized alloy wheels have developed stains that look awful. What should I use to clean them off?

To avoid scratching the wheels, use a mild cleanser, such as Bon Ami®. Saturate a rag, spread the cleanser on the rag, and then use a gentle touch to rub the spots. Follow this by washing the wheels with a spray of water from a garden hose.

What you describe is typical of alloy wheels which have been balanced using uncoated wheel weights. An electrochemical reaction between uncoated wheel weights, which are lead, and alloy wheels produces stains and can also cause wheels to pit. To prevent the problem, the technician should have used coated wheel weights.

TREATING RECURRENT BRAKE FAILURE

The first time I had to replace the front brake pads on my 1987 imported car

was at 24,000 miles; the second time, at 45,000 miles. Less than 5,000 miles after that, the car developed a frightening shimmy when brakes were applied at freeway speed. I took the car back to the shop that had installed the pads and was advised that the calipers had frozen. New calipers and pads were installed. About 4,500 miles later, I lost half the brake pedal travel so again returned the car to the shop. The explanation was that the right caliper had jammed because of a rusted pin. This supposedly caused pads to wear to less than 20 percent of their thickness. Repairs were again made. Now, less than two months after the last episode, the high speed shimmy has returned. I need help.

It seems as if your problems began the second time you had pads installed. The job probably wasn't done properly, and things just snowballed from then on. Here's what should be done whenever new pads are installed:

- *Refinish discs.* This should be done to eliminate irregularities that can cause abnormal brake pad wear. To correctly refinish the discs of many cars (yours is one of them), they must remain in position on the car and be resurfaced using portable equipment.

- *Lubricate.* Many manufacturers call for application of a lubricant, such as Molykote M77®, on certain parts of the shims, shoes, wear indicators, and calipers. The particular areas that require lubrication are identified in the car's service manual, but care must be taken not to get lubricant on the pads.

- *Install parts correctly.* Components have to be installed as outlined in the service manual with care taken to position pads so wear indicators face up.

- *Tighten lug nuts to the specification given in the service manual (about 80 foot-pounds) when tires and wheels are put back on the car.* A torque wrench—not a power wrench—must be used. If lug nuts are overtightened or not tightened evenly, disc runout can result, and this will cause a severe shimmy.

- *Break-in new pads properly.* When the job has been completed, the technician should bring the car to a complete stop from 35 mph using light application on the brake pedal. This should be done about 20 times. The purpose is to make sure all pad surfaces are burnished to the discs. Otherwise, shimmy will result when brakes are applied.

There's one other important fact to consider when you have pads replaced. There could be a choice of two kinds. One is the vehicle manufacturer's original equipment pads. The other is a pad made of a softer material. Original pads will outlast the softer pads, but they might emit a squeal in wet weather. This squeal is normal and is not cause for concern.

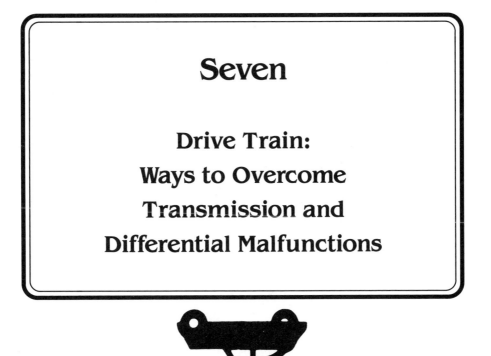

Seven

Drive Train:
Ways to Overcome
Transmission and
Differential Malfunctions

TELLING GOOD AUTOMATIC TRANSMISSION FLUID FROM BAD

Is the man who services my car correct when he says that as long as automatic transmission fluid is clear and doesn't emit a burned odor, it's safe to keep it in use? Or should this fluid be replaced periodically just as engine oil is replaced periodically?

Unless you use your car under severe service conditions, such as pulling a trailer, and you don't abuse the transmission by rocking the car back and forth trying to extract it from snow banks, it's usually not necessary to

change automatic transmission fluid on a regular basis. However, there's a simple test you can do to establish if fluid is contaminated and needs to be changed.

The test, which you can do as often as you wish (once every 10,000 miles of driving is reasonable), is done by pulling out the automatic transmission fluid dipstick and allowing a few drops of fluid to fall on a paper towel. After a few minutes, examine the stain.

If the spot is widely dispersed and red, pink, or light brown, the fluid is in good condition and need not be changed. If the spot is concentrated into a tight circle and the center is darker than the edges, the fluid is oxidized and should be replaced along with the filter in the transmission.

OVERFILLING A TRANSMISSION IS OVERKILLING

I had a local service station do a tune-up of the automatic transmission in my car. The work consisted of changing the transmission fluid and replacing the filter. I now find that the fluid level on the dipstick is about an inch over the FULL mark. The manager of the service station says not to worry about it—that the overfill won't cause harm. I'm not so sure and would like your opinion. Should I have this excess drained?

Absolutely! Overfilling an automatic transmission must be avoided to avoid damage. (See Figure 7.1.) Excess fluid causes moving parts in the transmission to spin like the beaters of an electric food mixer. This action leads to aeration; that is, it causes air to mix with the lubricant and produce foam that prevents fluid from reaching and lubricating moving parts of the transmission. In addition, foam causes a build up of pressure inside the assembly, which can force lubricant past gaskets and seals. In other words, you'll have a leak on your hands.

Take the car to a shop that specializes in transmissions. I suggest that you don't trust this assembly to just anyone. It's the most complex of all assemblies in a car, and it costs the most to repair if it's damaged.

BLACK PARTICLES IN AUTOMATIC TRANSMISSION FLUID

A shop I brought my one-year old car to for servicing almost gave me a heart attack by telling me the automatic transmission will soon need overhauling. This diagnosis was based on black particles found in the transmission fluid while checking the fluid level. I was told that these flecks are a sign that bands and clutches inside the transmission are disintegrating. I brought the car back to the dealer and had an argument with the service manager who says that the black flecks are normal and finally told me to get lost. I'm going to court to try and get a new transmission under the warranty. What I'd like from you is some ammunition I can use. Does this car have a history of automatic transmission failure?

No, it doesn't. Furthermore, you're arguing with the wrong people. Your complaint is with whoever told you that the black particles in the fluid are signaling transmission failure. That's utter nonsense.

The transmission fluid dipstick tubes installed in cars during manufacture are usually coated with black paint. Subjected to heat, this paint disintegrates and can cause particles to float into the transmission fluid. Most of these are trapped by a filter. Some aren't and show up on the dipstick.

Before you go off the deep end, have the fluid and filter changed. (See Figure 7.2.) Run the car a few hundred miles before checking the fluid. In all probability, black flakes will no longer be seen in the fluid.

HOW AUTOMATIC OVERDRIVE IS SUPPOSED TO WORK

My pickup truck is equipped with an automatic overdrive (AOD) transmission that won't downshift until the vehicle speed drops below 20 mph. The service manager at a dealership says I'm supposed to kick it down by bumping the

FIGURE 7.1. An automatic transmission requires a specific quantity of fluid—no less and certainly no more. The technician who replenishes the fluid must do it according to the specific requirements of the manufacturer as given in service instructions. These requirements differ from one manufacturer to another. Make sure the technician who does the job for you knows what he or she is doing.

FIGURE 7.2.   If you have the fluid in an automatic transmission replaced, be sure to have the filter changed, too. It filters out particles picked up by fluid as it circulates through the transmission. After thousands of miles, an old filter may be loaded with debris that can contaminate the new fluid.

accelerator pedal when the speedometer shows that vehicle speed has dropped to about 30 mph. Is he right? If not, what needs to be done to get this AOD to work as it should?

No, he is not right. But before I explain why let me describe how an automatic overdrive works. An automatic transmission without AOD has three forward gears and REVERSE. An automatic transmission with AOD adds a fourth forward gear, which some call the cruising gear.

The shifting quadrant of a car with AOD may display selections this way: PRN D321. D is automatic overdrive, while 3, 2, and 1 refer to third, second, and first gears, respectively. P is for PARK, R is for REVERSE, and N is for NEUTRAL.

When the transmission selector lever is placed in D, the transmission starts in first gear, and automatically upshifts to second gear and then to third gear as you accelerate the vehicle. When you reach the cruising speed at which you want to travel and level off on the accelerator pedal, the transmission automatically upshifts into fourth (automatic overdrive) gear. Fourth gear provides a gear ratio that puts the least demands on an engine, thereby keeping to a minimum the amount of gasoline the engine consumes.

Now, suppose you're cruising along in fourth (automatic overdrive) gear, and you allow the vehicle to coast down or you slow the vehicle down by applying the brakes. An automatic overdrive transmission is supposed to downshift automatically from fourth into third gear when vehicle speed drops to approximately 30 mph. It is supposed to automatically downshift from third into second gear at approximately 20 mph, and automatically drop from second into first gear when vehicle speed hits about 10 mph. There should be no need to "bump"

the accelerator pedal as the service manager told you.

Suppose, as you contend, the transmission in your car isn't shifting down until speed falls to below 20 mph. You would really know it, because an automatic overdrive transmission that sticks in fourth gear until vehicle speed drops to below 20 mph would make your pickup truck buck like crazy. You don't complain about this. Therefore, it's more likely that the transmission in your pickup is shifting so softly that you're just not feeling the downshifts as they're taking place. This is not unusual. "Soft" downshifting is characteristic of an automatic overdrive transmission.

There's a test you can do yourself that will reveal if the transmission is downshifting properly, albeit so softly that you don't feel it going through the motions. As you're cruising along the highway with the transmission in fourth (automatic overdrive) gear, take your foot off the accelerator pedal and let the truck coast down. When vehicle speed hits about 27 mph, draw the shift lever into third gear, represented by the numeral 3. If you don't feel a bump, it means the transmission is already in third gear, which is right where it should be. In other words, the transmission is operating perfectly.

REPAIR FOR A ROUGH-SHIFTING AUTOMATIC TRANSMISSION

My car is equipped with a V8 engine and automatic transmission. The transmission was shifting roughly when car speed was between 25 and 35 mph. The dealer told me, "They all do it," so I believed him. But now there's a new wrinkle. Recently, the SERVICE ENGINE light came on. When it did, the transmission started to shift beautifully. I brought the car back to the dealer who found that a faulty coolant sensor was the reason why the SERVICE ENGINE light came on. He replaced the sensor. That made the SERVICE ENGINE light stop glowing, but the transmission is shifting roughly again. What does one thing have to do with the other? Is there a repair for this rough-shifting problem?

The torque converter clutch, which is part of the automatic transmission, is controlled by the computer of the engine electronic control system. This system also governs the delivery of fuel to the engine. The coolant sensor, too, is part of the engine electronic control system. It feeds data to the computer. Therefore, the computer is the common denominator that links the coolant sensor with the torque converter clutch in the transmission.

When the coolant sensor in your car went bad, the computer activated the fuel system to provide a richer fuel mixture to prevent the engine from performing badly. It also released the torque converter clutch from its control to prevent stalling. Another thing the computer did was to turn on the SERVICE ENGINE light to warn that a problem existed.

Let me sum it up this way: The purpose of a computer-controlled torque converter clutch is to increase fuel economy. Your car would perform splendidly without a computer and with a torque converter that operated mechanically, but it would use more gas. This is exactly the way it was performing when the coolant sensor went bad and caused the computer to release its hold on the converter.

In light of this, you may wonder if you shouldn't just have the coolant sensor disconnected altogether. No, you shouldn't, because without a properly performing coolant sensor, the engine will run hotter than nor-

mal. Over a period of time, this will cause damage to the catalytic converter and engine.

AUTOMATIC TRANSMISSION WON'T SHIFT EASILY IN COLD WEATHER

My car has a V8 engine and an automatic transmission that has a hang up about cold weather. When the temperature hits 10°F or colder, the transmission won't shift out of first gear unless I press down on the accelerator pedal to rev the engine. At warmer ambient temperatures, shifting is normal. A technician has already installed a new governor. Now, he wants to have an open-ended charge account to track down the trouble. He says he doesn't know why this is happening and will have to do a series of tests. I would appreciate any information you can give me so I can tell him where to look.

There may not be a thing you can do about this condition since it may be normal for your car. Some automatic transmissions have a tendency to demonstrate a higher first-to-second gear shifting point in cold weather. But assuming the cold weather-induced higher shifting point is not normal for your transmission, several areas become suspect. Unfortunately, there's no way for a technician to pinpoint the cause of the trouble without doing a series of services. That's why he can't be specific as to cost. Let me explain what's involved.

The technician will start by changing the transmission fluid and the filter. The wrong type of fluid or contaminated fluid may be gumming up the transmission valve body in cold weather, which would cause sluggish shifting.

Next, the technician will look for frost in the vacuum modulator line, if the transmission has a vacuum modulator, and for a servo accumulator seal that's shrinking because of the cold weather. A servo accumulator seal that is contracting causes a loss of pressure, which will make the transmission shift erratically. A test of transmission pressure under cold weather conditions will also be made to determine if the servo accumulator seal is being affected.

From this point, the technician will investigate the possibility that a check ball in the valve body is sticking, a condition that will restrict the flow of fluid and affect shifting. In order to rule out a sticking valve-body check ball, the technician has to disassemble the transmission and remove the valve body.

DEFANGING A DANGEROUS AUTOMATIC TRANSMISSION

On two occasions the automatic transmission in my car jumped from PARK into REVERSE. The first time was when I left the car with the engine running to get something from the garage. When I returned, I found the car 20 feet away with the rear end against a tree. A week later, I put the transmission into PARK, turned off the engine, and parked on a slight incline. When I returned, I found the car several feet from where it had been, with the shift indicator in REVERSE. What can I do about this threat to safety?

Make sure you're engaging the transmission shift lever properly. It's almost impossible for an automatic transmission to jump out of PARK since there is a positive lock in the transmission to prevent this. You should make certain this lock is engaged when you park the car by applying the parking brake *before* you shift into PARK; then by seeing to it that the shift lever is shoved all the way into the parking gear.

Even without the shifting situation you describe, it's wise to take safety precautions when parking on a hill by setting the front tire against the curb to prevent the car from rolling, and never leave a car unattended with the engine running.

ALMOST STUCK IN PARK

The automatic transmission of my full-sized model car is extremely hard to shift out of PARK when I park the vehicle nose-up on our steeply inclined driveway. Do you have any suggestions I can pass on to a technician?

When the weight of a large, heavy car such as yours bears down on the parking mechanism in the transmission, which is called the parking pawl, it takes muscle by the driver to pull the transmission out of PARK. It's for this reason that manufacturers suggest using a specific method when parking a car nose-up on a steep incline. Before removing your foot from the brake, set the parking brake securely, and only then shift into PARK. Doing things in the correct order will make it easier to shift out of PARK if the parking pawl isn't damaged. Therefore, try this before you have the transmission disassembled unnecessarily. There's time to do that if shifting out of Park remains difficult, which then confirms the existence of a damaged parking pawl. The only repair for a damaged parking pawl is to replace that part.

NO PASSING GEAR

When I had the automatic transmission in my car serviced recently, a technician found that the passing gear didn't work. This is the one that drops into a lower gear when the gas pedal is stomped on. I didn't realize it, because I never use the passing gear. The transmission performs normally otherwise, but the technician is trying to sell me on making a repair that will cost hundreds of dollars. Is it worth it?

The trouble with the passing gear is probably centered in the valve body. The detent valve that controls the kick-down or passing gear is sticking because of sludge, or the solenoid that controls the detent valve may be defective. But what's the difference? The defect is not going to affect the other parts of the transmission, and you've been doing without a passing gear. So why repair something you're not going to use?

CLUTCH FAILS TO RELEASE

The clutch pedal in my car doesn't come up all the way. I fear that this is putting wear on the clutch. Can you tell me what has to be done to correct the problem?

If the clutch in your car operates hydraulically, air trapped in the hydraulic system may be causing the problem. Most hydraulic units have a bleed screw in the slave cylinder or master cylinder to dispel trapped air. After the screw is opened, pumping the clutch pedal up and down a few times will cause air to be pumped from the hydraulic system and allow the pedal to return to a normal position.

Air trapped in the system, however, might not be the reason why the clutch is failing to release. To find out, a technician should measure the travel of the slave cylinder rod. If the rod moves 15/16 to 1 inch, the technician should check the clutch fork (it may be bent), the ball pivot in the bell-housing on which the clutch fork rides (it may be worn), the throw-out bearing (it, too, may be worn), and the clutch pressure plate (it may be shot). These conditions also apply to nonhydraulic clutches which have pedals that aren't releasing fully.

UNABLE TO SHIFT
A MANUAL TRANSMISSION

I've had a problem with the manual transmission in my van, which I bought new, since practically the first day. On occasion, I've not been able to shift the transmission when the engine is running. I have to turn the engine off, shift the transmission, keep the clutch depressed as I restart the engine, and then let the clutch out. The trouble can occur several times a day; then again, it may not happen for a week or two. The technicians in the dealer's service department have replaced the master and slave cylinders three different times, but they have yet to figure out how to fix this trouble. Help!

This problem should have been solved the first time you complained about it. There's a defective part in the transmission, probably a poorly machined synchronizer. On those occasions when you can't shift the transmission, you happen to be catching the synchronizer when it's in position where the damage is causing gears to bind. The trouble

---

**SERVICE TIP:
GETTING THE MOST OUT
OF A CLUTCH**

Clutches fail, because they're misused. Furthermore, manual transmissions often sustain unnecessary damage when clutches are misused.

To obtain the maximum life from the clutch in your car and to prevent possible transmission damage, follow this advice:

- If your car has a mechanical (non fluid) clutch, be sure clutch pedal travel (free play) is adjusted to manufacturer specifications. Have free play checked when you have engine oil changed.
- Reduce the amount of clutch slippage by engaging and disengaging the clutch quickly and smoothly. Clutch slippage, which occurs as the clutch is engaged creates heat that hastens wear; therefore, keeping slippage to a minimum helps to lessen wear.
- Never rev the engine as you shift gears or lug the engine in a gear too high for a given engine speed.
- When accelerating from a stop, don't "pop" the clutch in an attempt to increase acceleration.
- When shifting gears, pause for a fraction of a second in Neutral before engaging the next gear to give synchronizers a chance to catch up and provide a smooth shift.
- When stopped on an uphill grade, don't use the clutch to prevent the vehicle from coasting backwards. Use the parking or foot brake.
- To start smoothly without rolling back when leaving a parking spot on an uphill grade, set the parking brake, depress the clutch, and engage first gear. Hold the steering wheel with one hand, slowly release the parking brake with the other hand, and simultaneously engage the clutch.
- Never rest your foot on the clutch pedal. Riding the clutch will cause friction material to wear away, leaving you with a burned-out clutch in only a few thousand miles.
- Never rest your hand on the gear shift knob. This practice causes increased wear to the synchronizers.

---

can be cleared up only by replacing the transmission or disassembling the gear case and replacing the damaged synchronizer or synchronizer and gear which may now be chipped. If the service department can't do the job, ask the service manager to request help from the manufacturer.

**MANUAL TRANSMISSION
GRINDS GEARS**

My problem concerns a manual transmission that frequently grinds gears when I shift into REVERSE. I've been told that this is normal. Is it?

Let's see. Start the engine, hold the clutch pedal one inch off the floor, and count off two seconds. Now, shift into REVERSE.

If you get a clash of gears, the clutch has a warped plate or disk, or a bad pilot shaft bushing. If you don't get a clash of gears, then you've been shifting into REVERSE too quickly.

Reverse gear is not a synchronized gear. This means that gears which are synchronized have to come to a stop in order to mesh with the nonsynchronized Reverse gear. This spin-down time, which allows the shift to take place without gear clashing, takes about two seconds. So, when you shift into REVERSE from now on, count to two before moving the shift lever from NEUTRAL into REVERSE.

REPAIR FOR A VIOLENT JERK

My car, with 55,000 miles on the odometer, has a five-speed manual transmission and a terrible problem with a slipping clutch. A violent jerking occurs as the engine is accelerated with the transmission in first gear. A technician replaced the clutch, release bearing, and pressure plate. He also turned the flywheel. The problem is still with me. Furthermore, since he's done the work, there's a loud squeak that disappears only when I press the clutch pedal down 1/2 inch or more. What's wrong?

It seems to me that whoever worked on the car has been treating the victim and not the culprit. You describe the condition as a slipping clutch which, were it true, would justify what the technician has done. However, I don't think you have a slipping clutch. I think the condition is a chattering clutch, which is the term applied to a violent jerking like the kind you mention. A chattering clutch makes this a whole different ballgame.

The cause of a chattering clutch doesn't have to be the pressure plate, clutch disk, flywheel, or release bearing although it could be. There are other possible reasons for this problem, including:

1. Oil on the clutch disk that causes a burned or glazed clutch disk face. When he replaced the disk, did the technician check for oil leaking onto the clutch from the engine or transmission? If not, oil may have again contaminated the disk.

2. A loose engine mount. Did the technician check each engine mount for cracks, and did he tighten each to the specification cited in the service manual?

3. A worn transmission input shaft. Did the technician inspect the splines of the input shaft to determine if there is wear?

As for the loud squeak, since it wasn't there before the technician worked on the car, the fork shaft of the new clutch, when assembled, may not have been lubricated or was installed improperly.

STUCK IN FIFTH

My mini-van has a five-speed manual transmission. The shift lever sticks in fifth gear, requiring much more than normal effort to shift. This occurs once or twice a day. All other times, shifting out of fifth is easily done. I've had the car to the dealer several times. He's greased and adjusted cables and connections, and now says he's done all he can. Is this true?

No. He can do more. There are two reasons for a manual transmission to get stuck in any gear. The first is a selector-shift cable that's hanging up. The dealer should see to it that the selector-cable is routed so it isn't interfering with any other component. If the cable is bent, it should be replaced.

The second reason is a synchronizer-strut retainer plate that is causing hit-or-miss lockup of the synchronizer spring and gear. It's not as terrible as it sounds. All the dealer has to do is replace that synchronizer-strut retainer plate with a new one. In your case, that's the fifth-gear synchronizer strut retainer plate.

4WD U-JOINT FAILURE

Can you explain why a universal joint (U-joint) of my four-wheel drive vehicle failed after only 11,000 miles? My dealer is blaming me for not having this part lubricated properly and is refusing to honor the warranty. But the part *was* lubricated. What should I do now?

Who did the lubrication? If it was the dealer's service department, then it's the dealer's responsibility and you should take the matter up with the manufacturer of the vehicle. If it was an independent technician and you have verification in the form of a receipt that the lubrication was done, who's responsible depends on whether the lubrication was done properly. Here's what I mean.

The U-joint at the transfer case end of the front propeller shaft of many four-wheel drive vehicles—yours included—has at least two grease fittings, possibly three. (See Figure 7.3.) This is called a double-cardan universal joint. If a technician doesn't realize that a four-wheel drive vehicle has a double-cardan U-joint, that second and third grease fitting can be overlooked.

Failure to lubricate all the grease fittings of a double-cardan U-joint will eventually result in premature failure of that part. Furthermore, lubrication has to be done at the interval recommended by the manufacturer in the owner's manual. If you use your four-wheel drive vehicle in off-road backwood areas, that interval may be as often as every 3,000 miles.

Considering these facts, do you believe the vehicle manufacturer, as represented by the dealer's service department, to be responsible for this U-joint failure? If so, air your grievance to the manufacturer. If lubrication was done by an independent technician, take the matter up with the manager of that service facility.

THE CHUGGLE PROBLEM

Driving at around 45 mph, it seems as if the engine in my 1986 car bucks. This constant back-and-forth movement is very annoying. After doing a tune-up and testing the engine, my technician now says he's stumped. Do you have the answer to this problem?

The sensation you feel is probably chuggle, which is a term that's been coined by General Motors. As you describe it, the engine seems to buck. The sensation, however, may really be the result of the transmission converter clutch (TCC) engaging and disengaging. The most common cause of this is an inappropriately calibrated electronic engine control module.

The TCC is under the control of the module. If it gets mixed signals from the module, it can't make up its mind whether it wants to

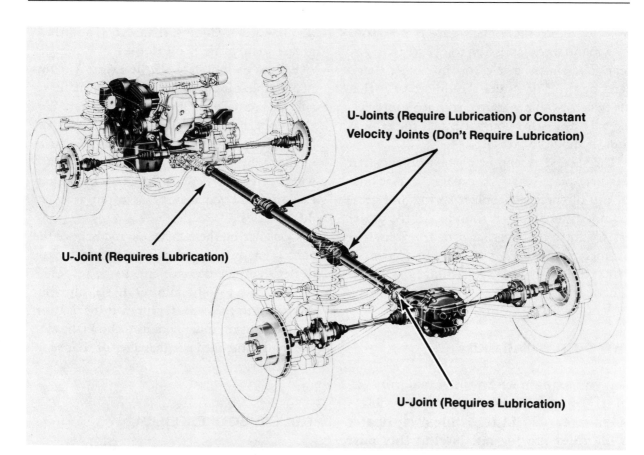

U-Joints (Require Lubrication) or Constant Velocity Joints (Don't Require Lubrication)

U-Joint (Requires Lubrication)

U-Joint (Requires Lubrication)

FIGURE 7.3. Four-wheel drive vehicles have as many as four universal joints. All require periodic lubrication. Ask a technician to check manufacturer service literature to determine how many grease fittings there are at each U-joint. Applying grease to every fitting is a "must" if the part is to last.

SERVICE TIP: HAVE CV JOINT BOOTS INSPECTED

Be sure to have the boots covering the constant velocity (CV) joints of your front-wheel drive or four-wheel drive vehicle inspected whenever you have the oil changed. There are four CV joints—one at each end of the two shafts that extend from the differential to the front wheels. If a boot develops a crack, which is apparent if there is lubricant oozing from the boot, grit can enter the boot and attack the CV joint. That joint can literally be ground to death by grit.

Have a damaged boot replaced immediately. It is far better to spend $20 to $30 for a new boot than $200 to $300 for a new CV joint.

---

engage or disengage. The back-and-forth sensation this produces is usually felt between 40 and 49 mph.

Chuggle and the condition called engine surge are often confused. Surging is the result of an engine malfunction, such as a contaminated oxygen sensor, deficient exhaust gas recirculation system, dirty fuel filter, or damaged spark plugs. Your technician, therefore, may not be able to put his finger on the cause of the trouble, because he's barking up the wrong tree.

If the problem is chuggle, replacing the chip (brain) of the electronic engine control module if it is a replaceable part, or the module itself, may be the only way to make the repair. I suggest you contact the service department of a dealer who sells your particular make of car to find out if the manufacturer has issued a technical service bulletin relating to the problem. When complaints that a vehicle is displaying a chuggling condition are received by a manufacturer, that manufacturer usually redesigns the electronic engine control module to eliminate the continual switching of the TCC between engagement and disengagement. An independent technician is often not aware that such a bulletin

exists since independent technicians aren't privy to technical service bulletins.

IMPORTANT FACTS ABOUT LIMITED-SLIP DIFFERENTIALS

A friend of mine bought a pickup truck and paid about $1,200 extra for a Posi-Trak® rear end. He doesn't know what it is. Neither do I, and we can't find anyone who does. So what is Posi-Trak? How does it work? How can you find out if a car or truck possesses the thing?

Whether it's called Posi-Trak, Positraction, Traction-Lok, Anti-Spin, Twin-Grip, or some other elaborate name used by a manufacturer, the limited-slip differential (the technical, generic term) has been around for many years. Its job is to provide traction when one rear wheel of a vehicle is on ice and the other is on dry pavement. The limited-slip differential is a piece of optional equipment you can order when buying a new car, utility vehicle, or pickup truck that has the differential in the rear to drive the back wheels.

To understand how a limited-slip differential works, first let's talk about a vehicle that doesn't have a limited-slip differential that gets stuck with one rear wheel on a patch of ice and the other rear wheel on dry pavement The wheel on ice will spin at twice the speed of the ring gear, which is the largest gear inside the differential and the one that passes torque onto the wheels. When both wheels are on dry pavement, the ring gear divides torque equally between them. But in an icy/dry pavement situation, with the ice-bound wheel spinning at twice the speed of the ring gear, the wheel lying on dry pavement gets no torque. Therefore, it won't move and the vehicle goes nowhere.

The main difference between limited-slip and nonlimited-slip differentials is that clutches are added to the former to reduce the amount of slippage of the ring gear when an icy/dry pavement condition is encountered. Clutches that grip the ring gear allow some torque to be made available to the wheel lying on the dry patch so it can rotate. The wheel, therefore, can provide enough traction to get the vehicle moving and the other wheel off the ice. A limited-slip differential is identified by a tag attached to the assembly.

The most important thing for an owner of a vehicle to keep in mind about a limited-slip differential is that the unit requires a special lubricant. Therefore, when you take the vehicle in for servicing, such as an oil change, tell the technician that the vehicle is outfitted with a limited-slip differential—just in case the unit needs replenishment. The type of lubricant that should be used (it differs from one manufacturer to another) is spelled out in your owner's guide.

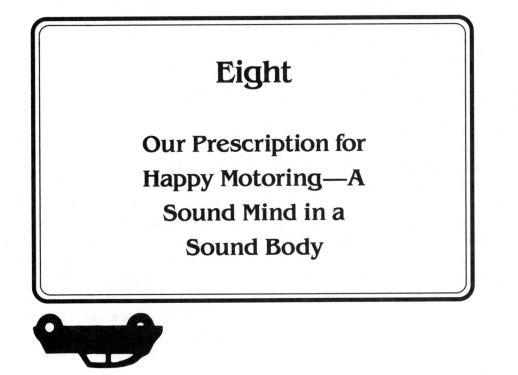

Eight

Our Prescription for Happy Motoring—A Sound Mind in a Sound Body

SHOULD YOU WAX YOUR CAR?

I've been advised that most cars manufactured since the mid-1980s have an acrylic paint that is similar to a no-wax floor, and that it makes waxing unnecessary. Is this true?

Paint containing acrylic resin has been used on automobiles since the 1950s so there's nothing new about it. The paint system I believe you are referring to consists of a color-coat, which is called a basecoat, over which is put a clearcoat. The system, called basecoat/clearcoat, contains acrylic resin, but it is not a no-wax finish.

The basecoat is an enamel containing acrylic resin or a lacquer containing acrylic resin that has pigment mixed into it. The clearcoat is an acrylic enamel or an acrylic lacquer void of pigment. The purpose of the clearcoat is to give the basecoat a specific aesthetic effect—a "wet" look.

Contrary to what you heard, "most" cars produced since the mid 1980s don't have a clearcoat. Far from it. Most cars manufactured since the mid-1980s are painted with pigmented acrylic enamel or acrylic lacquer without a clearcoat.

As for wax, its purpose is to protect the finish of a car against chemical spotting caused by industrial fallout, including acid rain, and road salt. Chemicals and road salt that get on auto paint that is left unprotected will cause that paint to chalk and discolor more rapidly than a wax-protected finish. The protection provided by wax is effective for about six months. In other words, maximum protection of the finish on a car is attained by using a polish to remove old wax and "dead" paint and applying a fresh application of wax semiannually. This is true whether or not that finish is basecoat/clearcoat.

Keep in mind that a single application of wax is enough. Applying a second or a third coat is a waste of time. Additional coats of wax will not protect a finish any better or to any greater extent than one, well-applied coat.

HOW TO TREAT A CLEARCOAT FINISH

I just purchased a new car that has a metallic blue finish covered by a clearcoat that was sprayed on by the dealer. I asked a fellow in the service department how long I had to wait before waxing the car. I was told six months to a year. When my brother bought his new car from the same dealer a year ago, a different member of the service department told him to wax the body two weeks after he drove the vehicle from the showroom. His car also has a metallic finish, but it was clearcoated at the factory. Which of these technicians is correct about this?

They both are. The apparent contradiction is the result of the clearcoat on your car having been applied by the dealer and that on your brother's car having been applied at the factory. The factory uses high-powered equipment that bakes the clearcoat finish onto the

metal a lot more tenaciously than the heat lamps used by the dealer.

The hard-baked factory finish can be polished and waxed 30 days after the finish is applied. With your car, the dealer seems to be allowing ample leeway for the finish to harden since polishing a "soft" finish can damage it.

Once the waiting period is over, you can keep the finish on a car that's protected by a clearcoat looking showroom new by washing it often using a nondetergent soap that's applied with a soft cloth. Turkish towel is best, because it won't scratch the finish. Keep the car in the shade as you wash it. Remove water with a damp chamois or Turkish towel.

If some stains caused by splattered bugs or road tar prove impervious to washing, there are spot-removing products available in the auto departments of retail stores and in auto parts and accessories stores for you to use. But first try removing these stains by mixing three capfuls of a concentrated heavy-duty liquid cleaner, such as Mr. Clean, into a quart of hot tap water. Apply the solution with Turkish towel. Rub hard. Then, rinse it off with a spray from a garden hose.

To protect the finish of your car, apply a coat of wax every six months.

RESTORING A CAR'S PAINT

The body of my car looks crummy. I intend to have the vehicle repainted, but I've gotten so many different estimates that I'm confused. They range from a low of $125 to about $1,000. What's the story here?

The first question you should ask yourself about buying a paint job is this, "Does the car really need one?" Many people repaint cars sooner than necessary. Even the most faded looking paint may be resurrected.

The only way to find out if repainting a car can be postponed for a year, two, or even longer is to rub out the surface to see if paint still has gloss. There are a variety of rub-out agents at auto supply stores. Select one that's abrasive enough to remove all the chalk—a term that refers to the powdery residue paint develops as it ages. If the rub-out agent isn't sufficiently abrasive, the good paint will stay masked. This will make the finish look like a goner although it really isn't and might cause you to repaint the car unnecessarily.

Conversely, avoid a rub-out agent that's too abrasive. It will remove good paint along with chalk and may cut into the primer, which is the chief agent that protects metal from corrosion. Once this happens, the car will have to be reprimed as well as repainted at almost double the cost.

Rub-out agents are either liquid or paste. Liquid rub-out agents, which may be designated on their packages as liquid cleaners or liquid polishes, are mildly abrasive. Paste rub-out agents, which are commonly called compounds, are either moderately abrasive or highly abrasive. In its moderately abrasive form, the agent is usually referred to as a polishing compound. In its highly abrasive form, it's often called a hand-rubbing compound.

To determine which agent is abrasive enough to remove chalk without taking off an excess amount of good paint and disturbing the primer, start with a section of one body panel—door, fender, roof, or hood. First try a liquid cleaner. If this doesn't bring up the luster, use a polishing compound. Finally, if that doesn't work, try a hand-rubbing compound. (See Figure 8.1.) Once you pinpoint the rub-out agent to use, complete the panel. Then, repeat the procedure at the next panel. This method is called selective rubbing out.

A more abrasive agent is usually needed to revive paint on body panels that are directly exposed to the sun's rays—roof, hood, tops of fenders, and trunk lid. A less abrasive rub-out agent often brings back the gloss on the sides of fenders and doors.

Caution: Follow instructions accompanying the product. If you do something you shouldn't, such as using an electric buffer, you could cut through paint into the primer.

If rubbing-out a car using the selective rub-out method restores the paint, apply wax to protect the finish. One coat of wax is sufficient—applying two coats is a waste of time and energy, because in applying the second coat you wipe off the first.

If after a month the finish on the car regresses to what it was, the car is a candidate for a new paint job. On the other hand, if only one or two body panels don't respond well, you can have only those repainted. This less costly method is called selective repainting. In doing it, a paint shop matches the new paint to the old; then, hand-works the new paint to get it to blend in with the old paint.

If the paint is shot and you decide to repaint, first determine whether the factory-applied primer is intact. Primer not only affords protection against corrosion, it also provides a base to which paint adheres.

No body shop has the equipment to apply primer the way it's applied by car manufacturers. The present factory priming process is called electrodeposition—E-coat for short. It's an electrostatic method that uses a positively charged polymeric binding agent in the primer that is attracted to metal that's pretreated to act as a cathode. The 0.8 to 1.2 mil primer thickness clings tenaciously to the back side, edges, and face side of metal as no primer sprayed on by a paint shop can. A mil is a linear measurement that equals $1/1,000$ inch.

If the factory-applied primer is damaged, much of its sealing qualities is lost. It is then necessary for the body shop to strip the surface of that panel to bare metal, so new

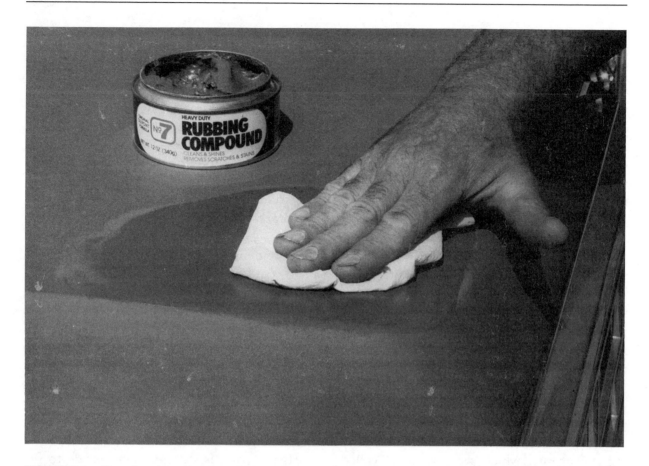

FIGURE 8.1. By using the selective rubbing-out procedure described in the text, you may be able to restore a vehicle's finish to a like-new luster and avoid the expense of having to have a paint job done.

primer can be sprayed on. However, since a body shop can't apply a primer coat as good as the factory, the wise course is to have only those body panels reprimed that need it.

If a body panel is dented or rusted, assume that the primer is damaged. If panels aren't dented or rusted but have scratches in the paint, it's necessary to determine if scratches penetrate the primer. To find out, a chemical paint stripper is used to remove paint from the surface around scratches to examine the primer. The chemical stripper is applied, and the residue is removed with a plastic squeegee as soon as paint begins to blister. If stripper is left on too long, it will eat into the primer.

After wiping off residue, the area is washed, dried, and inspected with a magnifying glass. If a scratch extends into the primer, the primer has to be stripped from the panel and the panel reprimed before it's painted.

Before turning attention to picking a paint, let's discuss a repair procedure that may let you avoid having to repaint an area of your car that's been surface-scratched or has been spotted by airborne chemicals or bird droppings. The procedure has been devised primarily for cars painted with a basecoat/clearcoat. If done carefully, it is intended to get rid of imperfections without the need for touch-up paint.

Buy No. US 1200 (ultra-fine) sandpaper from a store that sells auto body supplies.

Caution: Do not use No. P1200 sandpaper, which is a European grade and is coarser.

Put the abrasive in a sanding pad and dip it into a pail holding a quart of water to which you've added one tablespoon of rubbing alcohol. Sand the scratched area by lightly moving the pad in straight strokes. Go in one direction only. Wash and wipe the spot dry after two or three strokes to see if the defect is gone. If not, repeat the procedure.

Important: Keep the sandpaper saturated and avoid deep-cutting.

When you have to select a type of paint for your car, remember that the kind you select depends on how long you want the paint to last and dictates how much that paint job will cost. For example, if you have a car you want spruced up for sale, it calls for the cheapest paint job, so have the body shop use an alkyd enamel.

Alkyd refers to the polymers modified with oils that go into the paint. Application of alkyd enamel, which is frequently referred to as a baked enamel paint job, usually entails drying by a bank of high-powered lights that raise body surface temperature to about 150°F.

Since additives that give paint gloss and durability are not added in abundance, if at all, to alkyd enamel, the paint starts to lose whatever gloss it has in a few months. Depending on how often it is polished and the environment in which the car is used, the paint will weather away in one to three years.

The next step up in paint jobs is acrylic enamel or acrylic lacquer. The main difference between alkyd and acrylic auto paint is the addition of a chemical to acrylic that gives it gloss and durability.

Acrylic enamel provides a somewhat higher gloss than acrylic lacquer, but to the untrained eye the difference between the two is difficult to discern. Another difference between the two involves the method used by the body shop to dry the paint. Acrylic enamel, which dries relatively slowly if left to natural means, is usually subjected to heat. Faster drying acrylic lacquer can be dried by heat; however, many body shops allow a car painted with acrylic lacquer to dry by air.

To get maximum gloss, an acrylic lacquer finish has to be buffed. This extra work makes painting with acrylic lacquer costlier than repainting with acrylic enamel; however, don't off-handedly opt for acrylic enamel if you already have acrylic lacquer on the car. Acrylic enamel sprayed over acrylic lacquer or vice versa may result in the new paint wrinkling. It is, therefore, safer to repaint a car with the same kind of paint it now has.

A car properly painted with acrylic enamel or acrylic lacquer will retain its gloss for five to seven years if kept clean and polished.

The next best paint job is the wet-look finish (basecoat/clearcoat). A top-notch body shop can apply the finish and make it look every bit as good as a factory finish.

The two-part system consists of a basecoat of acrylic enamel or acrylic lacquer over which a clearcoat is sprayed. (See Figure 8.2.) The clearcoat protects the basecoat and gives the finish its wet-looking gloss. From the standpoint of durability, a basecoat/clearcoat paint job should hold its sparkle for 7 to 10 years if properly cared for.

The *creme de là creme* of paint jobs is done with urethane enamel. If properly cared for, a good quality acrylic urethane enamel will retain its gloss for longer than 10 years. The paint costs over $100 a gallon, but it provides the most durable coating and maximum protection against weathering, road elements, airborne chemicals, dirt, and acid rain.

In addition to selecting a paint, you may have some other decisions to make. For instance, are urethane bumpers and moldings faded? The body shop can restore their finish by sanding and coating them with a flexible primer (a special type for plastic); then, painting them. When paint has dried, a protective clearcoat should be sprayed on.

If bumpers are chrome-plated, it's expensive to restore their appearance. Rechroming costs about $200 per bumper.

There are two other things to consider as part of giving your car a new paint job:

Having the shop repaint flat black areas around windows and doors, and having pinstripes put on. Both are relatively inexpensive procedures. Prices I've gotten range between $50 to $100 per task.

No matter which paint you select for your car, it will last the longest possible time if you wash it frequently, and polish and wax it when necessary. A new paint job shouldn't need polishing and waxing for at least six months, but if you want to do it in less time than this you need not fear that you'll ruin the paint. A new paint job can usually be polished and waxed 30 days after it leaves the body shop.

As for the paint shop you deal with, let's not beat around the bush. You can get several estimates, but they are no indication of the kind of job you'll get. Although you may assume that the shop submitting the highest estimate is the one that will give you the best job, this is not always the case.

When it comes to a high-quality paint job done by a shop that won't cut corners in procedures or the products that are used, rely on the reputation of the shop. In addition to opinions of acquaintances and a check with the Better Business Bureau, an indication of reputation is the length of time the person owning the shop has been in business. Another indication is his or her willingness to put in writing everything promised to you verbally.

REPAIRING CRAZED PAINT

The blue paint of the new car I purchased three years ago is cracking on the hood, roof, and trunk lid. The car is kept in a garage when it's not in use and has been driven only 33,000 miles. A technician at a body shop I brought the car to refers to the damage as "crow's feet." Has there

FIGURE 8.2.   The type of paint you select dictates how long the new paint job will last. It doesn't make sense to paint an old car you're planning on selling in a year or two with a product that can last 10 years and which will cost over $1500, when a paint that will last three or four years at a cost of $150 will suffice.

been a problem with this color? Is there a recall?

There hasn't been a recall. Neither has there been a problem with blue. Therefore, I suggest you work through your dealer to bring the matter to the manufacturer's attention.

It's unusual for original factory paint to develop crow's feet, which is also called crazing. The primary reason for crazing is applying paint when the temperature in the area is too cold. Crazing is a condition more prevalent with repainted finishes than with original paint jobs. If the condition is some other form of cracking that the body shop technician has inaccurately termed "crow's feet," it's possible that it may have resulted from an excessively thick film of paint being applied at the factory.

Whatever type of cracking has taken place, the manufacturer of the car will want to know about it and take action to correct it as long as it can be established that the problem is the result of a poor paint job. In other words, if the manufacturer determines that application of an excessively thick film of paint is the cause of the cracking paint rather than some environmental condition, such as acid rain, the manufacturer will probably help to defray the cost of a new paint job.

RED PAINT IS TURNING MILKY WHITE

The red metallic paint on the hood and roof of my car is turning milky white. I've tried various polishes and compounds, but they haven't helped. A dealer, who says the problem is caused by acid rain, wants $600 for a paint job. Are there alternatives?

What you're experiencing is called chalking. Just like with house paint, it's a natural phenomenon that takes place as paint ages. Chalking occurs because paint is exposed to sunlight. Another cause is prolonged exposure to chemical fumes.

Chalking is not the result of acid rain. Paint affected by acid rain is characterized by spotting of the paint where rain drops have fallen and have eaten into the paint.

Some shades of red chalk more rapidly than others. But this doesn't mean that the paint on your car has chalked to a point where the only way to restore its appearance is to strip the old paint and repaint the hood and roof.

A detailer, one who specializes in cleaning cars, can use a professional rubbing compound (the most abrasive compound of all) to remove some of the chalked paint and determine if a thick enough film of paint remains on the hood and roof to restore their appearance. If so, spending $100 to $150 to have the entire car detailed would be a worthwhile expenditure.

Rx FOR BLISTERED PAINT

Six years ago I purchased a new car from a dealer in Colorado. Three years ago I moved to Texas. A year ago I began to notice blisters in the paint on the hood and roof. The explanation I'm getting from paint shops is that beads of water left after it rains act to magnify the intense rays of the sun, causing the clearcoat to be drawn off the metal. Can this be true?

Beads of water that magnify the sun's rays may be contributing to the deterioration, but they aren't causing it. The primary cause of blistering is dirt specks left on the surface as the car is being painted. Specks retain moisture. When exposed to the sun, moisture expands, builds up pressure, and breaks the coating. Other reasons for blistering include application of an excessively thick film of paint, and using a reducer or thinner that isn't compatible with the finish coat.

Although it's been six years, it may not be too late to have the manufacturer of your car share in the cost of repainting the vehicle. Repainting is the only way to get rid of the damage. The body shop that does the job has to strip off all the paint down to bare metal, so this is a major project. I suggest you contact the customer service department of the manufacturer and describe the condition and history of the car. A service representative who is sent to examine the vehicle may agree that the problem is the result of a deficiency that occurred during the manufacture of the vehicle.

REMOVING TREE SAP FROM A CAR'S BODY

Before I could get to it, tree sap that fell on the hood of my car hardened. Now, I can't get it off. Please help.

Hold a rubber spatula against sap buildup and push to break off lumps. Then, treat the spots of residue that remain with a sudsy mixture of laundry detergent and hot water (the hotter, the better). Put on a pair of heavy work gloves to avoid a burn, and scoop the sudsy solution on a soft cloth. Rub the residue with it as hard as you can. Repeat the procedure until stains disappear. Then, spray the area with cold water from a garden hose. When the metal has dried, polish the entire hood with auto-body polish.

REMOVING LABELS STUCK ON YOUR CAR

The dealer I bought my car from stuck his name tag on the trunk. How do I get it off?

With a hair dryer and a lot of patience. Set the hair dryer on HIGH, aim it at the label, and move it slowly from side to side as you use your fingers to roll the label off the trunk. That spot is going to get pretty hot, so wear a glove.

If you bought a used car, there will be a noticeable difference between the shade of paint under the label and that on the rest of the trunk. Therefore, unless you intend to have the car painted, you may want to leave the label just where it is and give the dealer a little free publicity.

REMOVING HARDENED WAX FROM PLASTIC BODY TRIM

Can you tell me how to remove dried spots of hard discolored wax from the plastic black bumpers and moldings of my car? I hesitate using an abrasive for fear of scratching the surface.

Park the car in the shade; then, mix baking soda and mineral spirits to a tooth-paste consistency. Apply the compound to the entire bumper or length of molding. Don't treat only the spots. If the whole unit isn't cleaned, those parts of it that receive care will end up appearing brighter than the rest of it. Rub hard as you apply the mixture. Then, use a clean piece of Turkish towel to remove the cleaner while it's still wet. If one application doesn't work, give the bumper or molding two more treatments before turning to a more drastic method which involves using caustic wax and grease remover.

Wax and grease remover is available in stores that sell auto supplies and accessories. Follow directions on the can and be sure to wipe the remover off while it's still wet. More than one application may be needed.

Caution: When you do this job, wear work gloves to protect your hands.

REPAINTING PLASTIC BUMPERS

Is there a way of restoring the black color of plastic bumpers? Those on my car have faded to a pale gray.

Start by lightly sanding the bumpers with No. 320 sandpaper to remove residue. Then, wipe the surfaces with a cloth that is dampened with an automotive wax and grease remover. You can buy this product in a store selling automotive supplies and accessories.

Before you spray on paint, cover areas adjacent to bumpers with masking tape to keep paint overspray from getting on them. Now, spray the bumpers with a satin black paint made for plastic. The paint, which is available in 11-ounce cans, can also be purchased from a dealer of automotive supplies and accessories.

As you spray on paint, hold the aerosol can about 12 inches from the bumper. Apply the paint with a single sweep of the can. In other words, don't move the can back and forth. One pass is all you should make. And don't hold the can stationary while your finger is on the trigger. Too much paint will run and sag.

Let this light coat of paint dry. Then, inspect the result. If the bumper doesn't have sufficient coverage to suit you, apply another light coat of paint.

REATTACHING A LOOSE MOLDING

The molding strip on the left front door of my car has come loose and is flapping in the breeze. Is there a glue I can use to reattach it?

Don't use glue. It won't hold molding to the door for long, if it holds at all. Besides, it's messy.

Reattaching a loose molding strip isn't difficult. Here's how to do it:

1. Peel the loose strip off the door.
2. Dampen a clean rag with an adhesive remover that you can buy from an auto parts and accessories store, and clean off the adhesive on the backside of the molding. Then, use the cleaner to remove adhesive from the surface of the door.

Caution: Wear rubber gloves and goggles. Adhesive remover is a caustic substance.

3. Lay strips of masking tape on the door to outline the location for the molding and to serve as a guide when you reattach the strip. To get things straight, align the masking tape with the top and bottom edges of the molding attached to the fender and rear panel adjacent to the door. Make sure the masking tape runs in a straight line.
4. Attach two-sided tape, such as 3-M Mounting Tape® or Manco Automotive Foam Mounting Tape®, to the backside of the molding. Before peeling the backing paper off the side of the tape that will go against the molding, hold the molding and tape between the strips of masking tape and against the door to see that the molding will fall into the exact position you want it.

5. Peel off backing paper on one side of the two-sided tape and attach the tape to the moldings.

6. Peel the backing paper off the other side of the tape; that is, the side that is to go against the door. Using the masking tape as a guide, carefully center and align one end of the molding and press it firmly against the door. Then, working down the length of the molding, press the rest of the molding firmly into place.

REPAIRING A HOLE IN CARPETING

One of my friends riding in the rear of my brand new car accidentally let a cigarette drop on the floor. Before he noticed it, the glowing tip had burned a hold in the carpet. My insurance policy has a high deductible so the cost of replacing the carpet isn't covered. Can it be repaired in some way?

You can do it yourself and have it come out looking brand new. Here are the steps to follow:

1. Using a sharp pair of manicure scissors, cut away the burned fibers. Then, use a utility knife to scrape off any black remnants so the area is clean.

2. Apply a small amount of a clear, waterproof cement to the spot. Be sure the entire area is covered.

3. Using the manicure scissors, cut off enough carpet fibers from a hidden section, such as from under a seat or door sill, to fill the bare spot. If you want to get fibers from under the door sill, you'll have to loosen the sill by removing the few screws that hold it and pulling out the carpet from beneath the sill.

4. Using tweezers, set one fiber at a time upright into the cement. Work from the outer rim in toward the center. Be patient and work carefully to make sure that each fiber stays straight. Fill the section with enough fibers to gain a density that equals that of the carpet around it.

MAINTAINING THE APPEARANCE OF SIMULATED WOOD PANELS

The minivan I recently purchased has simulated wood panels along the sides. The polishing products I've looked at are not recommended for simulated wood. What can I use to keep panels looking new?

The product to use should be a clear silicone, such as Armor All Protectant® made by Armor All Products Corporation of Irvine, California, or Brillianize made by Chemical Products Company of Omaha, Nebraska. Avoid any product that contains a petroleum derivative. It will cause simulated wood (vinyl) panels to fade. (See Figure 8.3.)

RESTORING THE APPEARANCE OF SIMULATED WOOD PANELS

My station wagon has simulated wood panels which have discolored. Is there a way to revive them, or do they have to be replaced?

Buy an auto-body liquid cleaner from an auto supply store and use it as directed. If discoloration is caused by a buildup of wax, the cleaner will remove the wax and restore the color. If discoloration doesn't disappear, spread a coat of brown shoe polish (wax) on the panels; then, buff them with a soft cloth.

FIGURE 8.3. Attractive as simulated wood paneling appears to many buyers of minivans and station wagons, this siding can discolor or fade if it doesn't get special treatment.

If neither of these methods proves satisfactory, you can remove the panels which are glued on. Beneath them, you'll find metal that's painted the same color as the rest of the car.

You have to use a chemical to remove the panels. 3M Company makes a stripper you can buy from an auto parts and accessories store. Apply it as directed. Then, start at an edge to begin peeling the panel off the car. After panels have been removed, clean off residue left by adhesive with an adhesive remover recommended by the auto parts and accessories store attendant. Again, 3M Company manufactures an effective product. The final step is to polish and wax the car.

SPOTS FROM A HOT WASH

I washed my car on a hot day and was not quick enough to get soap off the windows before it dried. This has caused spots on the glass. I've tried several glass cleansers, but spots won't come off. I'm surprised this happened, because the soap is made by a well-known company specifically for washing cars. Do you have any suggestion for getting spots off the glass?

You may be able to remove spots by scraping them off with a razor blade. The residue that remains can then be washed off. If this doesn't work, the windows can be polished with a commercial preparation that's made specifically to remove minor scratches in glass, but you should let an automotive glass shop do this job for you.

Don't blame the soap for your problem. Nothing is put into soaps made for car finishes that would adhere so tenaciously to glass without also sticking tenaciously to the painted surface of the car.

Minerals in water are the more likely culprits. When subjected to the sun, minerals can dry and cause crusty spots that are difficult to get off.

WHICH WASH CLOTH— CHAMOIS OR TURKISH TOWEL?

Someone told me it's best to use a chamois rather than turkish towel to dry a car after washing it. Is there any truth to this? I priced a chamois at an auto parts and accessory store and the cost for this rag is outrageous.

I've used both chamois, which is deerskin, and turkish towel and find that the chamois doesn't have any noticeable advantage over turkish towel. Both remove water so spots aren't left on the car, and neither one mars a car's finish. Whichever you decide to use, make sure that it's damp before you begin wiping water off the car.

REMOVING STAINS LEFT BY TAR AND BUG REMOVER

I hope I haven't ruined the white paint on my car by using tar and bug remover to get rid of tar. The stuff has left yellow stains about the size of a quarter in the paint. Is there something that will remove these stains or will the car have to be repainted?

Tar and bug remover leaves stains if you don't apply sufficient pressure as you wipe it and dissolved tar off the car. But take heart—you haven't damaged the paint. What you have to do now is apply another application of the tar and bug remover, but this time rub it in briskly and apply firm pressure as you rub it off. Use turkish towel, which won't scratch the paint. Don't use an electric buffer. It will leave swirl marks.

GETTING DIRTY WHITEWALLS CLEAN

The whitewalls on the front of my car get a black substance on them that's hard to get off. A mechanic told me it's disc brake residue, and that the condition is not unusual. Is this true? Is there any product that will allow me to restore whitewalls to pristine condition?

The black substance is, as you were informed, the result of finely ground powder that's given off by brake pads as they come into contact with rotating discs. The only thing you can do is try various tire cleaners until you find one that works for you. I've had good results with one called Westley Whitewall and Tire Cleaner®. Whichever product you use, follow accompanying instructions to attain acceptable results. Usually, the tire cleaner has to be applied to a dry tire and left on the tire for several minutes before it's washed off.

CURE FOR MISTY HEADLIGHTS

Condensation sometimes forms inside the headlamps of my new car. The dealer refuses to do anything about it, claiming it's normal. Is he correct or should I raise hell?

Headlamps of many cars built since the 1980s are of the composite design. One characteristic they have is the formation of condensation on the insides of lenses. That's why these lamps have a means of ventilation to keep condensation to a minimum.

Ventilation in cars like yours is through tubes attached to the headlamp housings. As long as these tubes aren't kinked or obstructed, condensation that forms when lenses are cool and the ambient temperature is warm is a normal occurrence and shouldn't be a cause for concern.

The way to tell if ventilation is taking place and condensation buildup is without bounds is to examine headlamps after they've been turned on for a few minutes, giving the insides of the lenses time to get warm. There shouldn't be any sign of condensation. If there is, ask the dealer to repair the lamp by clearing out or straightening the ventilation tubes. A problem such as this may entail the drilling of a tiny drain hole in the lamp housing. If so, there will be a service advisory issued by the manufacturer to this affect.

DEALING WITH CRACKS IN A VINYL TOP

Hairline cracks in the vinyl top of my car are beginning to join and form gullies. I've called several body shops for advice, only to be told that there's nothing that can be done to save the top. I find this hard to believe. Is there no way to repair a vinyl top?

There is no way to repair cracks in a vinyl top. The cracks that have formed are similar in character to cracks that form in a concrete driveway. Unlike concrete, however, cracks in vinyl can't be patched. Once the process begins, you may be able to stop its progress, but you can't repair the damage that's already taken place.

A vinyl top begins to crack when the plasticizer in the vinyl evaporates. You can delay evaporation by using a vinyl top care product on a regular basis. Used periodically, the compound retards the loss of the plasticizer and halts cracking. A one-shot application doesn't do any good.

KEEPING WHEEL COVERS IN PLACE

I keep losing the covers off the cast-aluminum wheels of my car. The dealer tells me this is a problem that hasn't been resolved by the manufacturer. Have you heard about this?

I've heard about it. Here are two possible solutions:

1. If you have to buy covers to replace any that are missing, ask the dealer whether covers put on wheels of cars built after yours will fit the wheels of your car. When a problem like this comes to the attention of the manufacturer, the parts involved are modified on the assembly line. In this case, the manufacturer may have modified wheel covers to keep them in place after learning of the problem.
2. To try and keep the covers you still have on the car in place so they're not lost, apply dabs of Roof and Gutter Instant Patch Tape made by Mortell Company at four equidistant points around the inside of each cover. Install covers by pressing them as firmly as possible against the wheels. This product has tremendous retention capability, especially when used to secure aluminum. Ask for it at a hardware store or a store that specializes in maintenance and repair products for the home.

PULLING OUT A DENT

I was leaning against the left front fender of my four-month-old car when I momentarily lost by balance and pushed my hand against the metal. This put a dent in the fender that will cost me $350 to get fixed. Is there a less expensive way to make this repair?

Find another body shop. $350 to have a dent straightened is outrageous. Even in the old days when cars were made with heavier gauge metal than they are now, we often straightened dents just by rapping them from beneath with a rubber mallet. Some dents can even be straightened by using a plumber's helper to pull metal back into shape. Press the suction cup against the metal. Then, pull the cup off the metal using as much force as you can muster.

TOUCHING UP NICKS AND DINGS

My fairly new car has several little scratches in the paint that I'd like to take car of myself. I can buy touch-up paint from a dealer who sells this make of car, but I need some advice about how to tackle the job. Can you help?

Follow these steps:

1. Buy a touch-up paint that comes in a jar and is applied with a small brush. Avoid a touch-up paint that is in an aerosol can. It is difficult to control the spray, which can get on areas of the car surrounding the scratches.
2. If there's any loose paint on the edges of a scratch, break it off using a putty knife. Then, smooth the edges using a fine-grit auto polishing compound. Take care to apply compound within the boundaries of the damage to prevent scratching the surrounding paint.
3. If the damaged area doesn't have loose paint, which means it doesn't have to be treated with compound, remove wax from the area with a wax and grease remover.
4. After cleaning the spot, shake the bottle of touch-up paint vigorously for at least

60 seconds—longer if the ambient temperature is below 65°F.

5. Pour a small amount of the paint onto a nonabsorbent pallet, such as the plastic lid from a can of coffee. Do not apply the paint directly from the bottle. Furthermore, if the area of damage is narrowly confined, do not apply paint with the brush supplied with the paint. Use a fine-pointed artist's brush instead.

6. Apply a single coat of paint. The coating should be thin and not a glob. Allow this to dry for 10 minutes. Then, apply another single, thin coat and wait another 10 minutes. Continue in this manner until the damage is covered. It shouldn't take more than three thin coats to do this. Try to keep paint confined to the area without getting it on undamaged paint adjacent to the area.

7. Allow the paint to dry overnight. Then, using a light touch, apply fine-grit automotive polishing compound to make the spot smooth.

REMOVING A SCRATCH IN A WINDSHIELD

There's a scratch in the windshield of my car, which causes an annoying reflection from the sun's rays. Is there a way to get rid of it without replacing the windshield?

Try jeweler's rouge having a fine abrasive grit to it. You can buy it from a jewelry store or a glazier.

Put a little on a cloth and rub it over the scratch; then, wash off the residue. If the scratch isn't deep, this will do the job. The only other alternative in trying to save this windshield is to have a technician at an auto glass shop use a commercial polishing agent to see if the scratch will disappear.

REPAIR FOR AN OCCASIONAL WATER LEAK

My car leaks water that soaks the carpeting on the front passenger side. Oddly, it happens only when the air conditioner is running. Before I take the car to a technician, I'd like your opinion as to what's causing this and how to repair it.

The part of the air conditioning system responsible for making water is the evaporator. When frost that forms on the evaporator coils melts, it has to have a place to drain so the case covering the evaporator doesn't fill with water. This drain is in the form of a tube that extends from the case. (See Figure 8.4.)

There is also a check valve plugged into the evaporator case. This value opens to let water drain out of the case through the tube when it reaches a preset level in the case.

When the evaporator is draining normally, you will often see water on the pavement near the car after you shut off the air conditioner and get out of the car. That drainage is coming out of the drain tube. If the tube is clogged or the check valve isn't working, water will fill the evaporator case, overflow, and run into the car. This is what's happening with your car.

By now you can pretty much tell what has to be done. The drain tube and check valve have to be removed from the evaporator case. The tube has to be inspected for an obstruction and the check valve has to be tested. One or both parts may have to be replaced.

On the remote chance that the tube is clear and the valve is okay, water is probably leaking into the car around a faulty seal between the evaporator case and cowl. In this instance, have a technician apply sealer to the surfaces of the case and cowl where the two meet.

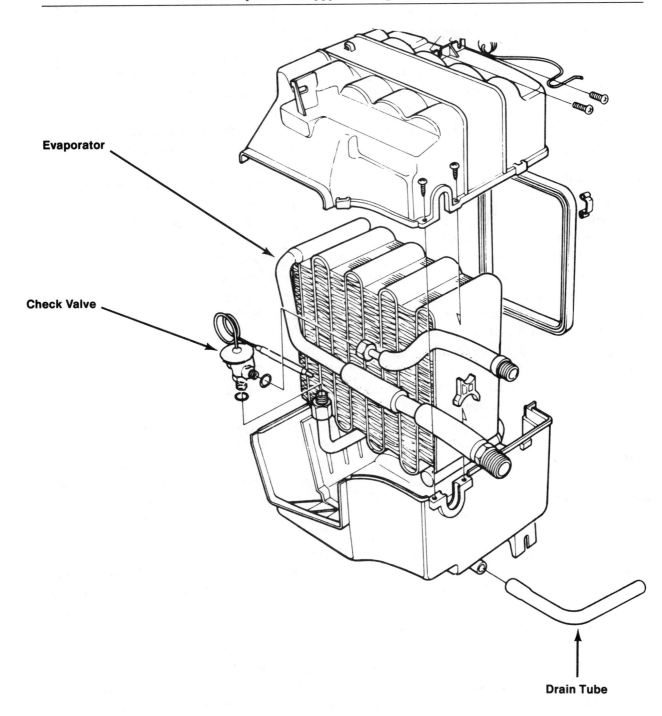

Evaporator

Check Valve

Drain Tube

FIGURE 8.4. Evaporators of automative air conditioners have to be equipped with drain tubes that allow water to drain; otherwise, water can fill the evaporator case and overflow into the vehicle.

TRACKING AN ELUSIVE WATER LEAK

My technician has not been able to pinpoint the spot where water is leaking into the interior of my car on the passenger side. It happens every time it rains. Can you help?

Has the car been tested for leakage using the time-tested, painstaking procedure that can take hours to do? This involves running water from a hose at a slow rate of flow over each possible leak area for a half hour at a time to see if the leak appears inside the car. This includes the top, sides, and base of the windshield, doors, fenders, and engine firewall.

If you're looking for a quick fix that might work to try and keep from paying the costly bill that this drawn out method might lead to, ask a technician to concentrate on the windshield. The windshield is the most likely of all areas at fault when a front passenger compartment water leak develops.

If the windshield turns out to be the trouble area, you'll have to decide whether removing and resealing the windshield would be a good bet. For a problem such as this one, I suggest you consult a specialist at an auto body shop and not leave the task to a general technician.

HAMMERING A RATTLE

There is an annoying rattle coming from the body of my car. It seems to be emanating from the trunk, but I've taken everything out of there and still have the rattle. Is there a method I can use to pinpoint the source of the noise?

A body rattle can originate from inside a door, from a loose fender liner, from inside the roof, from the trunk door, or from a loose bumper. The source of body noise is difficult to pinpoint, because noise travels. Therefore, it isn't often at the spot where the sound seems to be coming from. There is, however, this method to use to find its origin:

Gently bounce a rubber mallet over every inch of the body. When you hear a rattle, you've pinpointed something that's loose inside that panel. Have the panel opened and the repair made.

The only disadvantage to this method of locating the source of a body rattle is that it takes patience. You have to proceed slowly and meticulously. If you rush the process, you may skip just that spot where a loose part is located.

USING TAPE TO PINPOINT WIND NOISE

Is there any way for me to trace the origin of a wind noise my car is making when I drive at the highway speed limit? A technician wants to charge me $50 just to find the noise. He says an electronic air-leak detector is needed.

Although an electronic air-leak detector is an excellent instrument to use for pinpointing the origin of an air leak quickly, you can use ordinary duct tape to do the same thing—not as rapidly, of course, because you have to seal each spot one at a time, and drive the car between tapings to see if the leak has been zipped. Before doing this, though, make sure the wind noise isn't being caused by the radio antenna knifing through the air. Lower or remove the antenna and drive the car to see if the noise is still present.

As an example of how you would use duct tape when checking the windshield to see if the noise is coming from there, start by taping along the upper edge of the glass. Take the car for a ride. If the noise is no longer apparent, you now know that the molding has to be removed from this area to reseal it. But if the noise continues, tape and test the left or right side of the glass next, then the opposite side, and finally the base, road-testing the car between each taping.

Proceed in this manner around the car, paying attention to all joints where two parts of the car meet. Likely spots where an air leak can originate are between the tops of the doors and the base of the roof, around the edges of the door, between a body side molding and a door or fender, and around windows.

PREVENTING AN ELECTRIC SHOCK

I'm the only one in my family who gets a shock when I get out of our car and close the door. My husband installed ground straps, but they haven't helped. He has also treated the interior of the car, including carpets and door panel cloth trim, with an antistatic electricity spray he bought in the supermarket. That didn't help either. When I brought the car in for service. I mentioned the problem to the service manager who slid in and out of the car several times. He didn't get zapped. Why does it happen only to me?

The reason probably lies with the clothing you wear. Silky-type garments often generate and store static electricity as they rub against cloth upholstery. This electricity is released when you grab the metal door of the car, which acts as a ground. Even the methods your husband tried won't always succeed in diverting the electricity your clothes have built up.

I suggest you turn the tables on static electricity in this way: Open the door and keep your hand in contact with the side of the door so you are touching metal as you slide out of the car. Being in continuous contact with metal as you exit the car should prevent shock.

REMOVING HEAD RESTRAINTS TO INSTALL SEAT COVERS

I bought a set of seat covers for my car, but I can't install them. There's no way that I can see of getting the head restraints out of their sockets in the backs of the front seats. Can you help?

To remove the head restraints so you can install seat covers, get a 12-inch strip of thin-gauge flat metal, such as the type used as bands for securing cargo to a shipping pallet. Raise head restraints as high as they'll go and slip the metal strip down alongside one of the head restraint mounts. Search until you hit a pin. Maneuver the metal band around to trip the pin, which will release the head restraint and allow you to pull the head restraint out of the seat. Do the same on the other side. You can now install the seat covers.

Important: Be sure to reinstall the head restraints when you're done. They are needed to prevent a driver and/or front-seat passenger from sustaining whiplash in the event of an accident.

REMOVING HAZE FROM WINDOWS

A haze keeps forming over the insides of the windows in my car. When I clean it off, the glass streaks. What causes this and what can I do about it?

Your car probably has vinyl upholstery. If so, haze is a result of vapors given off by a plasticizer put into vinyl to keep it pliable. To remove haze without streaking the glass, wash windows with a mixture of four ounces of ammonia in a gallon of cold water.

You can prevent the haze from developing by washing vinyl upholstery with a mixture of one ounce of liquid dishwashing detergent in two quarts of warm water Rub the surface dry with cloth towels, and keep windows open so dampness dissipates. This procedure neutralizes vapors, but in time more may be emitted. Therefore, if haze reappears, repeat the procedure.

REPAIR FOR A HARD-TO-WORK WINDOW

Can the window in my car be fixed so it's easier for my wife to roll up and down?

Have a technician remove the door panel to inspect the gear teeth of the window regulator. If one or more teeth have broken off, a new regulator will have to be installed. If the mechanism is in sound condition, lubricating the moving parts will make it much easier for your wife to open and close the window.

KEY QUESTION

Will weight cause damage to an ignition switch if the ignition key is on a key ring that holds many other keys?

Weight will not damage the switch, but it could cause a brass key to sustain wear. Most ignition keys are brass. When a driver inserts an ignition key on a heavily weighted key ring into the ignition switch, he or she tends to insert the key on an angle. This puts stress on the key, which over a period of time will wear. If the key is then accidentally nicked or cut on this worn spot, it can break off at this point as it's turned in the ignition switch

when the engine is being started. For this reason, it's best to keep your car keys on their own key ring.

LOWERING A RAISED DASH PANEL

The dash panel in my car has risen so there's approximately a ½ inch gap between the panel and one of the sides against which it butts. Is there any way to draw the panel back down into its original position? The car, which I bought new, has been driven 25,000 miles.

I'm sorry to tell you that you'll have to have the panel removed and a new dash installed. The adhesive that was applied at the factory to hold the dash in place has undoubtedly been affected by heat. This shouldn't have happened, because manufacturers test adhesives to make sure the one that's used will hold panels at a temperature of at least 250°F. What you experienced, therefore, indicates that the adhesive was probably deficient to begin with.

Before you pay to have a replacement panel installed, contact the dealer who sold you the car. Let him inspect the raised dash, and ask him to notify the manufacturer. Although your car has exceeded the warranty period, the problem should be taken under advisement to determine if the cost of the repair will be assumed by the manufacturer.

REATTACHING A SAGGING HEADLINING

We have two cars with headlinings that sag. I've been told that headlinings have to be replaced at a cost of over $200 per car. Can you tell me if there's something I can do myself to fix this?

SERVICE TIP: PREVENT REAR DEFOGGER DAMAGE

If you reside in a state that issues a temporary cardboard license tag when you buy a car, be careful how that tag is mounted. Dealers frequently tape them to the inside of a backlite, which is the technical term for the rear window. If tape is put over a grid of the backlite electric defogger and you pull the tape off when your permanent license plates arrive, part of the grid can be ripped off with it. This will put the defogger out of action.

Remind the dealer to place the tape between the grids of the defogger. But don't assume that he has done it when you go to take the cardboard tag off the glass. Look to see if the temporary tag was mounted properly. If not, carefully peel the tape off the grid to keep from pulling it apart.

Whoever told you that a sagging headlining has to be replaced gave you wrong information. A headlining is a unit consisting of foam-backed cloth that's glued to a molded fiberglass panel. The adhesive holding the cloth-foam fabric to the fiberglass panel apparently has lost its grip, which is why the material is sagging.

You can reattach a headlining by taking it down, separating the material from the fiberglass panel, cleaning parts, and gluing them back together again. But this is not easy. You have to remove the courtesy lamp, sunshade-support brackets, coat hooks, upper quarter trim, side-roof rail moldings, windshield and backlite garnish moldings, shoulder-belt retainers and covers, windshield-side garnish moldings, and roof-mounted assist straps.

Where trim isn't held by screws, it is held by clips. If that's the case, pull trim away from its position and move the tip of a small screwdriver under the trim until you hit a clip. Press on the clip to free the trim.

When all trim parts have been removed, take the headlining assembly out of the car by releasing the fasteners that hold the assembly to the roof. Separate the cloth-foam material from the fiberglass panel. Use mineral spirits to clean off remnants of old adhesive.

Now, spread contact cement on the fiberglass panel and on the foam backing. When the cement has dried on both parts, place the cloth-foam material on the panel, but don't press it down until you have shifted it into position. Once it's down, it's down to stay. When the material and panel are in perfect alignment, press the two together. Work from the center toward the edges to prevent wrinkles.

Finish the job by reattaching the assembly to the roof and installing the trim.

RUSTPROOFING A NEW CAR

What's your opinion concerning rustproofing of a new car? Is it a worthwhile investment or a waste of money?

Applying rustproofing to the inner surfaces of a car's sheet metal is giving metal a capability it already possesses. As cars are manufactured, bare metal is dipped in an electrostatic bath of rustpreventing solution. Having more rustproofing added after you buy the car is a redundancy that doesn't increase the ability of metal to resist rust. (See Figure 8.5 and 8.6.)

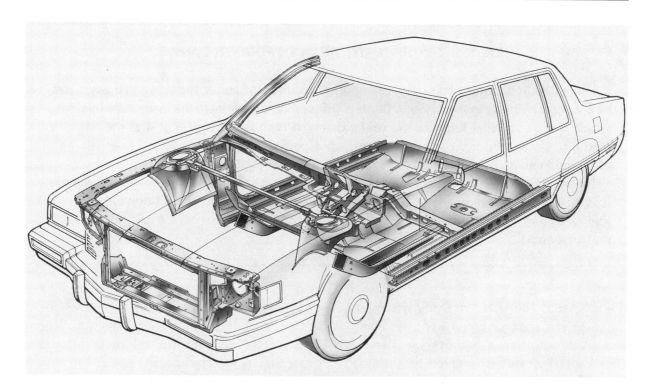

FIGURE 8.5.   Since the late 1970s, auto manufacturers have been using a process that coats the outer and inner surfaces of bodies and chassis with a rust-preventive solution. This procedure has permitted manufacturers to offer warranties against rust-perforation of metal for periods that range from 7 to 10 years. The only reason for having additional rust-proofing solution added after you buy a vehicle is as a safeguard against the unlikely event that an area of a panel missed treatment when metal was dipped into the solution during manufacture. But even metal that escaped coating is protected by drain holes. (Courtesy of Cadillac Division of General Motors Corporation)

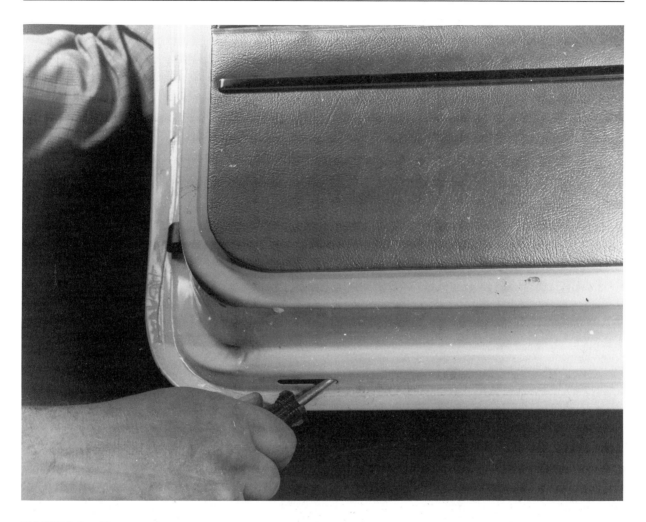

FIGURE 8.6.   The drain holes mentioned in the caption above are placed along the bottoms of doors and the bottom surface of a vehicle's body. Their purpose is to permit water to drain from between panels. If water, which can get between panels when it rains or when the vehicle is being washed, is trapped between panels because drain holes get clogged, it can attack metal that may conceivably have been left bare during the rust-prevention dipping process. It's suggested, therefore, that you have holes checked to make sure they're free of debris when the vehicle is on a lift having its oil changed.

Nine

Fixing Accessories That Blow Hot or Cold When You Want Them to Blow Cold or Hot

RESURRECTING A SLUGGISH HEATER

The output from the heater in my car recently took a nose dive, making it uncomfortable while driving in cold weather. I've had the thermostat replaced, but there's been no increase in heat output. What should I have done now?

The reason for low heat is almost always centered in the heater—not with the cooling system thermostat. The heater assembly consists of a heater core, control valve, control cable, and two hoses. Troubleshooting should pro-

ceed by making the least expensive attempt at a repair first. That's with the hoses.

If a technician working on the car had to remove the hoses and inadvertently reversed their positions when reconnecting them, you would get little or no heat from the heater. If this is the case, the hose carrying hot coolant to the heater is now connected to the output side of the heater core, which means that hot coolant is bypassing the heater instead of going through it.

Was the cooling system worked on just before you noticed the drop-off in heat? If so, have a technician take the hose off the intake side of the heater core and put it on the output end; then, put the hose from the output end on the intake side. Test the heater. If there's no increase in heat, the technician should reconnect hoses the way they were and continue troubleshooting.

The next component that should be checked is the control cable. Does it extend straight and true from the dash to the damper door in the heat duct? If the cable is bent or has come loose, it can't open the damper door all the way and there will be a reduced flow of warm air from the heater core into the interior of the car. That warm air is being blocked by the half-open damper door. While the technician is checking the cable, the damper door should also be tested to make sure it's operating freely. If it's binding, it can't open fully.

With these things out of the way, the only other malfunction that can result in little or no heat into a vehicle is a clogged heater core. If the heater core is plugged, it will have to be replaced.

HEATER BLOWS BOTH HOT AND COLD AIR

The heater in my car blows hot and cold air by itself without my touching the controls. When I slow down or stop at a stop sign or traffic light, air coming out of the heater duct gets cold. When cruising along the highway, air coming out of the heater duct is hot. This keeps happening during any one trip. The dealer has replaced the thermostat and now says the condition is normal. Should I believe him?

If you want to. I don't. A heater that alternately puts out both cold and warm air during a trip indicates that there's an air lock in the cooling system. To get rid of it, have a

technician bring the coolant level up to the designated mark on the coolant overflow reservoir tank; that is, to the HOT mark if the engine is warm or to the COLD mark if the engine is cold.

Then, with the engine running at idle, the technician should remove the threaded plug on the thermostat housing if there is a threaded plug. Many manufacturers provide this plug as a means for bleeding off air that's trapped in the cooling system. When coolant starts flowing from the hole vacated by the plug, air has been purged. After reinserting the plug, the technician should check the coolant level and, if necessary, bring it back up to the full mark.

If your engine doesn't have a plug on the thermostat housing, the technician should refer to the service manual to determine the procedure called for by the manufacturer to purge air trapped in the cooling system.

ERRATIC ELECTRONICALLY CONTROLLED HEATER

The only electronic climate control setting that gives us sufficient heat in winter to keep us warm is 90°F. But at this setting, it soon gets too hot in the car. The dealer replaced the electronic control unit, but that hasn't helped. What now?

A technician working on this problem should make sure that the cooling system is outfitted with the correct thermostat. It may not be the one that was installed in your car when it was manufactured. There may have been a change since then. Therefore, the technician should call the manufacturer's technical assistance number provided to dealer service departments. For example, if the thermostat presently in the car is rated at 180°F and a new one rated at 195°F is needed, this 15-degree variation can account for the inadequate heat at settings below 90°F.

The next step the technician should take is to make sure no air is trapped in the cooling system. Air can be purged by following instructions in the service manual. The amount of heat a heater gives off can be significantly reduced by trapped air.

Finally, the technician should test the inside and outside temperature sensors according to instructions in the service manual. These sensors send data to the electronic control unit (computer) of the climate control system. One or both may not be calibrated correctly. If that's the case, one or both have to be replaced to restore your heater to normal operation.

MAINTENANCE FOR AIR CONDITIONING SYSTEMS

Is there any service for a vehicle's air conditioning system that will help prevent a breakdown? I find none mentioned in the maintenance schedule printed in the owner's manual for my car.

There are two. One is to run the air conditioner three or four minutes at least once a week throughout the year. This practice circulates a lubricant that keeps the compressor sound, but there's another reason for doing it. The thin film of oil provides a seal against refrigerant seeping out of the system through hairline cracks. When the system is not operated for long periods, most of the oil drains away from potential areas of leakage and allows these cracks to open. This results in a loss of refrigerant.

Another reason for operating an air conditioner on a regular basis is to dispel any drops

of acid that form on the surfaces of parts. Left undisturbed, these can corrode surfaces. As the system runs, the turbulent flow of the refrigerant and oil circulating through the system moves the acid around before it has a chance to perforate the system.

The purpose for the second maintenance step is to get water out of the system. Water, which is the main reason why automotive air conditioners fail prematurely, builds up when air seeps into the system through tiny openings around seals and between joints. A canister full of desiccant, which is called the receiver-dryer, is installed in an air conditioning system to absorb and hold moisture so it doesn't cause damage.

Water can damage an air conditioning system in several ways. It reacts with refrigerant that's under pressure to form acid. Acid causes pinhole leaks, corrodes bearings, and mixes with lubricating oil to form a gritty sludge which abrades surfaces and plugs internal passages. Water may also freeze as it passes through an expansion valve or orifice tube of the system, blocking the flow of refrigerant.

To keep water from doing these things, the receiver-dryer should be replaced periodically. The frequency of replacement depends on the ambient temperature of the region in which the vehicle is driven, the frequency with which the air conditioner is used, and the mileage driven. A discussion with an air conditioner specialist will allow you to decide on how often to replace the receiver-dryer of your system.

BEEFING UP AN AIR CONDITIONER

The air conditioner in my pickup truck, which is an extended cab model, doesn't cool the truck's interior enough. When

---

SERVICE TIP: PREVENTING REFRIGERANT LEAKS

Auto air conditioning systems have threaded caps that screw onto valves that technicians use when servicing the system. One cap is on a valve for the high pressure line; one is on a valve for the low pressure line.

If a cap is left loose or isn't returned to a valve after the system has been serviced, refrigerant can leak from the valve and be lost. This leads to a reduction of air conditioning in the car. Refrigerant that escapes is also harmful to the environment.

Ask a technician to point out the location of these caps if you can't find them yourself. They resemble tire valve caps. Every so often give each a twist to make sure they're tight. Also, after you have the air conditioning system serviced, check to make sure the caps have been securely screwed back onto the valves by the technician.

---

the ambient temperature hits 105°F to 120°F during the summer, which it does in this part of Arizona, the inside of the truck is just bearable with the blower on HIGH. Two of my neighbors own the same model truck. They get great cooling with the blower set on MEDIUM. Yet, the dealer tells me the air conditioner in my truck is operating better than most. His testing indicates that the temperature of the air coming out of the air conditioner outlets is 45°F. So why isn't it cool in the cab?

The outlet test indicates that the air conditioner in your pickup is operating better than most. Most have a temperature of 52°F at the air conditioner outlets. Yours is at 45°F. So that's better than normal. Why, then, isn't the inside of your pickup truck more comfortable?

For one thing, the blower might not be up to speed. The dealer should check on this. If the blower is not operating at the speed specified for it in the service manual, it should be replaced.

Another reason for the uncomfortable condition inside the cab could lie with the damper door in the air conditioner duct. The damper door is also called the mode door or vacuum door. It may not be closing all the way when the air conditioner is on. A damper door that's stuck in a partially open position prevents all of the warm air from flowing out of the cab. What's left mixes with cool air, so the cab is kept at a temperature that's uncomfortably warm. The damper door is operated by spring-actuated levers. The springs may be anemic and have to be replaced with stronger springs so it will spring closed all the way when you turn on the air conditioner.

If neither the blower nor damper door is the reason for your problem, make sure the condenser is clean. (See Figure 9.1.) A dirty condensor acts as an insulator to prevent hot refrigerant that passes through it from throwing off that heat. Positioned as it is in the front of the vehicle, a condensor can accumulate debris. If it seems dirty, clean it off with water from a garden hose and a soft

FIGURE 9.1. Ensuring that the condenser stays clean is a good way to keep your air conditioner in good working order. Clean it off before the start of the air conditioning season with water from a garden hose and a soft brush. (Courtesy of Audi America, Inc.)

brush. There's nothing else that can be done except to block the sun. Call the local police department and ask if there's any restriction in your state that prohibits windshield and window tinting. Tinting the glass will reduce the intensity of the sun's rays shining into the cab, hopefully enough to keep the temperature at a comfortable level.

FICKLE AIR CONDITIONER

When that little green light in the center of the air conditioner ON/OFF button starts blinking, the air conditioner shuts down and there is no cooling. A technician couldn't find out what's wrong. Would you like to take a stab at it?

You have a foreign car, don't you—probably Japanese? The blinking green light is a warning that the air conditioner compressor has kicked off. Of course, when that happens, there is no cooling, because there is no longer circulation of refrigerant.

The electronically controlled air conditioning system in your imported car is equipped with a speed-safety sensor. The purpose of this sensor is to maintain control over the rotational speed of the compressor. When there's about a 10 percent difference in speed between the compressor and engine crankshaft, the sensor signals the computer that controls the air conditioning system to shut off the compressor. This feature is intended to prevent damage to the compressor that can result from overspeeding.

Something is causing the compressor in your car to run too fast. There are a number of reasons for this. One, the drive belt may be worn or improperly adjusted. Also, an air conditioner can switch itself off if the drive belt gets wet and starts to slip, causing an excessive variation between compressor and crankshaft speeds. Ask a technician to see if the drive belt is in a location where it might be affected by rain. If so, the technician can devise a shield for the belt. Another possibility is an air conditioner that's overfilled with refrigerant. Excessive refrigerant in this system will cause too much pressure to build up under certain types of operating conditions. A system experiencing high head pressure, as it's called, is designed to turn itself off.

Your problem could also be a result of a fault in the compressor electrical circuit. The circuit could be alternately opening and closing. This kind of intermittent action, which alternately causes a surging in compressor speed followed by a shutdown, is usually the result of a bad terminal connector.

LACK OF DEFROSTING ACTION FROM AN IMPORTED CAR

I recently bought my first Japanese-made car. The defroster in the vehicle seems to take forever to clear the windshield of frost. Even with the blower on high, the amount of warm air coming out of the defroster outlets isn't the kind of blast I got from any American-made car I ever owned. The heater works well enough, and the air conditioner is super even during the most merciless of summer days. What do you think—should I have the system disassembled to see if the defroster duct doors are hanging up?

Not yet. Since your former cars were American-made, you may be under the impression that the defroster in your Japanese car is turned on in a fashion similar to the way it's done with a GM, Ford, or Chrysler vehicle. It probably isn't. (See Figure 9.2.) Defrosters

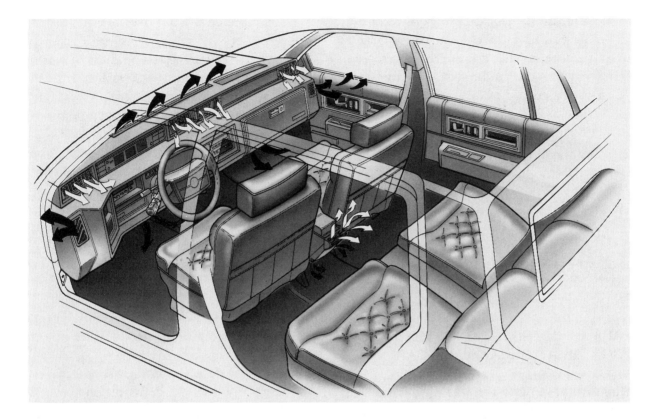

FIGURE 9.2.   A vehicle possesses many different outlets for keeping the passenger compartment warm or cool. Each outlet delivers either cool or warm air—not both. In this illustration, the white arrows indicate the air conditioner outlets and the black arrows are the heater outlets, except for those black arrows emanating from the top of the dash. These are defroster outlets. If you think the air in your vehicle is not cool or warm enough, insert a thermometer that has a long stem (such as the type used in a photographic darkroom) in one of the outlets in question. If you're testing an air conditioner, a temperature at the outlet of 50°F or lower with the air conditioner placed on its coldest setting and running is suitable. If you're testing a heater or defroster, a temperature at the outlet of 90°F or higher with the system on its maximum setting is passable. Before testing a heater, make sure the engine is warm. (Courtesy of Cadillac Division of General Motors Corporation)

in most Japanese-made cars work differently, so before you have the system torn apart on what may be a wild goose chase, take the following steps to find out if defroster output is increased:

1. Set the air intake lever to FRESH.
2. Turn the blower control lever to HIGH.
3. Set the air temperature control lever to HOT.
4. Set the air conditioner switch to ON (don't worry—you won't freeze).

How is defrosting now?

LACK OF DEFROSTING ACTION FROM AN AMERICAN-MADE CAR

Why don't I get enough warm air from the defroster outlets to clear the windshield of my American-made car? The output from the heater is more than enough. What's wrong with the defroster?

When you switch the selector lever from HEATER to DEFROST, you move a door that opens a path to divert warm air from the heater to the defroster outlets on the driver and passenger sides of the windshield. Getting sufficient heat from the heater, but a reduced amount from the defroster, makes me believe that there's a problem with the defroster door. The trouble might also be centered in the defroster ducts or with the defroster outlets.

To zero in on the part causing reduced defroster action, warm up the engine. Then, turn on the heater and set the temperature control for maximum heat. Place the blower motor on HIGH, so a maximum amount of hot air is flowing into the car.

Now, place your hand over one of the defroster outlets and move the selector lever to DEFROST. After feeling the amount of warm air flowing from the outlet, move your hand to the other outlet and check the flow coming from that. If you feel an equal amount of warm air coming from both outlets—no matter how little it happens to be—keep the selector lever on DEFROST, but move the temperature control rapidly back and forth between maximum heat and minimum heat.

Here's how to analyze what's going on:

1. If you get an unequal flow from the outlets, the defroster outlet on the side putting out the lesser amount of warm air is damaged or out of position.
2. If you get no air flow from either outlet when you switch from HEATER to DEFROST, the defroster door is stuck shut or there's a hole in the defroster duct which is allowing hot air to be diverted into the car instead of it being thrown against the windshield.
3. If you don't hear noise from the defrost door as you move the temperature control rapidly between maximum heat and minimum heat, the reason for lack of defrosting is a misadjusted or damaged defroster door.
4. If you hear the defroster door making noise as you move the temperature control rapidly between maximum heat and minimum heat, the defroster outlets are out of alignment with the windshield and have to be readjusted.

REAR "DEFROSTER" DOESN'T CLEAR THE GLASS

The rear window defroster in my car shuts off before the glass de-ices. I hear

a click when it shuts off, which I presume is coming from a thermostatic device. Can you tell me where this part is located in my car so I can replace it? Or am I barking up the wrong tree?

You're barking up the wrong tree. The unit serving the rear glass, which is called the backlite, is a defogger that also defrosts glass if it stays on long enough. The length of time it takes to defrost the backlite depends on the thickness of the frost.

Which brings us to this point: That clicking you hear is caused by points inside a relay which are opening and closing. When they are closed, electricity can get through the defogging grid attached to the backlite. Electricity heats the glass to clear off mist. When points open, the circuit is broken and the defogging grid cools off. A timer in the relay controls the length of time that points stay closed to deliver current. The timer keeps heat applied for 8 to 10 minutes. If they are closed for too long a time, heat will build up and crack the glass.

The fact that your defogger goes on and stays on indicates that there's nothing wrong with the unit. On the other hand, if you activated the ON switch and the unit went on, but turned off as soon as you released the switch, it would indicate that the relay was damaged.

Which leads us to the question of how to get additional heat to the backlite of your car to melt heavy accumulations of frost that are building up and aren't being completely melted before the timer turns off current. That's easy. When the timer causes the relay to open, shutting off electricity to the grid, wait 2 minutes and flip the ON switch back on again. That's all there is to it. The grid will apply heat for another 8 to 10 minutes.

FREEING A STUCK POWER ANTENNA

The power antenna for the radio in my car has stopped working. I can hear the motor running, but the antenna doesn't go up and down. What's wrong, and what's involved in getting it fixed?

The power antenna motor is apparently working, because you can hear it. This points to an antenna drive cable that has snapped, which means that the drive cable and antenna assembly will have to be replaced. If you didn't hear the motor, then that would be the part causing the trouble.

An antenna drive cable often snaps, because car owners allow dirt to build up on the antenna. Dirt causes the antenna to bind as it moves up and down, which puts stress on the drive cable. This means that the failure can be prevented. Here's how:

1. Every three months, raise the antenna to full height.
2. Using a cloth dampened with mineral spirits or alcohol, wipe the antenna clean. Lower and raise the antenna and repeat the cleaning procedure two more times.
3. With the antenna in the raised position, dampen a cloth with light household or sewing machine oil and wipe it over the antenna. Make sure every inch is covered with oil.
4. Lower and raise the antenna. Then, wipe the antenna dry with a clean cloth. Apply oil and wipe it off one time only. The reason for wiping off oil that remains on the antenna after it's been raised is to remove excess, which will attract dirt. Lowering the antenna the one time spreads enough oil in the tubes of the antenna to keep the antenna adequately lubricated until the next service.

PREVENTING LOST ANTENNAS

Believe it or not, I was driving along when the radio antenna fell off my car and was lost in interstate traffic. Do you have any comment about this strange occurrence?

This is more widespread than you might think. If the nut that holds the antenna to the car loosens, the antenna can fall off. Therefore, use a wrench to tighten the nut every few months.

ELIMINATING POPPING RADIO NOISE

From the first day I drove my new car, the radio has made an annoying popping sound. Although the dealer says a lot of radios do this, I'm ready to have the unit replaced. Before I do, I'd like to know if, indeed, "a lot of radios do this."

Are you kidding? Ask your relatives and friends if they have the same trouble. Then, tell your dealer to cut out the nonsense and take steps to find the cause of this trouble and fix it.

One likely place to look is in the distributor with the rotor. Car manufacturers coat the metal terminals of rotors with silicone grease to protect this part from corrosion between the time the car is manufactured and the time it's sold. The grease has to be wiped off before the car is delivered to a customer, because it can cause ignition noise which is transmitted through the radio. This noise, usually a popping sound, increases and decreases in frequency with engine speed. Therefore, ask the dealer to remove the rotor from the distributor and clean the terminal with emery cloth and grease solvent. If this fails to eliminate the noise, a new rotor should be installed.

Let's assume this doesn't work. Then, the radio is defective. Radio noise is not normal. Furthermore, radio repair or replacement in a new car is covered by the warranty. If your dealer refuses to act, get in touch with the manufacturer of the car yourself by calling the customer service department. The address and telephone number are printed in the owner's manual.

WHY CARS EAT UP HEADLAMPS

Although I rarely drive at night, my car eats up headlamps like they are going out of style. No sooner do I install new units than it seems that they fail. Is this the result of vibration?

Probably not. Headlamps will burn out quickly if the voltage regulator that controls alternator output or the relay between the alternator and headlamp circuit is faulty. These conditions will allow excessive current to surge through the headlamps, causing them to burn out. An automotive electrical technician, whom you can find by consulting the yellow pages of your phone book under "Automotive—Electrical," should be able to troubleshoot and repair this problem.

RESOLVING A PROBLEM
WITH HALOGEN HEADLAMPS

The high beam of the halogen headlamp on the right side of my car stopped working so I had the bulb replaced. But oddly enough, after a brief period, the high beam of the new halogen unit has stopped glowing. Yet, the low beam of

the new unit, like the low beam of the old lamp, is okay. What's wrong here?

Whoever replaced the old lamp probably damaged the new lamp as the exchange was being made. Halogen units are fragile and have to be treated with extra gentleness. A lamp can be damaged if it is jarred or if someone even keeps fingers on the glass for longer than a few seconds.

However, let's assume that the new halogen lamp installed in the car wasn't damaged by the person who installed it. Then, a malfunction exists with the connector into which the lamp is plugged, or with the wiring between the connector and the headlamp sensor or high-low beam switch. To find out where the trouble lies, the ring that locks the lamp into the socket has to be loosened and the lamp has to be disconnected from the connector to examine contacts. If contacts are corroded, try rubbing corrosion off with a pencil eraser. If this doesn't work, a new connector has to be installed.

Damaged wiring is more difficult to pinpoint. A troublelight has to be used to test wiring from one connecting point to the next. To do this, the wiring diagram in the service manual is needed.

REPAIRING VARIABLE-SPEED WINDSHIELD WIPERS

I'm having a problem with the variable-speed windshield wipers in my car. No matter at what position I set the wiper switch, wipers sweep once a second or once every 20 seconds. There is no variability. The dealer says the trouble is probably with a circuit board and wants to charge me over $100 to replace it. Before I give him the go-ahead, I'd like

to know if you think he's correct in his diagnosis.

The circuit board your dealer speaks of is called the pulse module. It's part of a control assembly that provides the variable delay. At the low end, that delay is supposed to provide a sweep of the windshield every 20 seconds. At the high end, it should allow wipers to sweep the windshield once every second. If a variable-speed wiper system is working properly, it should provide a sweep of the windshield at various time intervals between one second and 20 seconds, depending upon where the control switch is set. So, there is no question that a malfunction exists with your system.

The cause of the problem is probably the pulse module as the dealer indicates, but it could be with the selector switch instead. So before he replaces the pulse module, the dealer should make sure he's in the right spot by using an ohmmeter to test the selector switch as outlined in the service manual.

SILENCING WINDSHIELD WIPER BLADE CHATTER

The windshield wiper blades started chattering a few weeks after I drove my new car from the dealership, so I replaced them. Now, after being in use for only a few weeks, the new blades are doing the same thing. What's going on?

Residue left by dirt, insects, and wax sprayed on windshields at car wash facilities are the reasons why windshield wiper blades that are in sound condition will start to chatter. To "de-chatter" chattering blades, wash the windshield with a cleaner, such as Bon Ami® or GM glass cleaner sold by General Motors dealers. Then, moisten a cloth with full-strength windshield washer fluid and wipe residue from the blades. The final step is to rinse the blades with water.

TURNED ON WINDSHIELD WIPERS TURNS OFF CRUISE CONTROL

Why is it that when the windshield wipers of my car are on, I can't get the cruise control to engage? Technicians have given up trying to solve this problem. Would you like to take a crack at it?

I'll bet that as the windshield wipers sweep, one of the wiper arm linkages is hitting against the cruise control electrical harness, which is causing a short circuit that's preventing the cruise control from engaging. A technician can find out if this theory is accurate by examining the cruise control harness. Is it lying too close to the wiper arm linkage? If so, the technician should make sure the wire isn't damaged and then reroute the harness away from the windshield wiper linkage.

Another reason may be that the two are served by a common relay, which is damaged. Turning on the windshield wipers may be causing that part of the relay which serves the cruise control to shut down.

TIRE CHANGE CAUSES AN ERRATIC SPEEDOMETER

I switched tires on my 1990 model car from P185/80/R13 to P195/70/R13 in order to get a smoother ride. But now the car's electronic speedometer says I'm driving at around 65 mph to keep up with traffic going at 55 mph. Is this happening because the new P195 tires are larger than the old P185 tires? What has

to be done to bring the speedometer back into line?

You have things a little mixed up. Your new P195/70/R13 tires are smaller—not larger—than the original P185/80/R13. The important numbers are not 195 and 185, but 70 and 80, which are called the tire's aspect ratio. The aspect ratio of a tire denotes the tire's diameter.

As long as we're discussing tire numerals, let's digress for a moment so I can explain what that gibberish means. The P identifies the tire as a passenger tire. The three numerals following the P—195 or 185, for example—indicate the width of the tire in millimeters. The R identifies the tire as a radial tire. The last group of numerals—13—is the diameter of the wheel in inches on which the tire goes.

Now, let's get down to cases. The new tires you bought have an aspect ratio of 70—not 70 inches or 70 millimeters—just plain 70. As I mentioned, they are not larger but smaller in diameter than the tires you switched from, which have an aspect ratio of 80. Specifically, your new tires are 23.78 inches in diameter while your former tires are 24.65 inches in diameter.

If your new tires were indeed larger in diameter than your old tires, the speedometer would read lower than the speed at which you're traveling. But instead they're causing the speedometer to read higher—specifically $2\frac{1}{2}$ mph higher than it should, not the 10 mph difference you stated. You are either misjudging the speed at which your fellow motorists are traveling or the electronic speedometer in your car isn't accurate. But it doesn't matter whether the speedometer is providing an erroneous reading that's $2\frac{1}{2}$ mph or 10 mph higher than what it should be. You should bring the car to a dealer who sells your make of car to have the speedometer removed from the instrument panel and sent to a facility that specializes in electronic speedometers, where the instrument will be recalibrated to provide an accurate reading.

POWER DOOR LOCKS DON'T CLOSE AUTOMATICALLY

The power door locks in my car don't close automatically when I press the switch. Yet, they will open automatically after I push them closed by hand. A technician says he's never seen anything like this before. What's happening?

Tell the technician that there's a door-lock relay assembly located between the door-lock switches and the door-lock motors. One side of the relay assembly is the lock side. The other side is the unlock side. The problem lies on the lock side. The technician should look for a loose or broken wire that connects to this side of the relay. If that turns up nothing, the relay should be replaced.

POWER DOOR LOCKS WORK BY THEMSELVES

The power door locks in my van have developed the strange habit of locking and unlocking by themselves. No one touches the switch. Everyone I've talked to about this is stumped. Can you tell me what cosmothetic force is at work?

Nothing more ethereal than an electric wire serving one of the power door-lock motors that's short circuiting. It's happening, because insulation covering a spot on the wire has been rubbed off, leaving the wire bared. The bare wire is occasionally hitting against a metal part lying near it because of vibration caused by your van going over bumps and dips in the road.

To gain control over these phantom-like door locks of yours, have the door panels removed to find the bare wire. It can be repaired just by wrapping the spot with electricians tape.

KEYLESS ENTRY SYSTEM LOCKOUT

I drive a car that has a keyless entry system. One feature of this system is automatic door locking, which I'm not happy with. This thing has gotten me into trouble on more than one occasion when I inadvertently locked the keys inside the car and couldn't remember the code. Is there a way to disable the automatic door-locking feature, but maintain the other aspects of keyless entry?

Yes—by disabling the switch that controls the automatic door-locking feature, which in your make of car is located under the driver's seat. Have a technician pull the connector from the module that controls automatic door locking and wrap electricians tape around the connector terminals, so terminals don't come in contact with a metal part of the seat. If they do, the locks will close automatically, and you'll be in the same boat you're in now.

HERKY-JERKY, NOISY SPEEDOMETER

When driving my car at low speeds, the speedometer needle wavers back and forth and gives off a squeak. When I drive above 40 mph, neither condition occurs. Will lubricating the speedometer cable solve these problems?

Since the alternative can cost you approximately five times more than lubricating the cable, having this done is worth a shot. If in removing the cable from the car for lubrication, the technician finds that the cable is kinked and can't be straightened, it will have to be replaced.

Having the cable lubricated costs about $30; having a new cable installed, about $90. If the old cable is straight and lubrication doesn't get rid of noise and needle hop, the cause of the problem is a faulty speedometer head. Having a new one installed costs about $150.

REPAIRING BACKUP LIGHTS

The backup lights in my car don't go on when I shift into REVERSE unless I tap the gear shift lever with my hand. What's wrong?

The switch that controls the backup lights has to be repositioned or replaced. If the car has a console-mounted transmission shift lever, the transmission selector switch, which is usually mounted on the transmission, operates the backup lights. If your car has a transmission shift lever mounted on the steering column, the backup light switch is part of the PARK NEUTRAL switch and is mounted on the lower half of the steering column jacket. Repositioning or replacing the switch is a simple repair that should take about 15 minutes.

Rx FOR EXCESSIVE A/C COMPRESSOR CYCLING

When I run the air conditioner in my car, which has been driven only 2,500 miles, the compressor cycles on and off every 5

to 10 seconds. This is most annoying, but the dealer keeps brushing me off by saying that all new models do the same thing. Should I believe him?

You'd be wise not to. Only new models that have a problem such as yours do the same thing.

The service department's air conditioner technician should consult the service manual issued for the vehicle. It provides a chart that outlines the correct compressor cycling rate according to the setting on the temperature control. For example, with the temperature set at 70°F, a properly operating compressor of the kind you have in your car will make 3 to $4\frac{1}{2}$ cycles every 60 minutes, which translates into one cycle every 15 to 20 seconds.

The most common cause of an abnormally high compressor cycling rate is a low charge of refrigerant. Another reason is a clogged orifice tube screen.

AIR CONDITIONER REPAIR OVERKILL

I spent over $1,300 to replace the air conditioner in a 1984 sedan. The technician told me the system failed, because the compressor piston that is made of Teflon® disintegrated and particles jammed the system. He claims that once this happens, there is no repair other than replacing all parts. Is he right?

No. First of all, the pistons of air conditioner compressors are aluminum. The piston rings of most compressors manufactured since the mid-1970s are Teflon.

The second error he made was to replace all parts of the system. When Teflon rings disintegrate, only the compressor has to be replaced. The evaporator and condenser are protected from an invasion of particles by a fine-mesh screen in the orifice tube. But even if this screen failed to do its job, the system could have been flushed and the evaporator and condenser kept in use. The only reason for replacing the compressor is that the cost of a rebuilt compressor (about $300) is about the same as having the compressor disassembled to make repairs.

HOW TO REPAIR AN ERRATIC TEMPERATURE WARNING LIGHT

The temperature warning light in the instrument panel of my car comes on after about three hours of driving. The engine doesn't overheat, but even so I had a new thermostat and temperature switch installed to try and get the warning light to stay off. I'm still getting that accursed glow. What's causing it?

Most engines are served by two temperature switches. Each switch is actually a heat sensor. One monitors the temperature of the coolant. It's the one that technicians replace most often when there's a problem like the one you're having, because it's the obvious one to replace when the temperature warning light goes on for no reason.

The second switch, which is referred to as the engine heat sensor, is not as obvious and is usually overlooked. This sensor monitors the temperature of the engine cylinder head into which it's screwed.

The engine sensor in your car may be overly sensitive and allow the temperature warning light to come on although the coolant temperature is within limits. To determine if this is what's happening, have a technician take the engine heat sensor out of action by disconnecting the wire attached to it. Drive the car. If the "accursed glow" doesn't appear, have the technician unscrew

the engine heat sensor, screw a one-inch pipe fitting into the cylinder head, screw the sensor into the pipe fitting, and reconnect the wire. This will raise the sensor an inch or so off the cylinder head, thereby compensating for sensitivity.

What if the temperature warning light comes on when the wire to the engine heat sensor has been disconnected so the sensor is out of action? Then, it's possible that an air deflector which should be attached to the bottom of the front bumper has dropped off the car, if such a part was put on your car by the manufacturer. The purpose of this part is to deflect air toward the radiator and help in the cooling process. If an air deflector that's supposed to be there has been lost, the amount of air directed toward the radiator will be reduced, resulting in an increase in coolant temperature. This increase won't be enough to cause overheating, but it could be enough to make the temperature warning light glow. (Figure 9.3.)

TURNING ON ACCESSORIES KILLS THE BATTERY

Since installing a new battery in my car, I've not been able to turn on headlights, heater, air conditioner, or radio while driving in city traffic without running down the battery. As long as I don't use any accessory, the battery retains its energy. The new battery, alternating-current generator (alternator), voltage regulator, engine computer, and the rest of the electrical system have passed tests done by the dealer and three independent garages with flying colors. Help, I'm desperate.

My guess is that the trouble lies with that new battery. Does it match the reserve

Air Deflector

FIGURE 9.3.   This part is not installed to jazz up a vehicle. Its purpose is to divert cool air toward the radiator in order to assist in cooling down the hot coolant flowing through the radiator. If this air deflector drops off the vehicle, coolant temperature will increase. (Courtesy Ford Motor Company)

capacity and cold cranking amperage ratings of the battery installed in your car when the car was manufactured? The unit you have now may be a light-duty battery that isn't able to handle the combined load imposed by an accessory you've turned on while driving in city traffic.

Check the ratings of this battery against that of your old battery. The service department at a dealership that sells your make of car can help you.

There could also be an excessive drain being imposed on the battery by a bad resistor in the charging system, a loose wire, or a loose alternator drive belt. Have these been looked into by a technician who specializes in auto electrical systems? You can find one by checking the yellow pages of the telephone book under the heading "Automobile Electric Service."

HANDLING DIGITAL CLOCK FAILURE

One foggy day not long ago I accidentally left the lights of my car on while I tended to some chores. This resulted in a dead battery. I got a jump-start, but to be on the safe side I drove the car to a service facility to have the battery charged. After this was done, I noticed that the digital clock was no longer working. To make a long story short, I've been told that the clock has to be replaced. How did this happen?

The clock *may* have to be replaced if the service facility that charged the battery connected it to a fast-charger that jolted the electric system with 24 volts. Hitting an electrical system with this much voltage, which is done during a fast charge, can damage electronic components, including a digital clock.

The recommended way to charge a battery is by using the slow charge method. Some call this trickle charging. It takes a longer time to recharge a battery this way, but it's a much safer method to use in a car equipped with electronic components. If a technician has to use the fast-charging method because a customer is in a hurry, the technician should disconnect the cables from the battery before hooking up the battery charger.

If you're lucky, that 24-volt jolt the fast charger apparently pumped into your car's electrical system may not have killed the clock. It may instead have blown the fuse before the power surge hit the clock. On the chance that it did, have the fuse protecting the clock replaced. If the digital display comes alive, the clock is okay. If not, you'll have to install a new clock.

Ten

Questions About
Emergency & Safety
Problems

**JUMP-STARTING A DEAD BATTERY:
THE SAFEST WAY**

**Please explain how to jump-start a car
that has a dead battery. I've seen people
employ different procedures.**

There's only one safe way to do this job.
Here's how:

Caution: Remove jewelry and do not
smoke.

1. Maneuver the car having the strong
   battery near the car with the rundown
   battery. Don't let the two cars touch.
   Any metal-to-metal contact will create

a wayward ground, diverting current
that's needed to boost the dead battery
away from that battery.

2. Turn off the ignition switches, lights,
   and all accessories of both cars. Place
   transmissions in PARK or NEUTRAL and
   engage the parking brakes of both cars.

3. Connect a clamp of the positive jumper
   cable to the positive terminal (marked +
   or POS) of the weak battery. Attach this
   jumper cable's other clamp to the + or
   POS terminal of the strong battery. The
   positive jumper cable is a colored cable,
   most times red.

4. Connect a clamp of the black (negative)
   jumper cable to the negative terminal

(marked – or NEG) of the strong battery. Connect this jumper cable's other clamp to a clean metal part of the engine in the car with the weak battery. Get the clamp as far from the battery as possible. The alternator bracket or an engine bolt is usually suitable.

Caution: Do not attach the negative jumper cable to the – or NEG terminal of the weak battery. If you do, sparks may fly when the metal clamp of this cable comes in contact with the terminal of the battery. These sparks could ignite hydrogen that's being given off by the battery, causing the battery to explode and sending pieces of battery flying that can seriously injure someone standing nearby.

5. Start the engine of the car with the strong battery. Then, try starting the engine of the car with the weak battery. If it doesn't start, turn off the ignition switches of both engines and check that each jumper cable clamp is attached securely. Try starting the engine again.

6. When the engine starts, wait a few seconds to make sure it doesn't stall. Then, disconnect jumper cables in this order: (a) Negative cable from the ground connection of the car with the weak battery; (b) negative cable from the negative terminal of the strong battery; (c) positive cable from the positive terminal of the strong battery; (d) positive cable from the positive terminal of the other battery. (See Figure 10.1.)

FIRE UNDER THE HOOD

Have you ever heard of a battery ground cable catching fire? It's happened to me twelve times in the last six months. Please help. Buying cables is getting expensive.

Expense isn't your biggest problem. You ought to be more concerned about getting trapped inside a car as flames from the ground cable spread. You've been lucky so far, but don't press it. I suggest that you get the car to an auto electrical specialist at once to pinpoint the trouble and fix it.

A battery ground cable gets hot, starts to smolder, and erupts into flame when it develops resistance to the current flowing through it. The cause of this high resistance is one or more of the following:

1. A cable that may be undersized or constructed of aluminum wire. An undersized cable can't handle the load. Aluminum wire as compared to copper wire is unsafe, because it can melt under the heat produced by the flow of current. The parts department of a dealership that sells your make of car can provide you with the correct cable for the battery and electrical system in your vehicle.

2. Whoever is installing cables may be bending them. A gradual arc in the cable is acceptable, but an extreme bend will result in an increase in resistance.

3. Cable connections may be dirty and/or loose, which causes an obstruction to the flow of current. As the resistance increases, so does the temperature of the cable. To overcome this, remove the cable and use sandpaper to clean the spot on the engine to which the cable attaches. If that spot is coated with paint, sand it until bare metal is present. Then, use sandpaper or a wire brush to clean the ends of the cable, the screw that attaches the cable to the engine, and the screw (if one is used) that attaches the cable to the battery.

FIGURE 10.1. Carry a set of jumper cables in the car and learn how to use them properly.

Posts mounted on top of the battery should then be cleaned. If the battery has side terminals to which the cables connect instead of posts, the threads inside the battery and the bottom of the hole, which is often neglected, should be cleaned. Use a bottoming tap to do this, but the bottoming tap must be the right size for the hole and must not be tightened too much or the battery case may crack. Finally, secure the cable to the engine and battery.

WHERE TO STORE A FIRE EXTINGUISHER IN A CAR

I regard a fire extinguisher as an important piece of equipment to keep in a car, but I hesitate doing so. Every fire extinguisher I've ever looked at states on the label that it should not be kept where the temperature exceeds 120°F. The inside of my car often gets hotter than this during the summer. Is there any fire extinguisher that can be safely stored under such high heat conditions?

There is no fire extinguisher bearing the Underwriters Laboratories (UL) mark which states on the label attached to the extinguisher that it's rated to withstand temperatures above 120°F. But there's a caveat to this statement. Since 1980, UL has been exposing fire extinguishers to a temperature of 175°F for seven days to weed out those that rupture at this level. Every fire extinguisher manufactured since then that has the UL mark embossed on the canister has passed this 175°F resistance test.

If you decide to buy a UL-listed fire extinguisher to keep in your car based on this information, store it in the trunk during hot weather. The inside of the trunk stays cooler than the inside of the car, which is exposed to the sun's rays.

BLOWING APART MYTHS ABOUT AIR BAGS

Can you describe the concept behind air bags? The new car I'm thinking of buying is equipped with them, but I've heard that the gas used by the system is dangerous to breathe and that a person can suffocate by having his or her face pushed into the bag.

The air bag is one of the most effective automotive safety systems ever invented and poses none of the dangers you mention. On the contrary, air bags have saved thousands of lives and will save a countless number more as the system is installed by manufacturers in more and more new cars.

An air bag system includes sensors that detect the rapid deceleration which takes place during a frontal or near-frontal impact. The system goes into operation if that impact equals in severity the collision between a car traveling at 10 to 14 mph or more and a solid wall.

The sensors trigger an inflator module, which causes a solid chemical propellant (most systems use sodium azide as a propellant) inside an inflator to undergo a rapid chemical change. The reaction produces nitrogen gas, which inflates a woven nylon bag packed inside the hub of the steering wheel or in the instrument panel in front of the front seat passenger. The bag inflates fully in about $1/20$th of a second and then, almost immediately, starts to deflate.

Nitrogen makes up 80 percent of the air we breathe, so the nitrogen created by an air bag system and expelled into the car through pores in the bag during the deflation process is harmless. So much for that "dangerous to breathe" nonsense.

The reason for constructing air bags so they have pores is to make sure that the bag deflates at once to prevent a person whose face is pressed into the cushion during the collision from suffocating. So that takes care of that myth. Immediate deflation has another purpose, and that's to allow a person to exit the car as quickly as possible without being hampered by the billowy bag.

SOME MORE FACTS ABOUT AIR BAGS

I have these questions about air bags:

1. Is repacking an air bag after it deploys in an accident a job that can be done by the owner of the vehicle?

2. If repacking has to be done by a technician, how long does a customer have to be without the car?

3. Is an air bag effective in a side-impact collision?

4. Can I get an air bag installed in a car that's not equipped with one?

Here, in the order that you asked them, are the answers to your questions:

1. An air bag is not repacked after it deploys. A deployed unit is discarded and a new unit in the form of a module about the size of a cigar box is installed. This job has to be done by a technician using special tools. If the new unit isn't installed properly, it could deploy prematurely or not deploy at all if there's another accident.

2. Extracting the old module and putting in a new one will take a technician about 15 minutes. Keep in mind that many auto insurance companies cover the cost of replacing a deployed air bag.

3. Air bags are effective when there's a frontal or nearly frontal (within 20° to 30° of head-on) collision. They won't deploy when there's a side impact or a rear-ender, or if the car rolls over. They also don't offer protection against a secondary collision—that is, if a vehicle slams into another vehicle or stationary object following the initial crash. That's because an air bag is designed to deflate within milliseconds after the first collision, which will be before the onset of any follow-on crash. It's for these reasons—protection in a side or rear-end accident or in the event of a secondary collision following a frontal impact—that seat belts should be engaged although a car is equipped with air bags.

4. You can have your car outfitted with air bags if there's a unit made for the particular model.

FLAT TIRE, STUCK WHEEL

I had a terrible experience the other day in the form of a flat tire on a heavily traveled interstate highway. On the shoulder, with vehicles whizzing by, I removed the wheel nuts. But I couldn't get the tire and wheel off the car to put on the spare, because the wheel was stuck in place so solidly that it wouldn't budge. Hitting the wheel with a hammer didn't do any good.

To avoid being exposed any longer to danger from passing vehicles, I drove along the shoulder of the road on the flat to an exit and service station. Of course,

---

SAFETY TIP: DON'T SPIN YOUR TIRES

Gunning an engine and spinning tires to get a vehicle out of a snow bank or off an ice patch can cause tires to explode and send chunks of rubber flying through the air like shrapnel to strike a passerby. The practice can also result in severe damage to the transmission and engine.

As if these two reasons aren't enough to keep drivers from doing this, there's a third reason: Gunning an engine and spinning tires is not an effective method for extricating a car from snow or off ice. Rocking the vehicle back and forth gently is much more productive.

To employ the gentle approach, shift into gear and accelerate gingerly to move the car forward slowly. Come to a complete stop before tires begin to spin. Then, shift the transmission into Reverse and move the car backward slowly. Again, come to a complete stop before tires begin to spin. Employ this maneuver until the car breaks free.

I ruined a perfectly good tire and had to buy a new one. Tell me, in case this happens again, is there a way to loosen a stuck wheel so a flat can be changed quickly?

If you find yourself in the same spot on an interstate, stuck wheel or not, it's safer not to try and change the tire. Even if the tire is ruined, drive to a service station if there's an exit nearby or call a tow truck. Be sure to have your hazard warning lights turned on.

Suppose though that you face the same problem of not being able to remove a wheel from the car when you are on a road where there's little traffic. Here's what to do:

If you've taken off the wheel nuts, reattach and tighten them. Then, loosen each nut two turns. Lower the car and rock it from side to side. Get help if you can. Many hands rocking the vehicle are better than two. Now, raise the car and see if you can take off the wheel.

If you can't, lower the car, start the engine, put the transmission into a forward gear, drive ahead about 50 feet at a slow speed, and make a hard stop. Then, shift into Reverse and do the same thing backing up. This should loosen the wheel.

What you should never do is bang on a stuck wheel with a hammer, or use heat from a propane torch or similar tool to try and loosen it. You can damage the wheel, wheel bearings, and brake components.

HANDLING AN ON-THE-ROAD COMPUTER BREAKDOWN

What does one do if the computer controlling the engine goes bad as you're driving along? What tools should I keep with me to make an emergency roadside repair?

There are no tools to carry since nothing less than a new computer will overcome this emergency. There is no side-of-the road repair that a driver can make if the engine computer, which is also called the electronic control module or processor, blows itself out.

What you'll have to do is call a tow truck if the circuit in the computer that controls the *ignition system* fails. Notice emphasis on the words "ignition system." The circuit controlling this system is the only one that will make the engine stop running if there is a computer failure. Since without that circuit there will be no spark to ignite the fuel mixture, the engine won't run.

Such is not the case if any other circuit inside a computer goes bad. When this happens, the computer kicks into the limp-in mode, and the engine will continue to run, although roughly. You'll be able to drive the car home or to a facility where the computer can be replaced.

Important: If the computer of your engine electronic control system should ever go bad, remember that it is an emissions control system part and is covered by the 5-year/50,000 mile (whichever occurs first) emissions control system warranty (see page 11). It will be replaced free of charge if your car has not exceeded the 5-year/50,000 mile term.

WORRIED ABOUT FUMES FROM THE FUEL TANK

When I loosen the cap of my car's fuel tank to fill up the tank, a gush of pressurized fumes is given off. A dealer who sells this make of car claims it's normal, but I feel as if I'm sitting on a time bomb. I'd like you to tell me what's wrong so I can get it fixed before I blow myself and the car to pieces.

Relax. There's no danger of that happening. Gas vapor expands and contracts with changes in temperature. The fuel evaporation emissions system prevents these vapors from escaping from the fuel tank into the atmosphere and causing pollution. Instead, they are routed to a charcoal canister which

is a component of the fuel evaporation emissions system.

Are you in the habit of running your fuel tank nearly dry before refilling it? If so, the amount of vapor that will be expelled from the tank when you release the cap will be greater than if you fill the tank when it's no less than 1/4 filled.

There's another explanation for gushy fumes, especially in the summer. If the car has been in the sun and the fuel tank is hot, the amount of vapor given off when you loosen the cap to fill the tank will be greater. Therefore, you might want to fill the tank in the morning when it's cooler. Also, opening the cap slowly so pressure is released gradually should lessen the intensity of the gush.

Don't worry about the tank exploding. The cap has a relief valve which opens and vents the tank to the atmosphere if pressure within the system gets too great.

HOW TO FILL UP

The gas tank of my utility vehicle takes a year and a day to fill. I can pump in 11 gallons in one minute and 10 seconds. At this point, the automatic gas pump shuts off. If I took the time, it would take me seven minutes and five seconds to add an additional three gallons to completely fill the tank. The pump keeps clicking off unless I introduce gas at a trickle. This happens with every pump I try. The dealer from whom I bought the truck says, "They all act this way." I say, "Nonsense." What do you say?

It doesn't matter what I say or even what you say, because the authority is the manufacturer of the vehicle. Your owner's manual specifies a clearly defined procedure for filling the gas tank. That procedure is to put the pump on the high step of the automatic shut-off to pump in gas rapidly until the pump shuts itself off. Wait five seconds and add more gas by holding the lever in a position that's $1/2$ the full automatic speed. When the pump shuts off again, wait another five seconds and repeat the manual-feed procedure.

Now when the pump shuts off, don't add any more gas. As far as manufacturers are concerned, tanks are full at this point. The air space that remains in the tank is a safety margin to allow for any expansion of the gasoline that may take place, which can cause an overflow.

HOW TO TOW A CAR BEHIND A MOTOR HOME

I just bought a front-wheel drive station wagon that's equipped with a manual transmission. I'd like to tow the car behind a motor home by keeping all four wheels on the road. Will this cause a problem?

You can bet on it. This is not the way to tow any car. If you read the owner's manual for your front-wheel drive car, you may find that it states in no uncertain terms, "Do *not* tow for distances of more than 50 miles with front wheels on the ground." Doing so will cause gears in the differential to rotate, which puts them under stress that can result in premature gear failure.

To tow your front-wheel drive station wagon behind a motor home the correct way, rent or buy a dolly. Raise the front wheels and place them on the dolly. With the front wheels off the ground and the rear wheels on the road, you can tow the wagon as far as you want without causing damage.

If you were towing a vehicle with rear-wheel drive, you would reverse the procedure by backing up the car or station wagon so the rear end is nearest the motor home. Raise the rear wheels and place them on the dolly, allowing the front wheels to roll on the road.

If you were towing a four-wheel drive car, you would follow the procedure for towing a rear-wheel drive car with the additional step

---

SAFETY TIP: CLEAN OFF YOUR LIGHTS

Dirt that builds up on a vehicle's headlamps cuts down on the light case onto the road and reduces a driver's range of vision. Dirt-covered headlamps are especially prevalent in winter when vehicles in front of you toss up slush that coats lenses. Headlamps, however, aren't the only lights a car possesses. Neither are they the only lights that get dirty. Turn signals, brake and tail lights, and side markers are also affected.

So do yourself and the other people sharing the road with you a favor. Every week or so—more often if it's necessary—use paper towels to wipe surface dirt off all light lenses. Then, use glass cleaner and more paper towels or a rag to get off the dirt that remains. You'll be able to see better. Furthermore, others on the road will be able to see you better, which is a lot safer for everyone concerned.

of shifting the drive train out of four-wheel drive into rear-wheel drive.

TIGHTEN UP A SHOULDER SAFETY HARNESS? NO WAY

The three vehicles I own were manufactured by General Motors. They have shoulder harnesses which don't snap back to maintain tension across the chest if I lean forward to change a radio station or adjust the climate control system, or just to shift to a more comfortable position. I have to pull on the shoulder harness to get it to rebound tautly across my chest. Harnesses in other vehicles I've driven, such as the Jeep Wagoneer and BMW, stay tight under all circumstances. Can the mechanisms of the safety harnesses in my GM cars be modified to keep them tight?

Each auto manufacturer has its own a philosophy concerning the shoulder harness. In GM's case the "comfort-position" harness, as this design is called, is a feature that was adopted in the belief that the shoulder-chest restraint would be used by more people if the harness could be worn with relative freedom.

The way in which the GM shoulder harness is designed is the way it has to stay. There is no modification. If you want the harness held tightly across your chest after you shift position, pull on it until it snaps back.

Note: With the adoption by automobile manufacturers of automatic seat belts and shoulder harnesses, including GM, the comfort-position feature has been discontinued. The information given here applies to pre-1990 GM model vehicles.

SERVICE TIP: ONE WAY TO PREVENT AN OVERHEATING EMERGENCY

Examine the lower radiator hose of your engine to see if it has rub-marks on it. It's possible for this hose to come in contact with another part of the vehicle, such as an engine mount.

If the condition goes unnoticed, contact being made between the two components may eventually cause the hose to rub through while you're driving along. This will result in a rapid loss of coolant. The engine will overheat. You'll have to shut it down and have the car towed to a repair shop. If you find rub-marks on the hose, have it replaced and routed away from the other part.

SERVICE TIP: HOW TO CONTACT FEDERAL SAFETY AUTHORITIES

Write down this toll-free telephone number and put it in a place that you won't forget: (800) 424-9393. If you reside in the District of Columbia, the number you'll want is (202) 366-0123.

This is the auto safety hotline number for the National Highway Traffic Safety Administration (NHTSA) of the U.S. Department of Transportation. When you call it, you can get up-to-the-minute information of any current safety recall campaign for your particular vehicle. In addition, you can get the recall history for any make and model car, truck, motorcycle, or child safety seat.

A sad commentary relative to the recall program concerns the number of vehicle owners who disregard campaigns. According to NHTSA, "Only slightly more than half the owners of vehicles with safety problems have the recall work done."

This is a pity when you consider the fact that most repairs called for by recalls are designed to correct deficiencies that can lead to accidents that can result in serious injuries or deaths. Here's an example:

Approximately 36,000 1991 Chevrolet Beretta and Corsica sedans are suspected of having left the factory with incorrectly tightened steering wheel nuts. The deficiency could lead to the steering wheel separating from the steering column, which can cause a driver to lose control of the vehicle. The repair to be done by a dealer involves tightening this nut to the correct specification. There is no cost to the customer as is the case with all repairs required by recalls.

SAFETY TIP: CUTTING DOWN REFLECTION

Are you troubled by the rays of the sun reflecting into your eyes? If you are, then answer another question. Are you cleaning the instrument panel pad of the vehicle with wax or a cleaner that contains silicone? Wax or silicone can intensify the rays that strike the pad and bounce them into your eyes.

Not using wax or silicone will eliminate or reduce the reflection. But what should you use to clean the instrument panel pad? Plain warm, sudsy water will do nicely. Use saddle soap or mild soap flakes, such as Ivory.

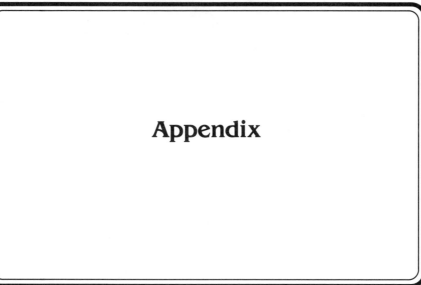

Appendix

Troubleshooting

The best chance you have of getting a problem with your car repaired properly the first time is to make sure that troubleshooting procedures recommended by car manufacturers are followed. Troubleshooting is the process of probing and testing all possible causes of a problem to uncover the reason for the malfunction before attempting a repair. As the lists presented in this Appendix demonstrate, troubleshooting should begin with the easiest-to-test and/or least expensive-to-repair possibility.

With this in mind, this Appendix is a compendium of how to troubleshoot the most common problems you may experience with your car. Use the appropriate information to make the tests and repairs you can do yourself and then as a basis for discussing the other possibilities with personnel at the servicing facility you employ. The lists are divided into the following sections:

- Section I. Tires & Wheels/Steering/ Suspension.

  These are handled as a group since a problem in one system (steering, for example) can be caused by a malfunction with another system (suspension or tires and wheels).

- Section II. Brakes

- Section III. Engine mechanical

- Section IV. Engine performance

- Section V. Automatic transmission

SECTION I.   TIRES & WHEELS/ STEERING/SUSPENSION

A. Lead/pull (on a level road with no pressure on the steering wheel, deviation of the car from a straight path)

1. Tires not inflated to manufacturer's pressure recommendation.

2. Mismatched front tires (check sizes and tread configuration).

3. Tire construction (switch front and rear tires to find out if lead/pull condition is altered).

4. Broken or weak front spring.

5. Wheels out of alignment.

6. Front brakes dragging.

B. Abnormal or excessive tire wear

1. Tires not inflated to manufacturer's pressure recommendation.

2. Not rotating tires to manufacturer's time period recommendation.

3. Hard driving and braking.

4. Overloading the car.

5. Tires/wheels out of balance.

6. Wheels out of alignment.

7. Damaged or worn-out suspension or steering component.

C. Scuffed tires

1. Taking curves at excessive speeds.

2. Wheels out of alignment.

3. Damaged suspension component.

D. Thumping from tire/wheel

1. Blister (bubble) on tire.

2. Tires/wheels out of balance.

3. Worn or damaged shock absorbers or struts.

E. Cupped tires

1. Wheels out of alignment.

2. Worn or damaged shock absorbers or struts.

3. Worn or damaged wheel bearing.

4. Worn or damaged ball joint.

5. Excessive tire/wheel runout.

F. Shaking (vibration) in steering wheel

1. Tires not inflated to manufacturer's pressure recommendation.

2. Blister (bubble) on tire.

3. Tires/wheels out of balance.

4. Worn wheel bearing.

5. Worn or damaged shock absorbers or struts.

6. Worn suspension ball joint.

7. Worn steering tie-rod end.

8. Excessive tire/wheel runout.

G. Noise from front end

1. Wheel covers not secure (remove covers and test for noise).

2. Noise from tires (drive car on different type of pavement to determine if noise is altered).

3. Lack of suspension/steering component lubrication.

4. Loose suspension/steering component.

5. Worn or damaged suspension/steering component.

H. Car wanders over road (lack of steering stability)

1. Tires not inflated to manufacturer's pressure specification.
2. Mismatched front tires (check sizes and tread configuration).
3. Lack of suspension/steering lubrication.
4. Worn shock absorbers or struts.
5. Wheels out of alignment.
6. Broken or worn spring.

I. Car leans or sways on corners

1. Tires not inflated to manufacturer's pressure specification.
2. Car is overloaded.
3. Broken or worn springs.
4. Worn or damaged suspension/steering component.

SECTION II.   BRAKES

A.   Brake pedal nears floor before brakes engage

1. Air trapped in brake system.
2. Low hydraulic fluid level in master cylinder (check for leak at master cylinder, caliper, wheel cylinder, and brake line connections).
3. Unevenly worn pads and/or linings.
4. Inoperative automatic adjusters.
5. Malfunctioning metering or proportioning valve.

B. Excessive effort needed to apply brakes

1. Vacuum loss with a vacuum-assisted brake booster (power brake unit).
2. Brake pedal sticks because of dirty or damaged linkage.
3. Glazed or worn-out pads and/or linings.
4. Damaged brake booster (power brake unit).
5. Sticking caliper or wheel cylinder pistons.
6. Malfunctioning metering or proportioning valve.

C. Sluggish brake pedal return

1. Brake pedal sticks because of dirty or damaged linkage.
2. Contaminated brake fluid.
3. Weak brake shoe return springs.
4. Sticking caliper or wheel cylinder pistons.
5. Malfunctioning metering or proportioning valve.

D. Brake drag (contact between pad and disc or lining and drum when brakes are not applied)

1. Brake pedal sticks because of dirty or damaged linkage.
2. Contaminated brake fluid.
3. Improperly adjusted parking brake.
4. Damaged brake booster (power brake unit).
5. Weak brake shoe return springs.
6. Malfunctioning master cylinder push rod.
7. Inoperative automatic adjusters.
8. Sticking caliper or wheel cylinder piston.
9. Malfunctioning metering or proportioning valve.

E. Brake pedal falls away under pressure

1. Low hydraulic fluid level in master cylinder (check for leak at master cylinder, caliper, wheel cylinder, and brake line connections).
2. Sticking caliper or wheel cylinder piston.

F. Brake grab (a sudden, uneven, almost violent stopping effect displayed by one wheel)

1. Tires not inflated to manufacturer's pressure specification.
2. Pad or lining contaminated by grease or dust, worn out, or glazed.
3. Incorrect wheel alignment (if the action is side to side rather than front to rear).
4. Sticking caliper or wheel cylinder piston.
5. Scored disc or drum.
6. Inoperative automatic adjuster.

G. Brake pedal pulsates

1. Damaged disc or drum.
2. Tires/wheels out of balance.
3. Wheel bearings incorrectly adjusted.

H. Squealing/squeaking noise

1. May be normal (see page 123).
2. Worn-out, glazed, or contaminated pads or linings.

3. Weak brake shoe return springs.
4. Lack of brake shoe guide lubrication.
5. Scored disc or drum.

I. Scraping noise

1. Damaged drum.
2. Same causes as H above, with the exception of "may be normal."

SECTION III.   ENGINE MECHANICAL

A. Engine seems to consume too much oil

1. Oil dipstick not being read properly (wait five minutes before checking oil if engine has been running; have car on a level surface; be sure to insert dipstick all the way into dipstick tube).
2. Oil viscosity is not one recommended by manufacturer (consult owners manual).
3. Continuous high-speed driving or other severe use, such as towing a trailer.
4. Engine leaking oil externally.
5. Inoperative positive crankcase ventilation (PCV) system.
6. Worn valve guide seals and/or valve guides.
7. Worn or broken piston rings.

B. Engine overheats

1. Complete loss of coolant because of a leaking hose, water pump, radiator, heater core, engine core plugs, or head gasket.
2. Broken or slipping water pump drive belt.
3. Clogged radiator.
4. Malfunctioning thermostat.
5. Defective radiator cap.
6. Inoperative fan.

C. Indication of low oil pressure

1. Oil viscosity is not one recommended by the manufacturer (consult owners manual).
2. Engine idling speed set too low.
3. Clogged oil filter.
4. Malfunctioning oil pressure switch, oil pressure warning light, or oil pressure gauge.
5. Worn or damaged oil pump.
6. Clogged or loose oil pickup screen.
7. Damaged or clogged oil pickup tube.
8. Damage to engine bearings.

D. Clicking/tapping noise

1. Low oil pressure (see above).
2. Improperly adjusted valves (mechanically operated units only).
3. Worn or damaged valve lifters (hydraulically operated units only).
4. Worn or loose rocker arm and/or push-rod assemblies.
5. Sticking valves or broken valve springs.
6. Worn valve guides.
7. Worn camshaft.

E. Heavy knock when starting a cold engine

1. Oil viscosity is not one recommended by the manufacturer (consult owners manual).
2. Noisy fuel pump (mechanical pumps only).
3. Loose flywheel.
4. Damaged valve lifters (hydraulically operated units only).
5. Worn piston and/or cylinder bore (consider wear to still be within operational limits if noise abates in less than two minutes).
6. Damaged connecting rod, crankshaft, or main bearing.

F. Heavy knock when idling a warmed-up engine

1. Oil viscosity is not one recommended by the manufacturer (consult owners manual).
2. Loose or worn drive belt or drive belt pulley.
3. Damaged bearing in air conditioner compressor or AC generator (alternator).
4. Noisy fuel pump (mechanical pumps only).
5. Damaged valves or valve components.
6. Damaged or worn connecting rod, piston, cylinder bore, or crankshaft.

G. Light knock when accelerating a warmed-up engine

1. Check causes for spark knock (see below).
2. Loose torque converter (automatic transmission).
3. Leak from exhaust manifold.
4. Worn connecting rod bearings.

H. Heavy knock when accelerating a warmed-up engine

1. Loose exhaust system part striking an adjacent component.
2. Damaged flywheel.
3. Worn main or connecting rod bearings.

SECTION IV.   ENGINE PERFORMANCE

Note the following concerning engine performance problems before making use of the lists below:

Since some problems are often referred to by different terms, each of those listed below is defined.

- If the engine in your car is equipped with an electronic control module (ECM) or processor (often referred erroneously to as a computer), a code which informs a technician of the cause of the problem may be stored in the memory system of the ECM. This code designates which part of the electronic control system (a sensor, perhaps, or the ECM itself) may be malfunctioning and causing the performance condition. The first thing a technician should do is to tap into the ECM and retrieve any codes which are there.

- Not every component specified in a list will apply in your case. For instance, some of the causes to be checked are for an engine that is equipped with a carburetor, while other causes are for an engine that is equipped with an electronic fuel injection (EFI) system. You engine has one or the other. Another difference is that engines equipped with carburetors have mechanical fuel pumps, while engines equipped with EFI usually have electric fuel pumps.

- Many of the problems listed below have one thing in common. They can all result from one of the following reasons, which call for a careful visual inspection by a technician before he or she turns to other possible causes: loss of engine vacuum because of a damaged vacuum hose; an air leak into the fuel system at the mass air flow sensor-to-throttle body connecting point (EFI) or between the carburetor and intake manifold; damaged ignition cables or wires; and corroded or loose battery or body ground cables.

- One of the most difficult problems for a technician to troubleshoot is an intermittent problem—one that happens sometimes, but not other times. For instance, sometimes your engine may cut-out, but not other times. Or sometimes the engine may stall, but not other times. If the problem doesn't appear when the engine is being looked at by a technician, there's little chance that he or she will find the cause. Do not allow the technician to replace parts with the hope of solving the problem. Most problems that occur intermittently are caused by an electrical malfunction. Therefore, to troubleshoot this kind of trouble, the technician should do the following:

1. Determine if there's a trouble code stored in the ECM memory.

2. Inspect all wire connectors for corrosion, bent terminals, and looseness.

3. Inspect the battery and body ground cables for corrosion and looseness.

A. Hard starting (engine cranks briskly but doesn't start promptly, or starts but dies and has to be restarted)

1. Improper starting procedure (refer to owners manual).

2. Damaged or worn spark plug(s).

3. Water-contaminated fuel.

4. Inoperative throttle position sensor, coolant sensor, or mass air flow sensor.

5. Malfunctioning exhaust gas recirculation valve.

6. Incorrect fuel pressure (EFI).

7. Faulty electric fuel pump drain valve (EFI).

8. Malfunctioning or incorrectly adjusted automatic choke (carburetor).

9. Defective mechanical fuel pump (carburetor).

10. Inoperative thermostatic air cleaner (carburetor).

11. Inadequate ignition system output.

B. Spark knock (also called ping or detonation—a mild or heavy sharp metallic-like knock that is most audible during acceleration)

1. Incorrect fuel (refer to owners manual).

2. Minor buildup of carbon in engine (treat with top engine cleaner—also see below).

3. Incorrect ECM memory chip (ask dealer to check for existence of a technical service bulletin announcing a change in this part.

4. Engine temperature higher than normal.

5. Inoperative exhaust gas recirculation valve.

6. Misadjusted ignition timing.

7. Incorrect fuel pressure (EFI).

8. Carburetor malfunction.

9. Faulty torque converter clutch (automatic transmission).

11. Damaged valve seals.

12. Significant buildup of carbon in engine (disassemble and remove carbon).

C. Poor fuel economy (amount used is noticeably higher than expected)

1. Poor driving habits.

2. Poor maintenance habits, such as underinflated tires and use of incorrect engine oil.

3. Incorrect estimate of fuel usage (test engine using an accurate miles per gallon gauge and compare result to manufacturer's specification).

4. Dirty air filter.

5. Damaged or worn spark plugs.

6. Brake drag.

7. Improperly operating torque converter clutch (automatic transmission).

8. Restriction in exhaust system.

9. Incorrect fuel pressure (EFI).

10. Fuel system leak.

D. Lack of power (less than expected power from engine, especially when accelerating)

1. Dirty air filter.

2. Contaminated fuel filter.

3. Air leak into fuel system.

4. Incorrectly set ignition timing.

5. Stuck exhaust gas recirculation valve.

6. Restricted exhaust system.

7. Dirty or binding accelerator cable.

8. Low alternator output.

9. Misadjusted engine valve timing.

10. Low engine compression.

11. Worn camshaft.

E. Hesitation (also called sag or stumble—a momentary lack of response by the engine on acceleration)

1. Dirty or binding accelerator linkage.

2. Fouled spark plugs.

3. Water-contaminated fuel.

4. Inoperative exhaust gas recirculation valve.

5. Binding throttle position sensor.

6. Air leak into fuel system.

7. Incorrect fuel pressure (EFI).

8. Malfunctioning injector (EFI).

9. Defective mechanical fuel pump (carburetor).

10. Dirty or damaged carburetor.

F. Surging (car feels like it's alternately speeding up and slowing down while cruising on the highway although there is no variation in pressure on the accelerator pedal)

1. Operation of air conditioner compressor or torque converter clutch (automatic transmission) operate (ask dealer if there's a technical service bulletin calling for readjustment, a different memory chip, or new parts).

2. Worn or damaged spark plugs.

3. Engine vacuum loss.

4. Dirty or clogged fuel filter.

5. Air leak into fuel system.

6. Damaged exhaust gas recirculation system.

7. Incorrect fuel pressure (EFI).

8. Defective mechanical fuel pump (carburetor).

9. Contaminated oxygen sensor.

G. Rough idle, shaking at idle, stalling (engine runs unevenly when idling; can may shake; engine may stall)

1. If condition exists only when air conditioner runs, check that system.

2. Engine vacuum loss.

3. Sticking or binding accelerator linkage.

4. Damaged throttle position sensor.

5. Defective idle speed control device (EFI).

6. Incorrectly adjusted slow idle speed (carburetor).

7. Damaged positive crankcase ventilation and/or exhaust gas recirculation valves.

8. Clogged or damaged fuel evaporative emissions control system.

9. Incorrect fuel pressure (EFI).

10. Defective mechanical fuel pump (carburetor).

11. Contaminated oxygen sensor.

12. Air leak into fuel system.

13. Low alternator output voltage.

14. Damaged ignition wires.

15. Fouled spark plugs.

16. Dirty or damaged fuel injectors (EFI).

17. Dirty or damaged carburetor.

18. Low engine compression.

SECTION V. AUTOMATIC TRANSMISSION

The most common conditions displayed by an automatic transmission that isn't performing properly are—

- Harsh shifting (a noticeable jerk or bump as gears shift)
- Torque converter clutch chuggle or shudder (a feeling that the car is alternately speeding up and slowing down while cruising on the highway although there is no variation in pressure on the accelerator [see Surging, above])
- Delayed shifting (gears don't shift when expected)
- Hunting (transmission shifts between gears as if it can't decide in which gear to settle)
- Slipping (noticeable increase in engine speed without car speeding up accordingly when transmission is placed in gear)
- Noise (whine, hum, or growl)

Before you allow a technician to take the transmission from the car for a major disassembly, you should make sure that he or she does the following:

1. Positively establish that the malfunction is with the transmission and not with some other system. Noise, for example, may be coming from tires, and "shifting" problems may be the result of suspension system damage or an engine problem.
2. Check engine and transmission mounts for looseness and damage.
3. Inspect transmission fluid color (must be red or green) and transmission fluid level under the operational requirements specified by the manufacturer.
4. Establish that cable and linkage adjustments are to manufacturer specifications.
5. Test the vacuum modulator (not all transmissions are equipped with this external part)
6. Establish that the cause of the problem is not the result of an electronic control system with those transmissions so equipped.

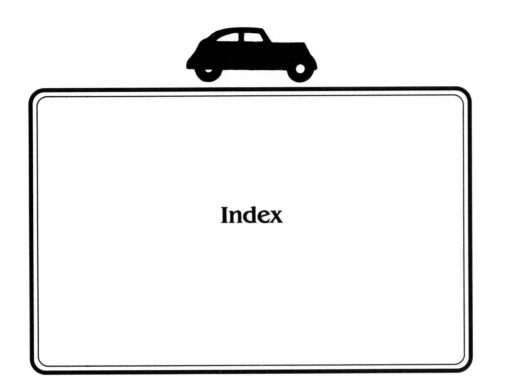

Index

Notes About Your
Car's Performance

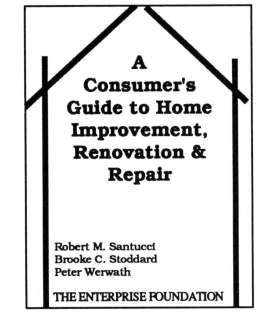